ACCESS
VERNACULARS

ACCESS VERNACULARS

Disability and Accessible Design in Contemporary Russia

Cassandra Hartblay

CORNELL UNIVERSITY PRESS   ITHACA AND LONDON

First published 2025 by Cornell University Press

Librarians: A CIP catalog record for this book is available from
the Library of Congress.

ISBN 9781501782824 (hardcover)
ISBN 9781501782831 (paperback)
ISBN 9781501782855 (pdf)
ISBN 9781501782848 (epub)

Contents

Figures

Note on Translation and Transliteration

The interviews described in this book were conducted in Russian. All translations are the author's own.

A standard simplified American Library Association Library of Congress (ALA-LC) system has been used to transliterate Russian words from the Cyrillic alphabet (the standard phonetic system for writing Russian). Certain names, place names, or other proper nouns appear as commonly spelled in English (including those originating in another language, for example, Finnish). For those unfamiliar with the ALA-LC system, it may be useful to note that symbols denote two Cyrillic letters that have no English equivalent. The soft sign [denoted by a single apostrophe] renders the consonant it follows soft, and the hard sign [appearing in transliteration as a double apostrophe] reinforces that the consonant it follows should be pronounced hard. The difference between hard and soft consonants in Russian may be hard to discern for those new to the language, but this difference is significant to Russian speakers and in some cases is essential to differentiate otherwise similar words; readers unfamiliar with Russian may ignore these notations, which will appear to most non-Russian-speaking readers like an oddly placed apostrophe. Additionally, Russian has more vowels than English; every transliteration system addresses this issue somewhat differently, and ALA-LC offers a consistent solution that is quite distinct from the typical Anglophone pronunciation of the same letters. Readers interested in pronunciation are encouraged to learn more about the Russian alphabet and to study the ALA-LC transliteration table. By way of authorly confession, I will also share that I'm absolutely horrendous at remembering transliteration rules, and any correctly transliterated spellings in this text are thanks to others who have helped me to fix them.

INTRODUCTION

I met Galya through an art therapy group for unemployed working-age adults with disabilities in a city in northwestern Russia. Galya carried herself with grace and sophistication and held herself a bit apart from the others in the group. A wheelchair-user following a spinal cord injury in her thirties, she was often in pain, but she did not like to discuss it, and I was not sure if her pain was related to her original injury or subsequent chronic concerns. She invited me to visit her in her apartment, a long bus ride from the city center, near the old bread factory, and fed me an elaborate lunch that she had prepared. Over tea after our meal, she consented to an interview, and I asked her questions about her daily life and about disability access in the city. Her apartment was up several flights of stairs and the building did not have an elevator, so Galya relied on her husband to carry her up and down. But, she pointed out, bringing me over to the window, she had a splendid view of the lake. Although she tried to stay occupied with housekeeping tasks and reading, Galya admitted that she was often bored: she sought routine, rigor, and discipline to keep herself from becoming depressed. What she missed was a feeling of being enmeshed in the social world. When I inquired about things she might do in her neighborhood, Galya explained that the residential district had few stores, and they were not very accessible.

Go and look, when you leave and go back to the bus stop, she told me. *Take a look at the corner store. You'll see they have a ramp there, but even with the ramp, it's a disaster to try to get through the door in a wheelchair.*

She explained that it was impossible for her to open the door, because it swung onto the stoop at such an angle that it cut off her approach; if she

1

managed to somehow circumnavigate around the door without falling off the stoop, there was still a metal threshold, a thin protuberance rising at least an inch from the floor (a type common in Russia and Asia) that is very difficult to roll over; past that, the aisles were narrow and tightly arranged. Galya narrated this litany of barriers in the built environment, describing infrastructural norms familiar to many who lived and traveled in Russia in the first two decades of the 2000s, and to many wheelchair-users elsewhere who have experienced poorly implemented accessible design.

The concept of *accessible design*, a technical-material strategy to promote the social inclusion of people with disabilities, emerged in the late twentieth century in Western Europe and North America.[1] It has subsequently been exported to a variety of global destinations as a distinctive cultural category and as part of the vernacular lexicon. In this book, I argue for attention to *global access friction*, moments when the intended purpose of accessible design fails as a result of cross-cultural disjuncture. I use "friction" here in two senses. First, the term *access friction* was developed in disability community and by disability studies scholars to describe moments when the varying access needs of different people in a group conflict, or, moments of inaccess that arise when the intended purpose of accessible design fails as a result of complex social barriers (Hamraie and Fritsch 2019).[2] Second, following anthropologist Anna Tsing's usage (2005), *global friction* describes the way that an object, task, or process may hold different (and sometimes incommensurable) meanings for different cultural actors. Tsing argues that friction arises when objects and concepts circulate in global economies. Yet, this type of friction is not always *bad*. Tsing argues that *global friction* is actually generative, and in many cases, the very mismatches in categories and the meaning that stakeholders ascribe to those categories that cause so-called friction are exactly what allows the practices, objects, and ideas to spread globally. In this book, I extend this concept of global friction to explain the spread of accessible design in Russia in the 2010s, in particular, in the ways that seemingly contradictory or corrupt implementation still allows elements of accessible design to proliferate, with mixed results for actually disabled people. I observe that the concept of *disability access* in common Russophone vernaculars rarely stood only for itself, but instead was bound up in broader social and historical conversations about the material politics of an imagined good life. Although the examples herein are drawn from my ethnographic research in one region of Russia to demonstrate the specific historical and cultural points of friction that arose around the meaning of accessible design elements like wheelchair ramps and handrails, the concept of global access friction and attention to local *access vernaculars* in global cultural contexts

FIGURE 1. A ramp in front of Galya's neighborhood grocery store in Petrozavodsk looks well-constructed at first glance. But, a second look shows that the final lip of the ramp is in disrepair. The door at the top of the ramp opens at an angle that is awkward for a wheelchair user to navigate. Upon entering the store, one finds the tight turns in the vestibule to be too narrow for a wheelchair or stroller, and inch-high thresholds. At first it appears that this storefront, unlike many others in the city, is accessible; however, Galya can enter the store only with great difficulty: She relies on the help of her husband to hold doors, push her through tight spots, and lift her wheelchair over high thresholds. As a result, she rarely goes grocery shopping. Photo by Cassandra Hartblay, 2012.

offers an essential tool for thinking about the future of global disability justice and the limits of a disability rights framework.

The ethnographic accounts in this book are drawn from my fieldwork with adults (in their twenties and thirties, and a few in their forties) with mobility and speech impairments. Ethnography as a research method prioritizes stories as a way to understand subcultural insider perspectives. Ethnographic research is useful in exploring global access friction and access vernaculars because the ethnographic vantage traces concepts, discourses, and design objects not only across cultural locations but also at different scales—from interpersonal interactions, to regional and national politics, to global geopolitics. At each of these scales, people develop discursive explanations about where inaccess comes from.

I call vernacular explanations for and mobilizations of access friction to various political ends *inaccess stories*. I identify two types of inaccess stories. One type are those stories that disabled people and their kin tell about their experiences of inaccessibility. Throughout this book, I call these stories, like the one related by Galya, the first type of inaccess stories. As speech acts, these inaccess stories establish a shared understanding between narrator and audience of the systematic nature of ableism as a systemic injustice. These inaccess stories center what I call *disability expertise*, the knowledge that comes from a lived experience of disability. These stories are told by a disabled person or someone close to them (Hartblay 2020; Galis 2011).[3]

A second, distinct kind of inaccess story circulates at a national and geopolitical scale that does not center disability expertise. These stories about inaccessibility in the built environment circulate independent of disability advocates, instead gaining political currency as discursive examples that mobilize accessible design as a metaphor. We can understand these two kinds of inaccess stories as threads running through this book. The next example showcases the second type of access story.

Inaccess Story 2: Disability Access without Disability

In 2019, a Russian artist group published a series of photos to Instagram depicting a young man seated in a manual wheelchair set on a platform that appears to be mounted on the side of a dilapidated Soviet-era apartment building, with a set of steps and rail-ramp leading nowhere, or rather, into thin air, apparently quite high off the ground. The angle of one of the photos in the series emphasized the stark drop-off and the implication of certain injury should the person go down

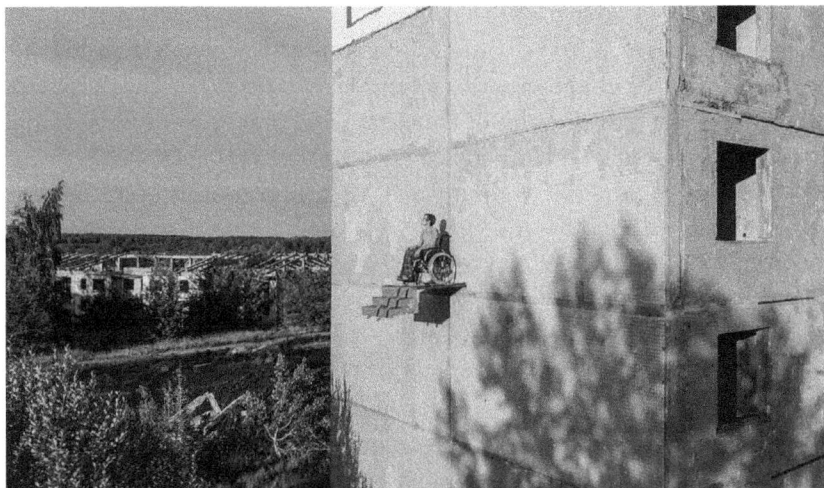

FIGURE 2. The photo here and in figure 3 of a wheelchair user seemingly stuck on a platform suspended in midair with nowhere to go circulated on Instagram and more widely as part of a digital art project. Yet, the artists' other works are unrelated to disability advocacy, and those sharing the images online were largely not connected to disability activism. There is no clear way that the person reached this platform, which has three steps and a rail ramp, as would a ground-floor door stoop. This photo shows clearly that the building is empty: windows have no panes and inside are blank concrete interiors; yet, the dilapidated siding suggests old, rather than new, construction. Photo by vreditel_li art collective, 2019, reproduced with permission.

FIGURE 3. Photo by vreditel_li art collective, 2019, reproduced with permission.

the ramp. The person in the wheelchair appears to be a young man wearing glasses, with nondescript brown hair pushed to one side. In one image, he leans forward, peering over the edge of the platform with an expression of neutral curiosity, incongruous with the absurdity of the apparent situation. The image was part of a performance art and photography series with a social message about how everyday people are trapped by aspects of Russian society (@vreditel_li 2019; Davies 2019). This wheelchair image, in particular, attracted coverage in a variety of media outlets following reposts by Russian influencers, including television personality and once-presidential-candidate Kseniya Sobchak (*Moscow Times* 2019; Sobchak 2019).

As a scholar writing about disability access in contemporary Russia, I was drawn to the image for the poignant depiction of an infrastructural failure. Considering elements of this image led me to ask a series of questions: Why use an access ramp as a metaphor in an artistic image? What kinds of meanings did the inaccessible accessibility ramp suggest to the viewers on the Russian-language internet (affectionately known as RuNet)? Although the ramp in the Instagram post seemed to be "about" disability, it was also an image without actual disabled people (the artist depicted was sitting in a wheelchair that clearly was borrowed for the occasion) and a design without actual accessible affordances. Although the artist released a statement in solidarity with the accessibility concerns of a "disabled neighbor," the content of the other images in the series—for example, a person (the same person?) relaxing with an inflatable palm tree on the ledge, and in another, a person impersonating a Buddhist monk in meditation—suggests that the wheelchair image was intended to entertain and provoke.[4] The social critique in the wheelchair image was one of several scenarios that the artists presented. The platform in midair served as a kind of stage to decontextualize and reframe, a way to point to absurdity. In this way, these images circulated widely as an example of an inaccessible accessibility ramp, interpellating *not* an audience of disabled users (whose experiences of inaccess need no hyperbole to inspire indignation), but rather an audience of nondisabled denizens of RuNet who might appreciate something about the absurdity of the Russian built environment provoked by the photo series. These images are at once about the injustice faced by disabled people and about all of the other kinds of infrastructural injustice the images index for Russian audiences.

In this example of the second type of inaccess story, the concept of disability access works as a vehicle to communicate other associated ideas—a symbol for something other than itself. Here, the absence of disability access stands for a failure on the teleological trajectory of modernity: an imagined post-Soviet future of convenience and mobility has failed to materialize. This formulation suggests a potent way that ideas unrelated to disability stick to the concept of disability access in contemporary Russian popular culture. The image and those reposting it suggest that good design is accessible design, and Russian design is inaccessible. Put another way, accessible design travels in global friction, serving as a metaphor for the abdication of the Russian nation-state's moral obligation to care for its citizens and provide a so-called "normal life," a turn of phrase that indexes imaginaries of Euroamerican postindustrial modernity.[5] In this example, although disabled people and their activism are actually left out of the story, accessible design as a discursive formation is still mobilized and proliferates as a concept and desirable material configuration through global friction.

On one hand, Russians are not alone in equating design and progress or modernity, suggesting what Lucy Suchman (2018, no page) calls an "uneasy question": "Has design now displaced development as the dominant term for deliberative, transformational change?" Anthropologists argue that infrastructure and technology have become a primary modality by which nation-states and other global power hierarchies index modernist teleologies of development. How might thinking with and about *design* expose social processes of a neoliberal conjecture bent on making these differences valuable, desirable or undesirable? After all, design is primarily an expert practice of producing value by rearranging configurations of matter. Who, then, are the experts? What kinds of material conditions are desirable? And what limits are there to the capacity of technology and design to address complex social issues?

On the other hand, there is something distinctly Russian and specific to this moment in time that led this image to go viral online and attract the commentary of cultural influencers. In this book, I attempt to understand this specificity, and, in doing so, argue that the legacy of Soviet ideology continues to influence how the first post-Soviet generation thinks about the sociopolitical impact of the built environment on daily life. Ironically, disability access, derived from Marxist ideology by British disability activists in the 1970s, is the closest shorthand for a critique of the social inconveniences of daily life that are structured by the material world. Understanding this historical confluence helps to explain how images of disability (in)access circulate in contemporary globalized Russia, and therefore, how people living with disabilities in Russia make meaning of life in an inaccessible world and imagine other possible futures.[6]

Inaccess Stories in Context

In the summer of 2010, not long after arriving in the city of Petrozavodsk for my first stint of fieldwork as an US graduate student (already proficient in Russian and having lived, worked, and conducted research in Russia previously),

I interviewed Nina Anatoliievna, a schoolteacher whose twenty-two-year-old daughter, Sveta, has cerebral palsy (DTsP, short for *detskii tserebral'nyi paralich*, in Russian) and uses a wheelchair.[7] Sharing her experiences parenting a disabled child, Nina talked at length about buildings with ramps. She described a theater that only had one ramp at a rear service entrance and a "renovated" university building that had an accessible ramped entrance to the first floor, so that her daughter could attend classes but could not access the bathrooms on the second floor. Other research interlocutors—Sveta's peers, adults with disabilities in their twenties and thirties—later told me about that same renovated university building, highlighting the fact that the entrance ramp made it possible for them to take classes and earn a degree. In Nina's case, however, she relayed this story as a kind of complaint.

Nina's story is what I have come to describe as the first type of inaccess story. This example emphasizes that with the concept of a personal *inaccess story*, I mean to identify a genre of speech act in which a disabled person (or someone close to a disabled person) recounts a series of specific events. Taken together, these stories illustrate the injustice of having to navigate a social world and built environment that was not built with disabled people in mind. Sometimes these inaccess stories focus on the attitudes of other people; other times, they focus on the long, bureaucratic processes that disabled people must undergo to arrive at a tenable result in an inaccessible situation.[8] Often times, these stories are recounted with varying measures of exasperation, humor, matter-of-fact resignation, and righteous indignation. At yet other times, they are told as long jokes, with a punch line at the end. The listener is expected to guffaw, chuckle, or share a similar story in return. In this sense, inaccess stories are a core element of what Carol Gill has called *disability culture*. Gill argues that disability culture is not only a "shared experience of oppression" but also an "emerging art and humor," the creation of a concept of shared history, and a "remarkably unified worldview" (Gill 1995, 18; cited in Kuppers 2014). Although it is impossible to imagine a uniform disability culture across global contexts, we can imagine inaccess stories as diverse, situated reactions to ableisms. Within the word (in)access is the word access; similarly, within the telling of an inaccess story is an imagined experience of access, of being able to move through a world without material traces of ableism. Inaccess stories rehearse and support disability communities' capacity to recognize and describe ableisms as they appear.

I noticed specific patterns to these stories recurring again and again. Some of the stories describe literal errors in the construction of accessibility elements in the built environment, like the one I just shared. Some described the details of navigating social attitudes of nondisabled people, while others described the difficulties of navigating bureaucratic systems to obtain a goal. A great many involved problems related to housing—that is, of getting in and out of one's home, of living where one would want, or of being trapped in living situations one did not want. Many stories involved a deep-seeded perception that the shifting services available to disabled people over the thirty years before my fieldwork took place—the collapse of the Soviet Union, the simultaneous marketization and globalization of the new Russia, and the reconsolidating of the centralized state under Putin's second presidency—meant that very little could be certain about state services for disability. In essence, these stories amount to an observation that Russia is not a "normal country," and as such, it is difficult to live a "normal life" in Russia.

One mismatch kept coming up. In the United States, it was almost always disabled people or their close friends or kin who told inaccess stories, whereas in Petrozavodsk, multiple nondisabled people told me inaccess stories. On the one hand, this makes sense: As an anthropologist new to the field, I told everyone I met that I was studying the social inclusion of people with disabilities, so they often told me the first thing that came to mind about social exclusion and disability (which was usually some story about inaccess, or else, about some newly installed accessibility measure). On the other hand, I began to notice that nondisabled people also told me stories about infrastructural failure whether or not they knew I was studying disability. Sometimes those stories of inaccess had nothing to do with disability, but rather, they were stories about how the chimeric Soviet-cum-Russian state had failed to provide a normal life (in terms of social attitudes, bureaucracy, housing, or social programs and reliable civil order) for both the narrator and the population in general. This style of *Russian talk*, as Nancy Ries (1997) calls it, at once a humorous anecdote, a social complaint, and a mode of building camaraderie, I realized, was in Russia not specific to the disability community. Instead, this style of speech act *and* the principle complaints of people with disabilities were deeply held across a variety of social contexts, transcending class and generation.

Recognizing a sort of echo of inaccess stories in anecdotes that had nothing to do with disability, at first I thought that perhaps Russian disability culture was more assimilationist than disability culture in North America. Instead, I realized, the issue was not assimilation, but rather that the complaints of people with disabilities, as well as the *register of complaint*—to borrow a term from Jocelyn Chua (2012)—were similar to the complaints and stories of nondisabled Russian people: In spite of the small city's vibrant cultural opportunities (music, nature, universities, community) again and again stories returned to the idea that it was *impossible to live a normal life in Petrozavodsk*. I realized that this created a particular problem for Russian disability advocacy. If the complaints of disabled people as a class or group were not distinct to that group, the case for change seemed tenuous.

Moreover, I realized, that one of the reasons that nondisabled people liked to tell certain inaccess stories that were literally about disability was that they understood disability access as a metaphor for a broader social condition. For nondisabled residents of Petrozavodsk who felt that it was impossible to lead a normal life in Russia, examples of inaccessible accessible design for disabled people served as a sort of metonymic figure to illustrate the absence of a so-call normal life, or *normal'naia zhizn'* in Russian. Likewise, disability access seemed to act as a symbol of what the general population understood to be a normal life. For instance, throughout my fieldwork, friends, colleagues, and acquaintances forwarded me memes and images of inaccessible disability access ramps that circulated broadly—far beyond the disability advocacy community—and often with comments that bemoaned Russian life in general, rather than the problem of inaccessibility in particular.

Metonymy: Inaccess Stories and Disability as Metaphor

Returning to the differences between the two types of inaccess stories, we can observe a difference of scale (specific versus broad discourse) and a difference of proximity to disability (whether the story includes the expertise of actually disabled people). I realized, as I began to write and talk about this work, that yet another important difference existed between these two kinds of inaccess stories—that is, whether the speaker was invoking disability access literally or figuratively. In the example of vreditel_li's photos, disability access is presented as a metaphor for something else that is open for interpretation. Disability studies scholars have argued that narrative descriptions of disability in art and literature can have the effect of crowding out actual disability experience from popular narratives, because audiences become accustomed to the idea that disability stands for something else (Mitchell and Snyder 2001). In the case of the second type of inaccess stories in Russia in the 2010s, disability might symbolize the failure of the state to provide safety, care, and infrastructure commensurate with an imagined ideal of modernity. Although some disability studies scholars have interpreted Mitchell and Snyder's argument about narrative prosthesis to suggest that disability should never be used a metaphor, because to do so crowds out the political assertions of actually disabled people, Mitchell and Snyder have argued that in fact, they did not mean to suggest that disability can never be used as a metaphor. As Sami Schalk (2018) demonstrates, literary uses of disability as a metaphor and intersectional identity can provide compelling, liberatory opportunities to imagine the world otherwise. What I suggest is that in some cases, when my interlocutors told inaccess stories about disability expertise, these stories were neither exclusively literal nor exclusively figurative. Rather, disability access was at once both a metaphor and a literal concern. That is, in some cases, calls for disability access in Russia in the 2010s were *metonymic* (wherein a metonym is a category of figurative language in which an object is both itself and a symbol of something greater or more complex).

Thinking of inaccess stories about inaccessible accessibility ramps told by disabled people and their kin as metonymic helps explain how these stories seemed at first to be assimilationist: the speaker was arguing that inaccessible accessibility was both a specific literal barrier *and* symbolic of corrupt negligence on the part of the government to deliver the infrastructural standards of modern life. Another example of this kind of metonymic or dual-type inaccess story is the case of the snow-covered ramp. The figure shows a well-constructed ramp that does not work because a snowbank covers a large portion of the ramp, thereby making it functionally useless. The image is both a specific complaint about not being able to access a swimming pool complex from the point of view of disability expertise, and a figurative complaint about systemic failures to ensure infrastructural function in Russia in general (such as, perhaps, the negligence that the ramp remained covered in snow, unshoveled). In this paradigm, elements of accessible design, like the wheelchair ramp at the swimming pool complex, allow access to index a sense of ease, a lack of difficulty, that stand for a desire for urban modernity. The images of a poorly placed, maintained, or constructed ramps suggest a politics of abandonment (Biehl and Eskarod 2005), wherein, as Robert McRuer (2013, 2016) argues in a consideration of such a ramp in Mexico City, the signifier of disability (the ramp) appears, but disabled people actually continue to be excluded from citizenship (in that citizens are imagined to move freely through public space), a sort of neoliberal commodification of the architecture of urban modernity that disregards disabled people. Attending to global access friction in this way allows us to see that accessible design elements and images of these elements in use are desired for many complex reasons that may or may not relate to advocating for disability access or to a crip commitment to desiring disability.

I argue that the social and historical context by which the concept of *disability access* entered the Russian vocabulary in the late twentieth century cannot be separated from the way that the idea of an accessible environment (*dostupnaia sreda*) came to stand for a particular notion of a modern, prosperous, and "open" society. In offering this analysis, I do not mean to promote this metonymic usage of symbols of inaccess to represent something about Russia in general or do I suggest that there is something good or useful about it. Instead,

FIGURE 4.   Snow covers an accessibility ramp at the swimming facility in Petrozavodsk, constructed in the early 2000s. The steps to the front entrance have been shoveled, but the ramp has not. Footprints show that some visitors have used the ramp anyway, but the deep-drifted snow along some parts of the ramp would make it difficult for a wheelchair user or someone pushing a stroller to navigate. The image tells a story of inaccess. This image was sent to me by a parent-activist whose daughter uses a wheelchair; she received the picture from a friend. "Why make the facility accessible if you're not going to shovel the walk?," the mother quipped. Photo submitted to author anonymously, 2012.

as an ethnographer, I can only observe that it exists and set out to understand how it came to be so, and to learn what, precisely, is going on in this context. Whether or not my North American disability studies politics agreed, inaccess stories were circulating in Russian as a specific type of vernacular complaint that did not neatly match up with Euroamerican understandings of disability access or minority justice advocacy.

Confronting this ethnographic quandary—that is, the mismatch between the Euroamerican concepts related to disability, access, and justice and the terms of debate and registers of complaint put forth by my interlocutors in Russia—meant that as I returned from the field, I found myself searching through my fieldwork notes, my interviews, and the secondary literature about Russia and global disability studies for answers to a few foundational questions: What is disability? What is disability access? What is accessible design? How and when does the concept of disability access *appear*, following Tanya Titchkosky's usage (2011), and when did it come to matter in contemporary Russian life?

Conceptualizing Disability Access Cross-Culturally

I turn now to the academic ground on which I base my understandings of some of the key terms that ground my argument: disability, design, and access. In doing so, I further explicate some of the concepts that I draw on to make sense of my findings: Disability anthropology, global disability studies, disability expertise, friction, and global postsocialism. Finally, I describe my research methods and outline how my arguments proceed in subsequent chapters.

Disability and Disability Anthropology

Disability, in anthropological terms, is a culturally contingent category that becomes meaningful through social worlds. A category must be understood as a set of ideas embedded in culture and history: Categories are how we understand the world as humans, and therefore, categories are cultural. The category of disability in one language may not match the category of disability in another language or, indeed, over time in the same place. Myriad social disagreements and legal battles emerge from the very question of what constitutes a disability in a given time and place, and what kinds of entitlements a disability ought to bestow. National and international taskforces work to create and revise legal definitions of disability, in the process nuancing who "counts" as disabled and who does not (Kohrman 2005; Washington Group on Disability Statistics 2017). This late-modern social practice of "making up" definitions works to establish firm boundaries between categories or kinds of people: normal and abnormal; able-bodied and mobility-impaired (terminology changes quickly every few decades); disabled and nondisabled; sighted, vision-impaired, and blind; deaf, hard-of-hearing, and hearing. Disability as a category is quite often bound up in sorting through definitions (Hacking 1986; Titchkosky 2011, 59). That is, whether some particular bodily or mental state fits into a legal, medical, or social policy's definition of disability is an enduring cultural concern of modernity. The question of whether or not a given person is "disabled" in cultural terms is in flux. The boundaries of these categories are complicated by the variations in vocabulary and sociomedical history across languages.

The boundaries that these definitions create also vary across cultural and political settings and over time, and they are frequently contested and remade by the very people they seek to define.

The process of creating and revising legal definitions of disability to nuance who "counts" as disabled and who does not is a time-consuming and ongoing project that is never finished. Like other global identity categories that become meaningful for governance, human rights, and justice, the complexity of creating transculturally relevant *metrics* for capturing rates of disability in different global populations lay bare the fuzziness of the category (Adams 2016; Merry 2016). The UN committee tasked with defining disability for internationally standardized questionnaires, originally intended as a short taskforce group to convene for a couple of years, has now been meeting regularly for more than twenty years (Washington Group on Disability Statistics 2017). This social practice of defining the category of disability is undertaken at the national level in every nation that seeks to proffer a disability pension, a standard element of the modernist welfare state. Inevitably, some people who self-identify or are characterized by others as belonging to a category of disability in social life do not "count" as disabled according to complex legal definitions (Kohrman 2005). That is, the question of how disability is defined in a given time and place suggests as much or more about the cultural world as it does about the body that is ostensibly being described.

Furthermore, disability is not just a bodily state or an "identity" in the rote sense. Such a view objectifies the body, when in fact, we know that bodies are not just objects but also are our *selves* as sensing beings (Overboe 2016, 23); we live in bodyminds, in that our self-perception relies on the very apparatus (our senses) doing the perceiving. Moreover, cognitive difference, then, creates a set of problems for a discipline like anthropology that is premised on a shared social world. As Michele Friedner (2018) observes, the world as perceived is not stable between interlocutors or ethnographers, but rather is contingent on diverse embodied sensory experiences. Observations are filtered by sensorium cast with neurodiversity, pain, uncertain mobility, and varied auditory and visual perception. So, how then, should we study disability anthropologically, if it is at once a changing, manifold cultural category and complicated as a sensory experience of the world?

Thinking about how the concept of disability develops as a meaningful cultural category requires a particular approach to understanding what disability is as well as a model for thinking about how disability appears in the world. Categories come to live social lives of their own and are shaped through social practice by the people who claim these categories as part of their social identity. As Ian Hacking has argued, definitions and categories "make up" the existence of differences and of kinds of people, and, in turn, the bearers of these identities "make up" what it means to belong to these categories. As the sociologist Tanya

Titchkosky writes, "It is in culture, in the midst of others, that disability is made; in this way, we are never alone in our bodies" (2011, 59). That is, we can only know the category of disability through comparison and through relationships among people, society, and the environment, a perspective on disability that Alison Kafer (2003) calls a *relational model*. A relational model of disability builds on the foundations of the social model of disability, which rejects the medical approach to disability that locates disability-as-difference as pathology belonging to an individual body. Instead, according to this model, bodies may have various impairments, but the disabling effects of the impairment actually come from elements of the social world (e.g., stigma and the built environment). Considering critiques that the social model is too reliant on the idea that impairments are not disabling and fails to fully capture intersectional considerations, disability studies scholars have sought other ways to frame a model of disability. Anthropologists tend to be wary of models of thought, given that it can be difficult to transpose static models across the diversity of human cultural relations and sociopolitical and economic ways of living. Instead, we might examine what work a particular category is doing in a given cultural setting.

I argue that *disability anthropology* is a specific scholarly conversation. In my formulation, disability anthropology has several characteristics. First, it overlaps with but is not limited to the questions that medical anthropology asks about how health, illness, and disability—and culturally located medical responses are shot through with socially and historically specific politics and power. Second, it is in conversation with the interdisciplinary field of disability studies (sometimes called critical disability studies) in terms of citational praxis, scholarly exchange, and changing political horizons. A defining characteristic of this discourse is a concern with understanding and undoing *ableism*, the historically and culturally constructed system of oppression that privileges nondisabled people and perspectives. Third, disability anthropology centers *disability expertise* as both an object of study and as an essential element of research praxis. One goal for disability anthropology is to understand disability expertise ethnographically as the specific knowledge about particular domains of embodied social life that come from lived experience of disability or proximity to disability. Some kinds of disability expertise may be thought of as shared knowledge passed down through disability culture. The project of naming and cataloging disability expertise is important for disability anthropology for two reasons: First, the ableism inherent in medical practice and charity models of disability have often denied the expertise of disabled people and have discursively constructed disabled people as passive recipients of care and pity, rather than as agentive creators and political actors. Second, anthropology has often implicitly excluded disabled people from ethnography studies, by focusing on cultural norms or on average members of a given society, or simply by following the ableist assumption that disabled people are socially marginalized—at the edges rather than the centers of social networks.

Within disability studies as an interdisciplinary field, anthropologists and sociologists work in conversation with historians, literature scholars, cultural studies scholars, activists, and others. Disability anthropology is well-suited to produce global ethnographic accounts that trace disability, ableism, and access as they function in different cultural contexts around the world (Ginsburg and Rapp 2013; Ingstad and Whyte 2007; Friedner 2015, 2022; Nakamura 2006, 2013; Phillips 2011; Mol 2002; Stiker 1990. This approach contributes to inter-disciplinary conversations in transnational disability studies and US studies (e.g., Mitchell and Snyder 2019; McRuer 2018; Kim 2011, 2014, 2017; Erevelles 2011; Hunt-Kennedy 2020) and likewise offers critiques of the normative frame of Euroamerican disability studies pioneered by Black disability studies and disability justice advocates (Puar 2017; Schalk 2018, 2022; Bell 2017; Berne 2020) and anthropologists (Ralph 2014). Where disability as a category of difference has gained a certain primacy in some political movements, scholars and activists have called for more attention to the ways in which debility, injury, and sickness are the product of historical systems of oppression, colonialism, and imperialist violence. The ethnographic approach revolves around the project of working to center the voices of interlocutors, and thereby, the subjectivity of diverse disabled people.

More specifically, a disability studies perspective, here taken up as a manner of doing disability anthropology, suggests looking "back at society" from the point of view of people with disabilities (Linton 2005) and considering what it is about society that could be altered to create a better fit for disabled people. Rather than follow the bodies of disabled people as objects of research, the project of disability studies is instead to follow the ways in which ableism, or multiple ableism, works to produce disability as a category of exclusion, separate from a dominant "norm." As such, I understand disability as a marker of ableism: a category that comes into being and becomes useful, apparent, or unavoidable in certain situations in which the latent social system of ableism is made apparent. As Titchkosky (2011) argues, we can learn much by considering when disability appears. That is, scholars have demonstrated that disability is a category of the modern welfare state; therefore, its invocation is inherently political and it serves as a modality by which people claiming disability call for social benefits as a political class. The use of disability as a concept may also be implemented as a tool to justify and implement segregation and social exclusion by designating some bodyminds as "too much"—that is, to assert that a bodymind ought to be designated as disabled is to produce the characteristics of that person as somehow in excess of the norms of social inclusion.

Just as feminist studies have investigated patriarchy, disability studies scholars have often sought to study ableism. Where feminist studies encountered the limits of the universal in terms of the myriad, incommensurable ways to be "woman" globally and to configure iterations of patriarchy, the very category of disability has been unstable over time and across cultural contexts, and ableism, when considered globally, is better described as ableisms. This is especially evident when we compare the variegation of words for disability and disability diagnoses.

Vernaculars of Access

The concept of disability access has emerged in multiple social contexts. It is a technical-legal concept defined in laws, codes, and standards. Underlying the content of those standards are the folk concepts developed collectively by activists in disability advocacy movements who describe how disabled people move, communicate, and thereby participate socially and politically. These frameworks are informed by and contest medicalized concepts of rehabilitation technology as well as by ideological principles of citizenship and political participation. In this way, "access" is a concept borne of the twentieth-century modern national state, which specifically links public infrastructure with the rights of citizenship. The codified normative concept of access is continuously enacted and interpreted by disabled people and activists in daily life. The word *access* thus circulates—separated from the fuller phrases *accessible design*—as a shorthand for technosocial infrastructures of justice. So-called *disability access* may then dovetail, oppose, or be conflated with other kinds of access. By this, I do not mean to detract from the important work of negotiating the ways in which access needs are shaped by multiple intersectional identities (e.g., Hamraie 2020). Instead, I want to observe the way that—perhaps as an artifact of the strategic essentialism of the disability rights movement in North America—a distinct definition of access (of or pertaining to the social and political participation of disabled people, especially in relation to movement through space and the design of digital or physical infrastructures or consumer products)— emerged. Because the civil and human rights logic of "access" in (neo)liberal democracy requires that disabled people be identified as a protected class (or minority group), this identity must be artificially flattened into a classifiable (frictionless) entity, thereby belying internal diversity. As a result of this classification effort, however, to proceed as a legal category, disability is discursively separated from other identities (e.g., race, class, gender, sexuality, religion, language) even though this discursive separation does not reflect the lived experience of intersectional identity. Similarly, and this is the point I am getting at, disability access has thus emerged in contemporary North American English a rhetorical category that seems to be separate from other valences of justice. It had to be defined as such so that it could be legally codified in the particular legal systems of the United States and Canada. In considering disability access cross-culturally, however, the utility of distinguishing disability access from other valences of justice—material, economic, religious, and so on—may or may not be a rhetorically useful strategy. Disability access, as such, may not appear as a distinct endemic conceptual classification, or, it may appear as a translated phrase connoting a variation on the Euroamerican concept that moves in friction. In sum, vernacular descriptions of justice for disabled people may or may not align with the Euroamerican conceptual domain and political rhetorics.

To trace the knowledge practices of access in Russia, in this book, I follow fellow anthropologist Arseli Dokumaci's question (2018, no page), "How can we think of access, not as a monolithic entity but as a multitude of meanings and valances that may not always neatly cohere?" That is, to approach an ethnographic understanding of access, I pay attention to how access and its synonyms and attributes appeared in Russian daily life and how they emerged in my conversations and interviews with both disabled and nondisabled interlocutors. I hold in the frame the fact that this Russophone access (*dostupnost'*) exists in a global friction, following Tsing's (2005) meaning, as a word that is a container for a multiplicity of meanings that do not necessarily align, and whose differences may actually propel the concept into wider use.

I argue that an ethnographic examination of disability access or accessible design must attend not only to normative definitions and their genealogies but also to *vernaculars of access*. By vernaculars of access, I mean the myriad ways that culturally situated actors interpret, make sense of, and deploy the idea of access and the material objects of accessible design.

So what is the normative Euroamerican notion of access? Clarifying this will be necessary to distinguish how this concept moves in global friction, creating un/productive mismatches with other vernaculars of access. In daily life, the idea of disability access is typically glossed with simplistic symbols (e.g., a white figure in a wheelchair on a blue background; a handrail; a curb painted a particular color), but accessibility as a concept is a complex and evolving category. The meaning of access may vary from one user to another, across translations, or between contexts. Access is many things. It is the inclusion of minority or stigmatized groups in social and political life. It an unhindered physical and material movement through space. It is a relational concept of interactions between complex networks of heterogeneous actors. These core ideas of disability access build on precepts developed through disabled people's advocacy and activism in design and architecture and extend into political advocacy and the dynamics of sensory and social life.

As has been widely observed, the access needs of one person may not match and may impede the access needs of another. Rather than pursue a final, universal idea of access, critical access studies sets out to challenge the notion that access is a "self-evident good," instead investigating the politics of how "access-knowledge" comes into being (Hamraie 2017, 13). Instead, this critical crip approach seeks to understand access as a *knowledge practice*. Centering knowledge practice in the definition of access is an easy method for "asking who is served or empowered by such knowledge" (Hickman and Serlin 2018, 135). In Western Europe and North America, an "access industry" (Imrie 1996, 97) of for-profit business organizations has emerged to capitalize on the need for accessibility expertise and material infrastructure. As the idea of accessible design circulates globally, so too does the commodification of disability expertise. I argue that as access objects and knowledge become commodified and, like other commodities, travel through global supply chains, they create problems of uneven distribution; mismatches between production, distribution, and consumer desires; and friction. For example, access knowledge may be simplified and extracted to circulate in the form of checklists or objects, decontextualized from the activist cultures of care that created them. Commodified accessibility objects circulate independent of access knowledge.[9] This has led to inaccess stories like the ones that Galya and Nina in which an access ramp leads to a store with aisles too narrow to accommodate a wheelchair user. But a simple critique of this type of inaccess story as an instance of "bad access" misses the nuance of the culturally specific bricoleur practices, and the ways in which friction and mismatch may actually be generative, raising the profile of accessible design as a concept, commodity, and practice.

Attending to vernaculars of access, I contend, offers an important way to trace how these specific mismatches allow the concept of accessible design to travel in friction. I use the word *vernacular* in conversation with a tradition of ethnographic attention to vernacular architecture, which can be understood as architectural designs and structures created by laypeople working in specific local contexts outside of formal architectural expertise and practice. To be clear, vernacular (as a metaphor from vernacular language extended to material structures) does not mean non-Euroamerican, and it does not refer to some lesser rung on a civilizational teleology. Indeed, there are architectural schools and design expertise in locations cast by global hegemony as South/East. Instead, my use of vernacular refers to bricoleur manners of working, reworking, tinkering, and adapting: interpreting and making-do with what is available using the ingenuity of lived experience rather than formal training. I use the word vernacular to highlight the fact that I am not interested in, for example, the establishment of institutional rubrics for conferring accolades of expertise about disability access in Russia. Instead, I want to trace the ways that people with lived experience talk about access, literally, vernacular in the sense of common discourse. Attending to vernaculars of access ethnographically brings to the surface the situated knowledge and disability expertise—as well as the national, public, and mediated discourses about access—that may be missed by more prescriptive efforts that focus on defining access as normative and universal.

I consider the specific ways in which Russians in Petrozavodsk talked about access during my fieldwork from 2010 to 2016 to argue that access is both a metaphor and a literal expression of agency and of social worth or neededness. I argue that for adults with disabilities in Petrozavodsk, access is described as a state of affairs that is *peaceful* (*spokoino*) and *comfortable* or *convenient* (*udobno*). For my interlocutors as well as for a broader Russophone constituency (a primarily nondisabled public) access denoted an *idealized normal* (*normal'no*) and the imagined *not bad* (*neplokho*) that is at once an aphorism of sarcastic perseverance and a refusal to accept the livability of the status quo. Underpinning these iterations is a core concern with the livability of what the disability activists who created the British social model of disability called the *built environment* and what early Soviet avant-garde designers understood in Marxist terms as the *material conditions of daily life*. Like many complaints about infrastructure, complaints about (in)access as a result of the configuration and maintenance of physical objects in the world are deeply tied to how citizens understand the responsibility of the state to provide the minimum conditions necessary to lead a normal daily life.

This approach to accessibility requires setting aside the transnational definition of disability access, as laid out, for instance, in the United Nations Convention on the Rights of Persons with Disabilities (UN CRPD), as one modality among many. The UN CRPD's history suggests that its creation is a testament to diversity global advocacy, and its subsequent reach and derivation make this document a significant nodal point of friction between multiple global localities. I resist the common mode of understanding disability access in terms of checklists or minimum standards, although these checklists and minimum standards certainly make up one domain of access as a knowledge practice. Instead, I think of access, and encourage readers of this book to also think of access, as "an interpretative relation between bodies" (Titchkosky 2011, 3).

Anthropology Of Design: Technologies of Productivity and Ontological Pluralism

Studying vernaculars of access requires considering not only infrastructures and designs as they circulate in the world but also how to approach the domain of access as a social practice. Thinking about design anthropologically, we can observe that design, like access, refers to many things, including a set of practices or a particular process of concerted creation. To design an object, system, or process is to elaborate on a model for how something might work in the world, particularly in relation to human action. A doorknob, a staircase, a keyboard, or the interface in which you are reading this book (whether a book or a screen) is a designed object. Design, then, is both a sociocultural practice, and a "relational configuration between people, spaces, and things" (Murphy 2015, 32). The conceit of design—as opposed to art on the one hand and construction on the other—is that, as a discipline, design considers both form and function to optimize relations that its output creates in the world.[10] Design, in seeking to make the world better, Keith Murphy argues, always connotes an imagined good. To think with design, Arturo Escobar (2018) tells us, is to think with the question of how the world might be otherwise. Accessible design, then, as an idea, is a utopian hope for a different kind of relationship between disability and the world.

There are many ways of approaching the concept of design, and many modes of doing anthropology, and thus several intersections of critical praxis that may be understood in relation to design anthropology (Murphy and Wilf 2021). Perhaps most relevant to the present work, conceptualizing the anthropology of design as a subfield of ethnographic investigation opens the possibilities for understanding design as a field of human practice. Thinking of design as such "provides an ideal ground both to document the processes by which certain 'designed' objects are transformed into 'culture', and to refine the conceptual apparatus required for understanding how such processes function more generally" (Murphy 2015, 217). Defining design thus leads to the quandary of which kinds of human activities might fall into this category of design, to attend to how the boundaries of design expertise are established and enforced, and to determine how some designs or designers are thus rendered good, and others, bad (Murphy 2015, 2021).

This anthropological approach to design necessarily begins from a reckoning with the perceptions about the concept of design garnered through daily life. As global consumers, many of us think of design as an attribute of goods that we consider for purchase, or, if we pause to give it a bit more thought, as a kind of process that leads to the particular designed elements of our favorite devices and things. We are aware that certain brands produce their value through an attention to design—from Apple electronics to Nike sneakers—by which we understand this "attention" to be a concerted consideration of both the materials used to construct the item and the way that these materials are formed into a functional object. In this respect, at least, the colloquial use of design (and even designer fashion) shares a core element with the kernel of design logics taught to aspiring professionals in design school: that good design is a balance between form and function. At the same time, twenty-first-century consumer products often tend to suggest that even though all products are in fact designed (i.e., their shape, materials, and the plan by which they are made and manufactured was considered and detailed by someone with an intention for the execution to create a particular object or outcome or process), the design labor that goes into many of these products is obfuscated, and good design is equated with luxury, wealth, and value. Because good designs work better than bad designs, we might also agree that to have the financial capacity to access luxury designed objects also suggests a kind of ease and convenience that comes with both the disposability of the broken and the means to support maintenance work. In some contexts, a given form comes to carry a semantic meaning derived from its original function, even where the form no longer serves this purpose: the prestige conveyed by false columns on a building's façade, for example.

As we encounter objects in the world, we may or may not think of them as crafted, and as such, we may or may not imagine that human intention is present behind the form and fabric of their existence. Yet all cultural objects are designed, and all tools used by humans are cultural objects. In this sense, we must also differentiate between *vernacular design* and *professional design*. Vernacular design is the work of the layperson reorganizing the quotidian world (have you considered the order of the books on your bookshelf, designed a cataloging system; or purchased and installed a hook to hang a piece of artwork or to hang your bag or coat or bathrobe?). That is, vernacular design is all of the making and rearranging that we do with only our standard cultural training, but without thought for the expert training. Professional design is the work of a professional, usually in the sense that one has been trained into a particular practice of expertise and hired to do design work. In this way, professional design is tied to the concept of creating value—both for the design and for a client whose product or company will benefit. This distinction of vernacular and professional relies on cultural logics of expertise that may be contested.

The anthropology of design as an area of scholarly investigation dovetails with recent disciplinary conversations about *infrastructure*. Sociocultural anthropologists argue that tracing infrastructure ethnographically reveals that public elements of the built environment constitute a material iteration of the (modern) nation-state (and thereby modernity). Popular attitudes about infrastructure create a discursive arena in which to consider, critique, and assert complaints about a modern state's responsibilities to its citizens (Larkin 2013). Hand in hand with an anthropology of bureaucracy, the attention to infrastructure and the administrative processes by which it is made, maintained, and neglected make up an important domain of everyday political practice in early twenty-first-century human societies. In the context of the liberal democratic nation-states that make up the hegemonic global North/West, bureaucratic infrastructures have come to be understood, through the concerted lobbying efforts of disability activists and resulting legal measures, as a valence of sociopolitical inclusion and exclusion.[11] Moreover, accessible infrastructures are defined by the United Nations as a human right that nation-states ought to provide for their citizens. In this geopolitical context, infrastructural failure both literally results in and may be discursively mobilized metaphorically to represent sociopolitical exclusion of disabled citizens, and, by extension, a failure of the modern nation-state's liberal democratic contract.

Central to all of these ideas, however, is the observation that to design is a fundamentally human practice. To design something is to bring the materials into the world of human cultural logics by finding and refining its value to be or do, to appear and distinguish, or to create effects and provoke responses. All of these effects rely on the symbolic world of culture; without shared meanings, design cannot be valued, and without value, one design cannot be distinguished from another. At the same time, this property of valuing good design means that some designs may be more valued by one constituency than by another. The aims of what an object, building, place, space, tool, or virtual interface ought to do (and how) may be valued differently.

In an altogether different approach to considering the politics of design anthropologically, Escobar (2018) argues that we might consider liberatory political thought as an opportunity to design the world differently, not only in the sense of different leaders or forms of government, but ontologically differently, in the sense of what it means to be together in a world. That is, the ontological terms of reality are defined by the categories we think with, which shape the kinds of political futures that we can imagine. Escobar asks: How might we redesign our sociopolitical taxonomies to decolonize the future and live differently? Which ontological worlds are understood to be real and belonging to the present (rather than orientalized and belonging to the past)? Escobar argues for a world of multiple ontologies and for provincializing the Euroamerican worldview's grasp on ontological possibilities. Escobar's concept of *ontological design* speaks to this book's consideration of global access friction. Global friction arises in the mismatch between cultural ontologies linked by systems of exchange in global capitalism. Thus, an interrogation of ontological design following Escobar might lead us to ask which ontological ways of being together are understood as "accessible design" by capital, and which are cast aside as antimodern (i.e., belonging to the past)? What political possibilities for disability inclusion do these hegemonic ontological designs foreclose? And what other liberatory political possibilities might emerge by provincializing Northern/Western cultural ontologies that imagine liberal modernity (and its concept of rights-based inclusion) as the only viable path to the sociopolitical liberation for disabled people?

As a fundamentally human practice, design can also be understood to serve human interests, but, which interests? Design for whom? Whose bodies and lives are supported or excluded? How do the assumptions built into the physical world preclude or limit the participation of some bodies? In the "Crip Techno-science Manifesto," Hamraie and Fritsch write, "Disabled people are experts and designers of everyday life. But we also harness technoscience for political action, refusing to comply with demands to cure, fix, or eliminate disability" (2019, 2). This is part of the authors' "anti-assimilationist position that disability is a desirable part of the world" (2019, 2).

Although many disability studies texts have imagined communism as a liberatory alternative to capitalism, in which ableism is so potently manifested in relation to expectations of productivity and labor that marginalize those disabled people deemed less productive, I argue that the productivist and nationalist logics of design were prevalent (if different) in both Soviet and liberal democratic twentieth-century modernity (Hartblay 2014). Scholars of North American disability history show that design is a paradigm of modernity deeply tied to production and productivity and to the capacity of the human body to contribute to economic output (Serlin 2015; Hamraie 2017). In the mid-twentieth century, nations (as economic units) harnessed the labor power of their citizens and demonstrated their economic prowess on the world stage through innovations in design that improved productivity (Murphy 2015). In some examples, these innovations in productivity sought to harness the "lost" labor power of people with particular physical impairments. That is, the ways in which design, as a *technology of productivity*, did not necessarily leave out disabled people, but in fact sought to recognize and harness the labor power of the disabled citizen. Ironically, in spite of the many differences between the Western capitalist and Soviet ideological modes of considering work and the citizen, the thrust of technological advance was profoundly shared. Indeed, exhibitions of advances in the design of domestic consumer objects became a display of soft power (Murphy 2015, 28). In some social democratic nations, government investment in the design of consumer objects in the mid-twentieth century became as an arena for the advancement of social welfare more generally, in that good design might create more productive, more hygienic spaces, and, therefore, citizens. Murphy (2015, 39–41) argues that the politics of design in twentieth-century Sweden were tied up in complex attributions of agency that imagined some designs as being more or less democratic and socially equitable than others. At the same time, Soviet constructivist design imagined domestic design as an arena for the implementation of communist ideals; constructivist thinkers argued that aesthetics are influenced by and create political consciousness (Romberg 2018).

Today, post-Soviet Russia has been cast by the West as a failed project of modernity. Throughout this book, I argue that discursive evidence for this Russian failure of modernity is sometimes expressed through representations of design failures. Global media hegemony reproduces this perspective, building on generations of European depictions of Russia as backward and antimodern. Moreover, considering the specter of design as a symbolic expression of development and modernity, contemporary Russian design logics produce a logic of twenty-first-century assimilation that is familiar across global contexts. Thinking of Russia not in the former Cold War lens, but through the neocolonial lens of development economics, we can place 2010s Russia in its alphabet row among the BRICs: Brazil, Russia, India, and China. Although the evidence in this book focuses on Russia, I suggest that images of failed design circulate as a critique of national governments capacity for development, for example, stories of the unjust and poorly implemented Brazilian Olympic Village. In this reading, we consider the role of design as *display*—that is, a way of presenting a desired progress toward development (Irani 2019).

Accessible design—from the iconic white-on-blue icon to the shapes and aesthetic markers (e.g., ramps and handrails) characteristic of accessible design—comes to stand for the look of modernity. That is, the *parti*, or aesthetic characteristics, of accessible design announce particular political assumptions or aspirations. Murphy offers the concept of *cultural geometry* to describe the way that sociopolitical ideas come to be associated with the particular aesthetic characteristics of a school of design practice. The aesthetic characteristics that make up a cultural geometry are the expression of aesthetic preferences that index ideological claims about the relationship between form and function; particular kinds of lines (curved or straight), angles (sharp or rounded), and material finishes convey particular political leanings. Like the transnational futurism of international airport design, elements of accessible design taken together when clean, well-executed, and well-maintained communicate desirable mobility, imagined individualism, prosperity, and a kind of global professionalism. That is, accessible design as a cultural geometry becomes a container onto which ideas about a normal modern future are projected. Likewise, states mobilize urban infrastructure as a vernacular for the expression of sociopolitical values, economic power, and geopolitical prowess. Throughout this book, I argue that in Russia in the 2010s, the cultural geometry of globally recognizable accessible design features in the built environment carried a symbolic association with an array of ideas about a modern, democratic, middle-class European public sphere.

Global Access Friction: Provincializing Accessible Design

In the chapter opening, I introduced the concept of global access friction, in which the idea of disability access as a design practice and associated objects moves "in friction" across global cultural contexts. In common parlance, when something is said to be "in friction" it means that something is difficult, hindered, or likely to encounter challenges.

Anthropologists mean something specific when we use the word *friction*. Tsing proposed that we may think of friction metaphorically, as a productive force that occurs and produces heat or complexity. Things and ideas, Tsing argues, do not flow freely from one context to another. Tsing suggests that rather than think of cultural differences or the mismatches in the ways that given objects or ideas are passed from one cultural sphere to another as an impediment or imperfection, it may be useful to think as these mismatches and tensions of interpretation or meaning as productive friction. Or rather, where conventional wisdom reads mismatches or misunderstandings as troublesome, Tsing takes a more neutral perspective: The friction generated by the mismatch may be useful. This is one of the many ways that contemporary ethnographers talk about conflicting ontologies (e.g., Ries 2009; Mol 2002). One way to read Tsing is to understand friction as a critical intervention into popular narratives about capitalism and globalization, in which objects, concepts, and values are imagined to "flow" from a Euroamerican "center" to "all corners of the globe," suggesting unhindered movement into otherwise-empty landscapes and localities. Instead, she argues, the ways that supposed *universals* like prosperity, knowledge, and freedom move between localities is rife with points of traction, tension, and heterogeneous confluence—*friction*. With this concept of friction, Tsing crafts a possible solution to the problem of how to "do an ethnography of global connections" (2005, xi) in a time when anthropology can no longer imagine temporally and culturally bounded cultures. Historically, ethnography was characterized by an attention to small communities and to the local and specific, but Tsing takes this concern with the specific and moves it forward into a locale threaded with global connections. To do so, Tsing proposes "to focus on zones of awkward engagement, where words mean something different across a divide even as people agree to speak" (2005, xi).

Friction, in Tsing's usage, is a metaphor drawn from the science of physics: Although friction is colloquially understood as *difficulty* or resistance, in physics, friction is also a productive and necessary force in understanding how objects move in the world. Many things we take for granted, like tires gaining traction to propel a vehicle forward on a road, rely on the force of friction; when the vehicle hits a patch of ice, a low-friction surface, the wheels spin without traction. In this way, when we think of how the idea of accessible design circulates, we can consider that it may be propelled not only by alignment but also by mismatch.

Things that circulate:

bodies
minds
words
ideas
images
materials
toxicities
remedies
therapies
expertise
support/protection
stories
design styles
discursive formations
political logics

Thinking of friction as *useful* or generative also helps us to understand how to find meaning and create value in moments of mismatch and failure. The stories that circulate about disability access globally move in friction; the importance and meaning of one story may be very different to different stakeholders. Images and stories of inaccess circulate. Inaccess stories are often stories about friction: some thing or category has traveled in friction, and the roughness that is creating that friction is drawing attention, concentrating affect, and generating narrative.

Circulation is linked to productivity and value. The images that circulate in the example of discursive inaccess stories that opened this chapter are examples of making an inaccess story *valuable*. As Friedner (2015) has argued, technologies move in ways that produce disability and access industries as valuable to others, including nondisabled people and the nonperson collectors of capital known as corporations. The artist gained something of value—attention on social media—by mobilizing the value of images of accessible design in Russian popular culture. Because global friction in Tsing's usage is another way to talk about cultural hegemony in the context of global capitalism, this term, global access friction, is a useful way to get at the way that capitalist logics of exchange incentivize the movement of accessible design as both a discursive idea and a style of material infrastructure. Indeed, the contrast between the two types of inaccess stories I introduced suggests the layered complexity of designed objects and accessible design and the social relations it indexes.

Other Frictions and Russian Ablenationalism

In contrast to the concept of global friction in anthropology, the term *access friction* circulates in North American anglophone disability community discourse to describe situations that occur when people have opposing access needs: a blind person sharing space with two deaf people using sign language, for instance, as Jessica Watkin (2022) describes. The term operates as folk theory that describes both moments of disjuncture and that produces generative possibilities for mutual care and creative solutions to do things otherwise. By conceptualizing access friction as at once a problem rooted in mismatch *and* potentially (although not always) generative, disability community theorists imagine access as a process of intersubjective care that is constantly enacted and negotiated (Watkin 2022), rather than as a property of an object or artifact. Like global friction, access friction starts from mismatch and looks for unanticipated possibility.

Simultaneously, design studies scholars use the concept of design friction to describe "the ways in which tension, conflict, or disagreement" in the design process "allowed for [. . .] prototyping alternative possible futures and questions rather than problem solving for today's challenges" (Forlano and Mathew 2017, 20). In this usage, design refers to the iterative process of making, and friction refers to the way that members of design teams or stakeholders in consensus-building participatory design iterate new ideas by leaning into problems and disagreement as a generative way to develop novel designs (in the case of Unsworth et al., specifically, participatory design for public policy and urban technology). The design anthropologist Laura Forlano and Anijo Mathew (2014) argue that too often collaboration seeks consensus before moving forward. Instead, they suggest, prototyping without consensus allows problems and controversies to be part of the frame of the design brief. Following Chantal Mouffe (2003), Forlano and Mathew suggest that design prototypes need not solve a problem (as the concept of a design problem in design thinking suggests), but instead might raise questions, or serve to draw attention to unresolved dilemmas (2014, 17). Like the concept of access friction in disability arts circles, in this case, the concept of friction draws attention to liberatory opportunities exposed by mismatch.

In identifying global access friction, then, I am calling for attention to how accessible design travels and identifying the need to trace how the concept of accessible design moves in friction in different geographic and cultural contexts repositions. Thus, I examine accessible design not as a universal, but rather as a provincial vernacular design logic borne of a particular historical moment in North American and Western European political life. Another way to phrase this move is as a call to provincialize accessible design. This usage of *provincialize* (Chakrabarty 2000) refers to a scholarly methodology of subjecting the colonial metropoles mores, practices, and attitudes to the same scrutiny the colonizer uses to view the colonized. Instead of a predestined universal, metropolitan practices are cast as local, specific, and diminutive. This effort does not diminish its real impact on disabled people's lives, or the ingenuity, expertise, and radical political potential that disability rights and disability justice movements respectively have unleashed. Rather, it is a call to attend to the local specificity of disability access thinking, of political rhetoric, and of infrastructures of access.

Global access friction can also be understood in relation to the notions of ablenationalism and cripwashing. Following Jasbir Puar's concept of homonationalism as a conceptual framework that asks "why a nation's status as 'gay-friendly' has become desirable in the first place [and] how we are conditioned by and through" this conjecture (2013, 336), thinking with ablenationalism in turn means asking why a nation's status as disability-friendly, or, accessible, has become desirable in the first place. That is, following Puar, ablenationalism is the analytics of power. Mitchell and Snyder theorize ablenationalism in terms of state policies that treat disability "as an exception" in a manner that "valorizes norms of inclusion," especially in the context of neoliberalism's characteristic "celebration of a more flexible social sphere" that produces good feelings for the cultural normative by offering "evidence of an expanding tolerance" in a manner that fuses nationalist sentiment with evidence of disability inclusion (2015, 13). Where the United States imagines itself to be a "global leader" on disability rights, this expectation easily dovetails with widespread media attention in the North American press to Russian homophobic rhetoric and legal measures unfolding during the 2010s. Thus, an assumption of Russian failure to provide disability access and inclusion follows. Where Russia has persistently doubled down on homophobic policies and rhetoric, developing new ways to instrumentalize political homophobia, with devastating consequences for queer people in Russia (Healey 2018; Kondakov 2022), the very same Russian state has explicitly enacted its own policy of ablenationalism, celebrating disabled athletes and artists, and creating or proposing ostentatious highly visible elements of accessible design. This seeming discrepancy perhaps tells us more about the global hegemony of North American logics of minority rights in conceptualizing disability and LGBTQ politics globally than it does about the Russian state in the 2010s. The project of elaborating the specificity of Russian homonationalism and ablenationalism, however, offers an important frontier for scholarship and advocacy, to which this book offers a minor contribution. I argue that expressions of cripwashing—or perhaps access-washing—are an important valence of global access friction and access vernaculars in Russia, propelling accessible design into the Russian public sphere—even as actually disabled people continue to live in poverty on impossibly small pensions, and elements of accessible design form tiny islands of access in a sea of inaccessible infrastructure.[12]

In the evidence presented in this book, the Russian Federation's move to sign the UN CRPD and systematically enact federally funded programming designed to include disabled people in rehabilitation programs unfolds at the same time the Russian state was erecting Potemkin ramps in government and commercial spaces while leaving home spaces and educational spaces unrenovated. I argue that this represents an ablenationalist slight of hand, whereby the the Russian Federation deployed the symbolic meaning of accessible design to project an image of itself as a nation interested in inclusion and in the rights and well-being of its citizens, while failing to actually provide meaningful inclusion for all but the most assimilated, productive, and upstanding disabled citizens.

Accessible Design in Soviet and Post-Soviet Russia

A core argument of this book is that the Euroamerican concept of disability access moves in friction in the region of Russia where this fieldwork was conducted. Tracing how this friction gains traction requires attending to the specificity of historical concepts of the body and the politics of infrastructure in Russia. How do the historical specificity of Soviet political advocacy and complaints about social issues continue to affect the way that the needs of people with disabilities were conceptualized discursively? What vocabularies and vernacular logics of disability access and inclusion continue to influence post-Soviet disability access discourse? To interpret ethnographic evidence in relation to these questions, it is useful to situate the ethnographic and disability history of post-Soviet Russia.

The disability history of Russia is a growing academic area. At present, the existing studies have sought, first, to map in broad strokes the prerevolutionary, revolutionary, prewar, postwar, and late-Soviet periods; second, to address the experiences of particular interest groups based on materials in specific archives, including deaf people and war veterans (e.g., Edele 2008; Galmarini-Kabala 2016; Shaw 2017); and, third, to develop contemporary disability studies in/of Russia in the social sciences (e.g., Phillips 2011; Rasell and Iarskaia-Smirnova 2013; Borodina 2020, 2021, 2023). As this book goes to press, recent historical scholarship seeks to describe a distinctly Soviet socialist disability advocacy practice that has contributed to the constitution of a global disability advocacy movement in the twentieth century (Galmarini-Kabala 2024). One important thread of scholarship has considered representations of the body in Soviet culture (Krylova 2001; Kaganovsky 2008, 2024; Iarskaia-Smirnova and Romanov 2013; Kolarova and Winkler 2021). As an anthropologist, I am reliant on historians to produce secondary source studies of archival material, and my interpretations of these sources support and shape my ethnographic analysis. Sometimes this means working backward to imagine a historiography that does not yet exist. I have sought elsewhere to develop, first, a detailed discussion of the language used to talk about disability in Russia over time (Hartblay 2006); and, second, an account of how the moral concept of productivity has emerged (Hartblay 2014; see also Mladenov 2015, 2018).

While recent work on Soviet Blind and Deaf unions attend to disability advocacy (such as: Galmarini Kabala 2024; Shaw 2017), many scholars suggest that the Soviet Union largely suppressed or avoided politically legitimating widespread disability access discourse related to physical disability. However, scholars agree that injured World War II veterans enjoyed a special moral status that facilitated some public discussion of adaptive design and infrastructure. Additionally, changes to the Soviet legal definition of disability in the 1970s to include childhood disability and disability from birth (previously Soviet disability benefits only referred to adult capacity to work), and anecdotal stories, suggests that advocacy and organizing was taking place. In the 1970s, mobility access activism led by non-veteran disabled citizens emerged, and was suppressed by Soviet authorities as a dissident movement for human rights (Bernstein 2024; Dale 2013; Phillips 2011; Fefelov 1986). Most significant for the purposes of this book, it is necessary to differentiate Soviet disability history from the normative example (in anglophone disability studies) of Euroamerican history of disability access and adaptive design.

Design histories of disability activism in the twentieth-century United States identify individualism and private property as core assumptions underpinning disability access advocacy, these values are in direct contradiction to Soviet collectivism and communist ideals. Soviet disability imaginaries were distinct from their Euroamerican counterparts, as evidenced in representations of disability and public discourse. The logics of citizenship, care, and governance specific to the Soviet state led to both the stigmatizing and repression of the discursive position of disability in official culture (to the extent that a Soviet official once declared to an international audience that there "are no disabled peole in the USSR"! (Phillips 2011)), and therefore to creative activist strategies with disability advocacy vocabularies. At the same time, Soviet design, architecture, and rehabilitation projects created an unusual context in which people with physical and mobility impairments and their family members advocated for themselves. These strategies included campaigns for accessible sports (Iarskaia-Smirnova 2001) and first-floor apartments or accessible cars or working prosthetics for war veterans (Edele 2008; Tchueva 2008; Bernstein 2013, 2015). These strategies can be held in contrast to the deaf-organizing strategies described by Claire Shaw (2017). The categories of *disability access* and *barrier-free environments* emerged from Euroamerican twentieth-century activism. Subsequently, these categories were taken up, and developed transnationally, most explicitly in the context of global disability rights as defined by the UN CRPD and related agencies (e.g. United Nations Enable 2004). In this way, local, specific categories developed by social movements in Berkeley, California, and in the United Kingdom, as well as in North Europe, came to stand as universal categories.

In considering disability and access cross-culturally, a persistent source of friction arises from the overlaps and incommensurability between the translation of terms. The Russian word *invalidnost'* provides a cogent dictionary translation of the word *disability*, and indeed, both terms describe a category of the welfare state based on medical-psychiatric expert assessment and compensated through redistribution. The social meanings that adhere to the category, however, are not stable across these cultural locations. This is also true for the word *dostupnost'*, or access, which like the English term has long been used in a general sense and only recently has been applied to questions of disability and design.

To look for accessible design in the Soviet Union is an anachronism, in that the term and concept did not exist in Russian until the 1990s. Yet, by defining the concept of accessible design as a moral claim about the kind of collective relations that *should* be possible in relation to disability, we can observe how this moral claim circulated in Soviet culture, ideology, and material design. Even when the concept of accessible design per se did not exist, we can examine how ideologies of design and moral claims about disability and sociopolitical inclusion appear or are occluded.

Attitudes about design *in general* in contemporary Russia bear some traces of Soviet design ideology. The Soviet Union came into being as a political project of ontological design, seeking to imagine and create a better world, one defined by a vision of socialist utopia that required remaking relations between people, objects, and labor. This led to novel forms of design thinking—for example, the constructivist movement of the 1920s adapted avant-garde philosophy art practice as a way to think about how reshaping the material world by building new structures and exposing the working class to art and culture might reshape the political consciousness of individual workers and thereby the working masses. This movement led to a new awareness of the built environment as part of political life and was aligned with theoretical ideas at the time that imagined society as an organism in homeostasis with its environment (as in Friedrich Engels's extension of biological metaphors to society). This notion of the body-as-formed-through-labor emerged along with the political ideology that glorified labor (e.g., awarding medals of honor to shock workers who exceeded quotas) and a cultural politics that imagined the body as developing and growing as one with the structures their labor constructed (as in a well-known early Soviet poem about a man whose spirit soars and body grows metonymically with the iron beams he forges; cited in von Geldern 1995; see also Golubev 2020). In this way, to restructure the world was to remake the human form of the laborer. This dialectical materialist consideration of the role of the sociomaterial environment in shaping malleable human subjectivities was especially present in Lev Vygotsky's theories of child development (now familiar in Western education and psychology). Perhaps less well-known in the anglophone world was the influence of his theories on the founding of a Soviet discipline known as *defectology*, which sought to address childhood disability through social and material modalities (Knox and Kozulin 1989). This logic led to a popular Soviet political stance that disability is the result of poor social conditions (and thereby the assertion that there could be no disabled people in the Soviet Union). Stalinist repression beginning in the 1930s suppressed avant-garde art and architecture in favor of a style known as Soviet realism that sought to represent the purported glory of what the Soviet Union might bring about, immortalized in the form of statues of large, strong, robust citizens. Scholars have noted how the Soviet realist–idealized human form produced a representation of near superhuman citizens and erased the many injured, ill, and disabled members of the Soviet population (Iarskaia-Smirnova and Romanov 2013; Kaganovsky 2008). Design ideology in the Soviet Union continued to shift following the end of World War II, when war veterans and the aftermath of war brought debility and impairment into the public eye and popular culture (Dunham 1989; Edele 2008; Phillips 2011). Veteran movements and state projects created new opportunities, such as modern apartments with indoor plumbing and centralized heating, and mobility vehicles Soviet similar to to the small cars distributed to veterans in the United Kingdom and Europe. Unlike Western private enterprise, however, the planning and design for these innovations came from centrally planned social projects. The 1950s and 1960s brought a focus on domestic objects and a new consideration for the convenience of daily life to Soviet design practice. Late-Soviet experiences of scarcity, lack of available choices, and shoddy quality in consumer products undermined citizen trust in centrally planned design and manufacturing.

Anticommunist Western messaging about the Soviet Union imagine the political "ideology" of the USSR as a kind of totalizing, top-down authoritative manner of forcing citizens to think in a particular way; however, the concept of ideology had a different meaning in Soviet Russia, and historians have long argued for attention to the creative ways that Soviet citizens claimed agency and worked within the discursive limits of the Soviet state. The revolutionary socialists who launched the Soviet political experiment thought of ideology in a philosophical sense—that is, in terms of the Marxist understanding of the way that individual political consciousness is formed, in which ideology is dialectically informed by human action in the material world. This historical grounding in Marxist historical materialism informed three generations of social thought in the Soviet Union. The anthropologist Anna Kruglova (2017) argues that the lasting effect of Marxist ways of thinking and describing social phenomenon—not only during the Soviet era but also after—can be understood as *everyday Marxism*, a kind of casual and colloquial manner in which the secular cosmology of Marxist-Leninist thought remains salient in contemporary Russian conversations and casual discourse. By this, Kruglova does not mean to imply that contemporary Russians are intentionally invoking Marxist frameworks, but rather, that sedimented layers of history that have shaped political subjectivity and approaches to the problems of daily life. In this way, traces of Marxist ideology remain important for understanding how contemporary Russians make sense of the world, and the generational logics of politics and change.

Situating Petrozavodsk and the Republic of Karelia

The regional specificity and ethnolinguistic diversity of the Russia Federation are striking; to write about one region ethnographically requires orienting details to situate the project and to qualify the scope of claims. My fieldwork for this project took place largely in the region of Karelia in Northwest Russia, including the regional capital city of Petrozavodsk, as well as other small cities, towns, and villages nearby. A six-hour train ride from the major city of Saint Petersburg, and a long day's travel by car or minibus from Helsinki, Finland, Petrozavodsk is generally understood in Russia as an unremarkable regional capital city, nestled on the shore of Lake Onega among fir and birch forests, surrounded by Karelia's sweeping wilderness. My trajectory to this region began thanks to a high school exchange program; I later opted to locate research on disability advocacy in Petrozavodsk following the success of a parent advocacy group's civil legal suit that sought to allow disabled children to attend neighborhood schools (Hartblay 2012).

The territory now known as Russian Karelia shares its name with the region of Finland that it borders. Indeed, the border was redrawn numerous times in the twentieth century alone. Like many border territories, the ethnolinguistic history of the region is contested: The Karelian language is understood by Finns to be an Eastern dialect of Finnish, whereas Russian scholarship and documents refer to Karelian people and language as distinct. I never met anyone in Petrozavodsk who spoke Karelian in daily life, although several friends and acquaintances recalled hearing it as children from grandparents in rural regions. Some children studied Finnish or Karelian language in school; local filmmakers, ethnographers, and museums have worked to document the region's heritage; and local dance troupes perform Karelian folk dance in traditional costumes with traditional instruments (as defined by Soviet ethnography; see also Kurki 2013). I found that most of the urban residents of Petrozavodsk I met had been Soviet citizens from other regions whose parents or grandparents relocated to Karelia for work, and I traced their ancestry to a variety of Slavic and other Soviet ethnic origins, including Ukrainian, Polish, Russian, Jewish, and Tartar (Melnikova 2009 also documents this state of affairs). Russian was uncontested as the primary language of daily life. Minority ethnic groups included Caucasian and Central Asian migrant workers (typically employed informally in open-air markets, construction, and other trades, and regional indigenous minority groups, such as Veps, Karelians, and others (Davidov 2017).

The region's distinctive politics and character are partially shaped by its status as a border territory. During the 2010s, residents of Russian Karelia had special privileges in securing visas to visit Finland, which meant they had access to the European Union for travel and access to Finland's consumer goods (I heard stories of people taking weekend trips or visiting black-market shops in Petrozavodsk to buy everything from furniture to baby formula to dairy products). Underpinning these privileges was a darker history of contested political control and occupation, including harrowing whispered stories of Soviet labor camps to open the Karelian forest for lumber and build the Murmansk railway, and prisoner-of-war camps when the territory changed hands between Finns and Soviets during the Great Patriotic War (Gatrell 2005; Trotter 1991). Rumors persisted in the early 2000s that Karelia might seek independence from Russia, but the movement never gained traction and remained a fringe idea. During the 2010s, the local political scene was a site of struggle and contestation, as Putin's United Russia Party sought to consolidate political control; a mayor elected in 2013 affiliated with the liberal Yabloko party was under intense pressure, and she was ultimately recalled in 2015 (Turchenko 2017).

As a small regional capital, Petrozavodsk was at once a destination for those in surrounding rural regions and regarded as a sleepy backwater by those in Moscow and Saint Petersburg. The city attracted cultural practitioners to run the well-regarded theaters and musical conservatory, while the most ambitious young people in other fields tended to move to Saint Petersburg or Moscow, or make their way abroad. Many residents of the city had grown up there, whereas others moved from surrounding rural areas to attend university. Several new shopping centers opened in the 2010s, bestowing a sense that global commerce was at long last arriving in Petrozavodsk, twenty years after the end of the Soviet Union. The city's first McDonald's franchise branch opened in a central mall to much gossip and fanfare during my fieldwork; previously, the nearest option to get a Big Mac was in St. Petersburg, and I had a group of friends who made a tongue-in-cheek habit of bringing one another a snack from the global chain upon return from a trip to the big city.

Methods, Positionality, Scope

On a Wednesday in October 2012, I walked three-fourths of a mile down the hill toward the lake, along the busy city blocks, to a repurposed kindergarten where an art therapy group met. The group gathered in the room were my age, in their late twenties and early thirties. Three of those present were the professionals—the social workers and psychologists—who facilitated the program. The other eight attendees were people with disabilities and were unemployed. The brightly colored van had made its journey through the city, picking up those who used wheelchairs; a few others came by city bus. Inside the meeting room, Vakas was waiting for someone to take his coat off, while one of the social workers helped Alina, seated in her wheelchair, to remove her hat, gloves, and coat. Sergei had already hung up his coat and was moving around the table to a seat he wanted to sit in, using the backs of chairs to partially support himself as he moved.

"Vakas," I asked, when he shuffled over to me and gestured that I should give him a hand, "You can't do it yourself?"

"Of course he can't!" tut-tutted the psychologist, upset that I would present him with such a question, "his brain injury has left him with limited mobility!"

Vakas and I smiled at each other. We were both at the mercy of medical facts and professional expertise—he as an *invalid* (i.e., a person with a disability); me as a foreigner and outsider.

This scene unfolded as part of an art therapy project for unemployed adults with disabilities, which I was lucky to be invited to, and through which I met several people who became key interlocutors. I was also joining this group partway through their session for weekly arts activities, which ranged from drawing to performing a recital of Pushkin poetry. As a visiting ethnographer,

I was welcomed into the fold by the group members for the novelty factor—our American!

A core contingent of the art therapy group—Alina, Vakas, and Sergei—have been the target of social programming for *invalidy* in Petrozavodsk since childhood. I came to know these interlocutors through the art therapy group, and their stories, along with those of other mobility disability activists in the city, became central to my research. Through interviews and participant observation, I heard their inaccess stories and took part in their experiences navigating access from family apartments to activities around the city.

The central method of my study was rooted in my understanding of disability anthropology as at once sociocultural anthropology and critical disability studies. I have drawn specifically on crip theory as an analytic that asks how norms work and come into being as a nexus of power and how it situates ableism in relation to compulsory ablebodieness and compulsory sexuality (McRuer 2006; Kafer 2003). As such, the project attends to disability experience and to the norms, standards, and emergent hegemonic conjectures that influence disability experience.

Throughout this work, I also exercised a practice of thinking with metonymy. While I was in the field in 2012 and beginning to think about accessible design in relation to anthropological conversations about infrastructure vis-a-vis the point of view of the interlocutors I was interviewing, I came across the artwork of Jill Magid. In the description of her performance work *System Azure* (in which she persuaded the Amsterdam police department to hire her to bedazzle security cameras), Magid (2002) writes:

> While an old Chinese saying claims "When the wise man points to the moon the idiot looks at the finger,", System Azure upholds the reverse: The wise consider the finger. Why? Looking at the finger is more interesting. The finger is reality. In considering the finger you consider how moon is being represented. Who is pointing this finger? Toward what is my attention being directed and why should I look there? What does this finger want me to see? With these questions in mind one can choose to see as the finger sees, to look at the moon in another way, or to look at something else entirely.

Thinking with this unusual provocation (by which she described her artwork's intent to draw public attention to otherwise unassuming surveillance technology), I moved through my fieldwork and subsequent analysis with the intention to look both at the object indicated and the hand doing the indicating. Magid's mobilization of an aphorism transforms the meaning, inviting the audience for her work to be both the "wise man" and the "idiot" at once, considering how attention is directed, and how meaning is made. Sociocultural anthropology's enduring concern with meaning-making holds that as actors in social worlds, we are all always already engaged in the work of meaning-making, and, moreover, that meanings are multiple and manifold. Symbols refer to multiple concepts at the same time, across incommensurable scales. In the case of metonymy, semiotic meaning and material meaning are culturally linked. Like a finger pointing at the moon, both the act of pointing and the indicated object become meaningful through a single gesture. In this way, following the links between material and semiotic meanings has served as a persistent mode of inquiry and analysis throughout this project.

This book draws on several years and multiple periods of ethnographic research. Ethnographic fieldwork in Northwest Russia conducted in the summer of 2010, ten months of work during 2012 and 2013, and follow-up work in 2014 and 2016 formed the backbone of this project. I also conducted tangentially related research in Siberia 2005 and 2011. Throughout these fieldwork trips, and several additional academic visits, I benefited from the opportunity to connect with colleagues in Moscow and Saint Petersburg, presenting and receiving feedback on preliminary research. Research included participating in the daily life of the city, taking part in activities and community groups related and unrelated to the research questions, and conducting semistructured and unstructured, open-ended interviews with consenting research participants. I took copious fieldnotes and later analyzed those notes along with transcripts of the digital audio recordings of interviews. My mode of analyzing interview transcripts was influenced by my training in the Spradley (1979) method of analyzing ethnographic interviews, rooted in the symbolic interactionist tradition, which seeks to understand how subcultures create and recreate shared meaning in historically and culturally specific ways. This requires what I think of as *category work*: breaking down and reassembling attributes and belonging to conceptual categories, so that the ontological and cultural taxonomies of daily life in subcultural worlds can be explicated and held in comparison to dominant culture or a reader's normative categories.[13] Although my analysis of interviews and fieldnotes is rooted in this exploration of situated knowledge, those perceptions are in turn considered in relation to global power structures, and to broader social discourses. I collected objects, paper ephemera, news media articles, headlines, shows, popular culture, and memes related to disability access, and I analyzed this archive as part of my ethnographic record.

Methodologically speaking, I have situated this book as disability anthropology and critical disability studies in the queer feminist crip tradition. The book is also in conversation with ethnography of postsocialist Russia, particularly considerations of design and infrastructure, on the one hand, and medical anthropology, on the other. The shape of the argument and the arrangement of evidence is structured to offer a relevant intervention in these scholarly conversations at the specific moment of the book's writing.

The scope of the study in an ethnographic project is invariably linked to research interlocutor recruitment. The ethnographic research for this book entailed leveraging my preexisting acquaintanceships and scholarly contacts to build early foundational relationships with disability advocates, nongovernmental (NGO) workers, and others with professional or personal ties to disability issues in Northwest Russia. Not all of those who supported the project are represented in the book (some specifically requested not to be represented). Some of those represented are referred to using pseudonyms; others preferred to be referred to using their real first name; a few are identified using their full name given their role as public figures. Out of respect for the privacy of those who wished to obfuscate their identity, I have not differentiated herein which names are pseudonyms and which are not. Because of the relatively small size of disability communities in the region, it is likely that some of the stories would be recognizable to others in overlapping circles. That said, there is a degree of anonymity in this approach: there are relatively few common first names in Russian, some of the experiences relayed herein could have happened to any number of people, and given that some names are pseudonyms, readers from the region may be unsure if they know the person whose experience a particular passage describes.

The scope of this project is based in my political convictions about the importance of the category of disability as an object of study in its own right, but this also reveals important limitations. I simply do not know, for example, all people in the disability community in Petrozavodsk and the Karelian Republic, and those people may or may not find affinity in the stories in this book. Moreover, this book describes the situation in a particular region of Russia during a particular time period; the situation there was markedly different from the situation in Moscow and Saint Petersburg or in other Russian regions at the same time. I often relate my interlocutors experiences to national discourses, and use words like "Russophone" or "in Russian" throughout this text, but I do not intend to suggest that all of Russia is uniform or that my few interlocutors can be understood as representative of the broad diversity of Russian experience; that is decidedly not the case. My research is based largely on conversations with young adults with disabilities who grew up in the 1990s, meaning that they have memories of the Soviet Union but came of age in post-Soviet Russia. Many of these young adults were identified as disabled from birth, and others became disabled after emergent impairments in childhood or adulthood. Although *disability* is a diverse and capacious category, I intentionally did not bracket the subjects of the study to a particular medical diagnosis, instead seeking to uncover a socially meaningful local category. Over the course of the research, the category of mobility-and-speech impairments emerged as the group that I came to have the most contact with. Based on local educational and social services groupings, this group was distinguished from blind, deaf, and mentally disabled people, each of which received specialized educational and social services. Diverse diagnostic categories fell under the category of mobility-and-speech impairments, including paralysis, traumatic brain injury, cerebral palsy, conditions like muscular dystrophy, and dwarfism. This research was also mostly conducted in cities, and therefore it does not substantively engage with the experiences of disabled people in villages.

My own positionality also influenced the shape and scope of the project in both knowable and unknowable ways. As an American who learned Russian in high school, university, and a career prior to joining the academy, I conducted the majority of the interviews and participant observation in Russian. Although colleagues and professionals in Moscow and Saint Petersburg sometimes opted for English, very few people in Karelia did so. I had some acquaintances and friends with strong English skills, but in most cases, my Russian was better (if accented and imperfect) and was therefore our primary language of exchange.[14] Throughout the course of this study, I identified personally as nondisabled. Having been singled out for testing as a child (I was identified by my mother and teachers as not typically developing), even though I never received a diagnosis, I was deeply affected by this early experience of neurodiversity-as-otherness. As a result, I came to identify with my disabled peers (mainstreamed in Massachusetts public school in the 1990s), and I later became an ally and advocate in high school, before discovering disability studies as an undergraduate, and with it a vocabulary to describe the experiences of disability community.

Overview of the Chapters

In the next chapter, I narrate my arrival in the field and introduce the reader to a group of young adults with disabilities who, in 2012, were embroiled in global access friction in terms of the specific ways that disability access discourse moved into their city in their post-Soviet childhood. I argue that contemporary disability politics in the region are deeply tied to the ways that post-Soviet geopolitics transformed social life in northwestern Russia through the first decade of the twenty-first century. Interspersing ethnographic vignettes and analysis of NGO literature, I observe that Putin's return to the presidency in 2008 and the

Russian foreign agent law in 2012 at the outset of fieldwork for this book set the stage for a shifting landscape of disability services as the NGO era waned and as social services were reconsolidated under hierarchically controlled state programs. At the same time, I trace the way that the now widely critiqued 1990s Euroamerican disability rights concept of independence entered the third sector as a term and goal of disability programs in post-Soviet civil society, which was at odds with Soviet-era politics of collectivity (as well as with subsequent feminist and crip-of-color politics of interdependence).

In chapter 3, I return to the question of friction and extend the metaphor in a different direction—thinking about the physics of ramps as a tool for access in public space. Drawing on examples from Petrozavodsk and the Russian internet, I observe that in spite of the obvious intention, the presence of an accessibility ramp does not always produce access. In this way, the ramp's form and function are in friction, and the concept of access circulates as a desirable commodity, even where ableist social norms characterize the presence of actually disabled people as undesirable. Attending to the ethnographic present (the core fieldwork period of 2012–2014), interlocutors with mobility and speech impairments narrate experiences of (in)access in the infrastructure of the urban built environment. Tsing's (2005) concept of global friction helps explain instances of inaccessible accessibility infrastructure and the uneven implementation of wheelchair ramps as an infrastructure of access.

Chapter 4 continues the broader consideration of inaccess stories centered on disability expertise by attending to interlocutors' stories about domestic spaces. Ethnographic analysis of the inaccess stories that interlocutors tell about the places where they live demonstrates that the material afterlife of Soviet infrastructure continues to affect the specificity of lived experience of mobility disability in Petrozavodsk. My interlocutors point out mismatches between legal codes that supposedly support access and the actual needs of disabled people and demonstrate a distrust of legally codified accessibility mandates in favor of interdependence and kinship networks. The maintenance and communal use of aging structures thus emerges as a central concern for disabled people who understand their homes as islands of access in a sea of inaccessible infrastructure.

Chapter 5 turns to the way that inaccess stories circulate beyond disability communities as political claims about failures of governance. Tracing the history of Russophone lexicons of mobility and access in public space, I argue that the vocabularies of ease, comfort, peace, and good governance that have long been part of how Russian speakers describe good passage on roadways are also used as implicit synonyms for globally derived vocabularies of disability access by disabled interlocutors.

In the final chapter, I revisit the concepts introduced throughout this book to describe the way that access vernaculars move in global friction. I consider how interlocutors described what the future might have in store for them to reflect on what a normal life and normal future might entail when imagined from the subject position of a disabled Russian body. I close by considering how (in)access stories are a speech genre that build community by establishing a shared recognition of ableism, thus offering a sort of universal crip concept that hinges on historically and culturally rooted claims about what is required to live a normal life.

Rooting the Story

Sometimes, walking to the subway, or lying awake at night in my bed in Toronto, I find myself back inside the stories of my interlocutors. After many years of living in the interstices of these stories, rereading and translating interview transcripts, or flipping through social media, I will be confronted with a photo from my fieldwork. A curious side effect of the slow pace of ethnographic research is that we as ethnographers grow into and along with the stories we tell. The inaccess stories of Russia in the 2010s live in me, and they make up my worldview as much as any other poignant social experiences. To determine where this story starts requires peeling away layers of sediment, making the stories new again, and setting them down in their historical context. And so, the next chapter begins from the question of what it means to be a member of the first Soviet generation, tossing us back into the moment of fieldwork in 2012. To root our story in the northwestern corner of Russia at a particular historical moment, I rewind to the 1990s to sketch the scene. In doing so, I trace the ways that the politics of disability may be at once part of the structure of daily life and subject to the caprices of geopolitics.

"I CAN DO IT MYSELF"

The Politics of Disability Politics, 1990–2008

> By virtue of their differences from capitalism all other forms of
> economy fail to conform to true economic specifications. In a
> way that is entirely familiar but nevertheless theoretically quite
> intractable, difference is rendered as "absence" or lack rather than
> as autonomous being.
>
> —J. K. Gibson-Graham (2006, 35)

Aina (pronounced *EYE-nah*) was one of the first people I met who was a disabled person my own age in Petrozavodsk. A fast-talking, whip-smart, quirky woman with a limp, Aina drove a customized Soviet-era car with hand-lever controls. She drove me home one afternoon in 2010 during a preliminary research trip. I was curious about the car's accessible design, but she quickly obviated my inquiries, saying that a mechanic had built it for her, and moved on to more interesting topics. She wanted to know more about my project and to tell me more about her journalism projects. Aina's dark hair was cut close, and her eyes behind her wire-rim glasses had the sharp quality of someone who moves quickly to avoid a nagging pain or to avoid discussing a difficult subject. She had a scar on her scalp under her dark hair. With the dusty summer wind blowing through the windows, Aina spoke quickly, and I tried to watch her and keep up with the conversation, while also looking where we were going to avoid getting car sick on an unfamiliar route rutted with potholes and curving roads. We were on our way back to Drevlyanka, the neighborhood where she lived and where I was staying with a friend that summer, following my first visit to the Weekend School. Although it was called a school, the Weekend School was more like a nonprofit support group for families of kids with disabilities, holding open-house hours and various activities each weekend in a friendly two-room space filled with toys, instruments, games, and a long table with folding chairs that could be put away to make space for children in wheelchairs to pull up.

Downshifting her old vehicle as we traversed a roundabout, Aina explained that the Weekend School started in the 1990s as a nongovernmental organization (NGO) for families of kids with disabilities and was still operating. Aina had spent several years of her teenage life going each Saturday to the ground-floor suite of four rooms near the city hospital. It was a simple concept—families would gather, mostly just to have a place to go with disabled children, given that most spaces in the city were unwelcoming and inaccessible. As an adult in 2010 Aina was now volunteering there. The families at Weekend School had kids of all ages, with all kinds of impairments. Charity organizations from Finland or Switzerland donated toys, books, and musical instruments. They had sing-alongs and celebrated birthdays and holidays. Some occupational therapists from abroad visited and created a sensory room for kids who had autism or significant mobility impairments.

In this chapter, I consider how access vernaculars changed with the landscape of disability services in the post-Soviet transition years of the 1990s and early 2000s. In these years, the lexicons of disability and disability access not only changed but also were deeply influenced by broader geopolitical events as the political stakes of disability inclusion shifted. Through this story of the Weekend School, I trace the changing landscape of disability services from the end of the Soviet era to the early 2010s, in the context of NGO literature from other disability third-sector and government projects and shifting state policy. Then, I consider how the inaccess stories and personal narratives that my interlocutors shared were inflected by the political changes in these years.

In thinking through how geopolitics influence the vernacular rhetorics of disability in my interlocutors' stories, I am also interested in how these disabled young adults coming of age in the post-Soviet era understand and claim disability politics. I use the phrase *disability politics* to describe the recognition that disability is a political position in relation to structures of power. This follows feminist crip scholarship; for instance, Sami Schalk, in conversation with Alison Kafer, defines the term as "engagement with disability as a social and political rather than individual and medical concern [. . .] not limited to policy or law" (Schalk 2022, 11; citing Kafer 2013, 153). Specifically, in this chapter, I sketch the way in which the specific rhetorical moves available to interlocutors claiming disability politics in Petrozavodsk shifted as broader geopolitical currents made available and then made dangerous discourses of civil rights and independence. Therefore, with the chapter title, the politics of disability politics, I point to the ways that orientations to disability politics are always already multiple, changing, and situated in historical context: There is no normative disability politics.

In 2012, when I returned to conduct longer fieldwork, two years after first meeting Aina, I was surprised to find that the Weekend School was closing.

Its closure reflected broader trends taking place in Petrozavodsk and around Russia at the time. Small NGOs were closing or growing dormant. NGOs had been so active in the region in the 1990s and early 200s that NGO-ization, the rise of the third-sector economy and professionalization in the 1990s and early 2000s, became a major theme in ethnography of postsocialism, and came to define disability services in Russia, as in other global regions (Katsui and Mesiäislehto 2022; Meyers 2016; Fröhlich 2012; Kulmala 2010; Hemment 2004, 2007). When the Russian Federation passed the so-called foreign agent law at the end of the first decade of the new millennium, however, foreign nonprofits and humanitarian organizations were prohibited from operating within Russia, and local nonprofits accepting grants from foreign organizations risked raids or closures if their activities attracted the attention of authorities. At the same time, city, regional, and other state-run disability social service programs had become increasingly stable and received significant investments from the federal government. This had the effect of shifting the disability services industry from family- and community-run nonprofits to professionalized social work agencies around the city.

Disability services, and therefore, the lexicons and conceptual categories of disability, inclusion, and access, changed rapidly over the course of the 1990s and early 2000s in Petrozavodsk. These rapid changes unfolded over the course of the coming-of-age years of the first post-Soviet generation, as my interlocutors gained a sense of themselves as social actors in the world. An emic—or insider—view of disability experience in Petrozavodsk therefore suggests a unique periodization of recent history. From the point of view of Aina and her cohort, however, the broader disability NGO landscape of Petrozavodsk featured three general periods. From the early to mid-1990s, disability services were characterized by localized, informal stop-gap organizing. Then, beginning in the mid-1990s through about 2008 or 2012, a growing professionalization of NGOs, bolstered by practical and financial support from international actors, sought to build civil society. Finally, the 2010s brought an increasing reconsolidation of state oversight of social service, a decrease of international funding with implementation of the foreign agent law, and the rise of therapeutic services instead of civil society programs. This chapter explores the era between the end of the Soviet Union and Putin's reconsolidation in the early 2010s.

Another interlocutor, Sergei, who was around the same age of Aina, reflected on the rapid pace of change he had experienced growing up with *DTsP* (*detskii tserebral'nyi paralich*, cerebral palsy) in Petrozavodsk. For him, the effect of these changes amounted to a sense of continuously shifting horizons and paradigms. As a recipient of and participant in services and programs for people with disabilities, this feeling of constant newness and change meant that everything felt like a giant social experiment with no one at the helm. In one interview, Sergei told me, "I feel like my whole life they've been doing experiments on me—I am always surviving experiments!" Chuckling, he added for emphasis the phrase *opytnyi krolik*, literally, "experiment rabbit"—the Russian for *lab rat* or *guinea pig*. Sergei did not mean that he had been abused like a lab rat, but rather, that for each stage of his life, people with disabilities like his were "the first group" to try some new thing. They were the experimental subjects on which the new social order was tested, and then altered again.

Many accounts of the post-Soviet transition draw out the tension between teleology of "improving" Russian civil society through democratization programs—in this case, disability inclusion—and a critique of the simple directionality and colonizing logic of Euroamerican interventions in post-Soviet Russia that "brought" new professional models shaped by a democratic ethic to the apparently deficient post-Soviet citizens. Although I started this research assuming that I would find evidence that postsocialism was never deficient, but rather, *other*, I found that what actually happened in terms of disability services in Petrozavodsk was more nuanced than an either/or story. Putin's reconsolidation of power in the 2010s at the time seemed to some interlocutors in Petrozavodsk to suggest the arrival of a longed-for stability after years of uncertainty and upheaval.

The End of an Era: Closing the Weekend School

In the summer of 2012, I arrived in Petrozavodsk for a long stint of fieldwork. Settling into a rented apartment on a wide boulevard at the edge of the city's downtown center, I was excited to rekindle relationships that I had fostered during preliminary research two years before. You don't foster a person, you foster a relationship. I had a spreadsheet of research contacts—email addresses and phone numbers for NGO organizers, parent activists, and special education professionals in the city. Before arriving, I had reached out to just a few by email, so, on a sunny day during an unusually warm July, having just arrived in town, I crossed the busy intersection to the new shopping mall near my apartment to purchase a Russian SIM card for my iPhone (an upgrade from the minimalist cellphone I had carried on previous trips to the field). The mall's exterior was an architectural conversation starter: following a new trend to use brightly colored siding, it looked like a Tetris brick, with bold green and purple blocks protruding from the wall. Inside, the mall looked like any sleek commercial interior, and only the Cyrillic script and fellow shoppers placed the space as Russian. Yet, there were few foreigners in town, aside from the usual smattering of Finnish tourists en route to lake vacations or looking for a cheap drinking holiday; when the twenty-something employee dressed in a yellow and black uniform shirt at the cellphone service provider store requested my documents to register a new plan, he was amiably surprised when I offered a US passport and local address. Back in my apartment, SIM card activated and internet working, dust from the road still clinging to my legs in the heat, I sat down to call Felix. He was out of town at the *dacha* but told me to call back on Saturday.[1] Sure enough, when I called back Saturday afternoon, I was invited to visit Felix and his wife Masha in their apartment at the opposite end of the downtown. I walked over, picking up snacks along the way, before spending more than two hours catching up.

I hoped that connecting with Felix and Masha would be the gateway to the vibrant disability community that I remembered from two years prior, but I was in for a surprise. Sitting in Felix and Masha's apartment again, instead of inviting me to join in at the Weekend School the following week, they invited me to help them move. The Weekend School, they explained, was moving. Or, more accurately, it was being ejected from the space it had occupied and that I remembered from my last visit. Several years prior, the organization had been granted space on the first floor of an old wooden building near the former city hospital, which it had happily used for a number of years, with no expectation of the arrangement changing. Earlier in the summer, however, city administration representatives had informed Felix, in his capacity as official director of the nonprofit organization, that the group would need to vacate the premises of the building. According to Felix, when they inquired as to the reason, they were informed that the building was a fire risk. Yet, Felix and Masha pointed out, raising their eyebrows meaningfully, many such buildings in the city continued to operate without questions. I asked if they meant to imply that they were being forced out on purpose, and if they had any chance of being relocated to a new space. They shrugged, pessimistically.

Later that week, I arrived at the Weekend School with my colleague, a historian visiting from Moscow and curious for a taste of life in Petrozavodsk, in tow. It was hot and sunny, and we had taken two buses to reach the Weekend School, but once we arrived, Felix and the others explained that they had already cleared everything out that morning. They were leaving to bring the items to a space that an acquaintance had offered for temporary storage. We were ushered into the car of one of the project members and found ourselves being ferried back across town where we had just come from, wending our way through traffic and arriving in a dusty courtyard ringed with slight birch trees behind a building that I had never visited before.

Near a garage in the parking area, we found several of the other Weekend School contributors, including Aina, who I had met two years before, and greeted amiably. Others were obviously friends or acquainted with Aina, all in their twenties, of varying unknowable disability designations and ambulatory to varying degrees. Given the day's task at hand, the group was feeling surly, from spending the morning moving in the heat, and feeling the dejection of knowing that the center was closing with no current hope of reopening. They were on smoke break as we arrived, and while we were being introduced, I quickly forgot the names of those I was meeting as I did not have a chance to write them down. One of them, tossing dark-dyed bangs out of his eyes, gallantly offered us cigarettes, which we accepted with thanks but smoked with the half-hearted motions of nonsmokers attempting to assimilate. The group grumpily bantered over subjects too far along for me to follow for the remainder of their cigarettes. They inquired about my colleague and I clarified that we worked at the same university when someone incorrectly assumed that he must be a fiancé. Then, reluctantly turning back to the unsavory task at hand, the crew appraised me and my colleague favorably, as two sets of fresh arms and legs capable of carrying haphazardly packed items, ranging from wheelchairs to boxes of musical instruments, up several flights stairs.

Before long, my colleague and I found ourselves on the stairwell leg of the moving relay, passing each other as we went up and down, accepting items from a group in the parking lot and handing them off to another group in the upper hallway or the room allotted to Felix for storage. The building was a late-Soviet construction in a state of semidisrepair, such that some rooms were in use, neatly outfitted and furnished with recently purchased office equipment and Chinese-manufactured furniture, and others were utterly unused and evidently had been for some time, with chipped paint and dusty floors. Most notably, the elevator did not work. The belongings of the Weekend School that we ferried up the stairs were stacked in one of the empty rooms with some manner of organization determined by Felix who received the boxes. I wondered why the school couldn't simply operate out of one of these empty rooms, and Felix explained that they weren't renovated, and the building's elevator was broken so Weekend School participants wouldn't be able to reach the third floor. In addition, the space hadn't been officially allocated and was lent only temporarily for storage on a personal and unofficial basis. Once the boxes were stacked and piled to satisfaction, Felix reluctantly closed the door. Those of us standing by took one last sad look before he shut and locked it, and then walked off slowly to return the key

In the moment, I was taken with the bustling activity of the day, topped off with a hearty meal of fish and potatoes and several rounds of vodka shots in Felix's apartment. But as time went on, I realized that the afternoon's move amounted not just to a temporary setback, but, seemingly, a final shuttering of the Weekend School and the end of an era in Petrozavodsk disability services and the life of my interlocutors. The camaraderie of the moving day was a moment of togetherness that—in spite of hopes stored in that dusty room—never again materialized for the Weekend School cohort during my fieldwork. I visited the vocational center several times for other meetings or activities organized by other disability activists, but I never again saw the inside of that locked room with the Weekend School's materials.

A few weeks later, after my colleague left and I was alone again in my rented apartment, I found myself feeling a little stuck. I had been planning to base a significant portion of my fieldwork around the Weekend School, based largely on the warm introductions and initial interviews that I had recorded with Felix, Aina, and others two years before. I found myself spinning as the "thing" I had been planning to study was literally no longer there. The Weekend School's furniture, toys, books, and instruments were packed away in the dusty unused wing of the vocational center. The box containing the Weekend School's dishes—the same dishes that had appeared in a promotional pamphlet that Felix had given me about the Weekend School, featuring a child with cerebral palsy washing dishes with the assertion "I can do it myself"—was packed up, out of commission. That afternoon, I felt like I was hitting a dead end: Without the Weekend School, there was no *there* when it came to independent disability advocacy in the city.

I set up a meeting with Svetlana, a sociologist and advocate who had introduced me to findings from her qualitative research on adults with disabilities in the region, and described the lay of the land in terms of disability organizations. She had promised to introduce me to other NGO directors, and we had made tentative plans to find a way to work together. But, at our first meeting that summer, she revealed that she was planning to move abroad, having fallen in love with a foreigner she met online. Her two daughters were already grown and in university. Then, Katya, a woman whose daughter had cerebral palsy, who had been instrumental in an earlier movement to assert the right for disabled children to attend general education schools in the city, explained hurriedly in an email that she was out of town on summer vacation; and, she went on, although the lawsuit she had described with a spark of excitement and possibility in 2010 had been won, her daughter still went to the *internat*, or specialized school, and there was not really much going on in terms of activism.

Typing up my fieldnotes, I wondered how exactly I would research disability advocacy organizations, when, it seemed, the organizations I was planning to work with no longer existed. I did not understand why Felix and the others were not relaunching the Weekend School; why Katya had shifted her activism from trying to take on the state to trying to work within it; or why Svetlana was leaving. Sitting in my rented apartment, feeling quite alone, I realized that it would not be enough to understand what people were doing, I would need to understand the backstory to understand what they were *not* doing. And, I would need to understand what larger political forces were at work that had led disability advocates, service providers, and NGOs in the city to change so dramatically in just two years.

The Russian Foreign Agent Law

On July 2012, the same month that I arrived in the field, and just a few weeks before I found myself schlepping boxes up and down the stairs with Felix and the cohort from the Weekend School, a new bill was introduced to Russian legislature by Vladimir Putin's United Russia Party and became law. Commonly known as the "foreign agent law," Federal Law No. 121 of the Russian Federation discourages Russian organizations from receiving funding from international sources (Human Rights Watch 2013b). "The law," asserts one policy study, "is designed to regulate the activities of NGOs (described as non-commercial organizations in Russian) that receive money from foreign sources and engage in political activity" (Tysiachniouk, Tulaeva, and Henry 2018). Although I had not heard of the law as I was preparing for fieldwork, it soon became major international news, and by the time I returned home to the United States, it was a major point of conversation in considerations of US-Russia relations.

This unfolded in the context of Putin's return to the presidency through a loophole in Russian federal law that allowed him to serve no more than two consecutive terms, but did not prevent him from reelection after another president served. I had conceived of this project and conducted my preliminary fieldwork during the preceding years of the Medvedev presidency. This interim between Putin's first two terms and his return to the presidency were widely considered to be an era of liberalization characterized by more openness in civil society and a strong economy. Putin's return to the presidency saw a reconsolidation of federal power on several fronts, including Law No. 121.

The foreign agent law offered a means for the Russian government to control the ways in which foreign organizations—from US Agency for International Development (USAID) to the Open Society Foundation (founded by George Soros)—incentivized particular kinds of civil society activity through grant-making programs. The late 1990s and early 2000s created a vibrant atmosphere of NGO-ization in Russia, but within certain sectors of the Russian government, these programs were emblematic of foreign soft power extending into

Russia and thereby violating Russian sovereignty. The 2012 law followed previous efforts to increase regulation and transparency in the NGO sphere (Benevolenski and Toepler 2017). As scholars have shown, foreign-funded programs played a significant role in shaping social mores in Russia in the early 2000s (Hemment 2004, 2007; Kulmala 2011; Bernal and Grewal 2014). Yet, in the years following the passing of the foreign agent law, NGOs with diverse orientations—feminist scholarship, labor organizing, LGBTQ advocacy, and more—were either slowly starved of foreign funds or were subjected to invasive and intimidating investigation under the charge of acting as foreign agents. For instance, a 2013 Human Rights Watch report, researched during the same period as my fieldwork, describes the rise and enforcement of the law, and observes that the law had the most significant impact on those NGOs deemed advocacy organizations—that is, those groups that are intentionally seeking to shift public opinion (2013b, 2). From the perspective of the United Russia Party, the NGO-era was a symptom of the Russia Federation's comparatively weakened geopolitical standing during the late 1990s and early 2000s. Scholars have observed that post-Soviet bureaucratic power is entwined with therapeutic and psychiatric power, and the reconsolidation of state authority was in part expressed through a reconsolidation of medical and rehabilitation services (Raikhel 2016, 8–9). As Putin's political machine sought a future for Russia as a major world power, free of the need for foreign assistance, and unbeholden to the influence of cultural norms from abroad. Expelling foreign funders in the nongovernmental sector paved the way for Russia to reassert itself as a world power in its own right.

From the vantage point of North America, the foreign agent law came to be perceived as one part of a "government crackdown" with Putin's return to the presidency, and a harbinger of worsening diplomatic relations between Russia and the West. For instance, in September 2012, USAID, the arm of the US government providing aid abroad, received a cease-and-desist order from the Russia government, closed its Russia office, and terminated activities in the country. The BBC reported: "The expulsion follows a government crackdown on pro-democracy groups. 'The decision was taken mainly because the work of the agency's officials far from always responded to the stated goals of development and humanitarian cooperation. We are talking about attempts to influence political processes through its grants,' the foreign ministry said in a statement" (Rosenberg 2012).

The foreign agent law was not the only element marking a shift in governance domestically. Russia-watchers and Russian liberal media bemoaned draconian legal response to the 2011–2013 protests for fair elections (sparked by the announcement that Putin would run for another term), the prosecution of Pussy Riot following their performance in a Moscow church, and other anti-US legislation, including a ban on adoption of Russian children by foreigners. These actions seemed to signal to the Euroamerican international community a break from so-called "reset" era politics, and a new unwillingness to bend to human rights demands coming from foreign governments. Some might say that, in retrospect, these domestic actions were precursors to the subsequent invasion of Eastern Ukraine. In Russian official media and popular under-standing, they were a reasonable reaction to US imperialism and chronic over-stepping of North Atlantic Treaty Organization. Yet, from the point of view of my interlocutors, Putin's return to the presidency was characterized by a recon-solidation of federal power over regional and local government, and, over the implementation of social services and civic agendas.

Were my interlocutors really at risk of being branded foreign agents by con-tinuing to work with foreign funders? But what, then was "foreign" cultural logic at work in disability NGOs in Petrozavodsk in the late 1990s and early 2000s?[2] How did Euroamerican ideology influence the disability services and advocacy in the city during that time period? What did disability access and inclu-sion have to do with democratization and transition, and what traces did those paradigms leave on disability culture and lexicons of access in Petrozavodsk?

Democratization and Disability Services: Talking About Disability and Access in NGO-Speak

My first introduction to the story of disability services in Petrozavodsk in the 1990s were stories I heard from Felix, the director of the Weekend School. I was first introduced to Felix and his wife Masha in 2010, through mutual acquain-tances. To my delight, when I visited them in their apartment near the center of the city that summer, I was treated like an old friend, perhaps a cousin or niece, and welcomed into an apartment bursting at the seams with memorabilia, handicrafts, tchotchkes including doilies and tiny glass animals, decades of magazines and newspapers, and other family keepsakes stuffed into dark wooden bookshelves. Lush green houseplants wound their way around the shelves, over stand lamps, and on and onto or away from the windowsill of a set of large south-facing windows that opened over the busy boulevard four stories below. Like many of us when we start trying to tell the story of something that has been central to our lives for many years, Felix and Masha started some-where in the middle of the story and worked their way out, often talking over one another, redirecting from one element of the story to another, or jumping to a seemingly unrelated detail. I was delighted watching their interactions, and felt like I was witnessing a comedy routine about an aging couple.

As the contours of their story emerged, I began to understand that Felix and Masha had somewhat unexpectedly found themselves in the midst of an emergent effort from the late 1990s onward to shift the way that children with disabilities in Petrozavodsk understood themselves and their role in society. This effort was driven in large part by the emergence in the late 1990s of a democratization paradigm that sought to build civil society in Russia, which included the translation of current disability rights discourses from Western Europe and North America. I watched Felix's voluptuous gray mustache bounce merrily as he talked, and furiously took notes, sipping my tea with cherry jam and honey, and furtively checked that my digital audio recorder was still working.

Felix and Masha's concept of disability inclusion and rights was premised on the idea that disabled children and teenagers ought to have the chance to pursue their goals and to recognize themselves and be recognized by others as capable, independent citizens. As Felix put it, the programming the nonprofit he came to run was devised to show that teenagers with disabilities "are also people, just like everyone else" (*chto oni takie zhe liudi, kak i vse*). A slide show that he prepared as part of grant reporting to funders included one slide that showed a child with an apparent disability (perhaps *DTsP*, similar to the English cerebral palsy) washing dishes with the assertion "I can do it myself!" under the image. This paradigm of independence echoed with strains of 1990s disability advocacy in the West, drawn from the independent living movement and the rise of new accessibility legislation that centered on the civil rights of the individual disabled person, which was quite contrary to Soviet paradigms of collective political futures.

During that first visit, Felix and Masha insisted that I try local Karelian specialties, including a tea made from an herb that grows in the region and two types of *bal'zam*, a herbaceous alcoholic beverage typically taken as a digestif shot. In this merry hospitality, I recognized that the couple was well practiced in welcoming Americans, and they knew quite well which local foodstuffs would be novel and interesting to me. They also insisted that I call them by their first names, no patronymics, per US custom (an aberration in Russian, as polite address to elders outside of one's own family would have me call them by first name and patronymic). Indeed, as I read back over the transcripts from Felix and Masha, I was struck by just how in touch with foreigners the Petrozavodsk disability community I encountered had been throughout the 1990s and first decade of the 2000s. Another woman, about the same age as Felix and Masha who ran a different NGO in Petrozavodsk, focused on democratization and civil society with a few disability-inclusion projects. She told me that she had so much ongoing contact with her US collaborator that two years after their last project she still had a suitcase of his winter clothes in her closet, stored for him should they get another project funded so that he could return.

Felix explained in our first interview that he started out working as any other afterschool or enrichment teacher at the city's palace of culture (a Soviet-era institution that ran programs for children). In the 1990s, he found himself working with children with disabilities in that context rather by chance. A state-department-funded citizen exchange program brought US citizens from Vermont to Petrozavodsk, and one of the legacies of that exchange was a new computer for the Palace of Culture. As part of a civil society initiative, it was proposed to Felix to begin a magazine authored by the disabled kids, and for several years they ran a magazine, with the kids writing and producing. The magazine project taught disabled children technical skills—computer use—and was formulated according to the principle that self-expression was good for disabled children, and interest-group citizen journalism was good for Russian society. Eventually, however, that project petered out as the participants grew up and the group lost cohesion. At one point, they had ambitions to develop the project into a permanent fixture by creating a print shop that would both produce the magazine and be a collective where the kids could work to fund the magazine; they had an idea for a radio program. By the time I was conducting the research for this book, the only remaining legacy of the magazine was in the stories I heard from those who participated, and the influence that its production had on several of the participants, including Aina and Vakas (who continues to write poetry).

NGO Publications: An Archive of Disability and Democratization Projects

Felix and Masha weren't the only ones taking part in the shifting field of disability services: Disability NGOs continued to grow and build power in the region throughout the first decade of the 2000s. Evidence of the array of disability NGOs in Petrozavodsk in this time can be found in the vibrant and plentiful publications put out by these organizations—from pamphlets to seminar reports to project summaries. I always collected these NGO publications while I was in the field, returning home with a folder full of colorful leaflets, CD-ROMs, and booklets with covers bearing the names of organizations and their projects in Russian and the logos of national and international funders. Perusing and cataloging their contents later, I found names I recognized from my time in Petrozavodsk, along with many names of people I had never met, including local government officials, visitors from other parts of Russia, and people from other countries, especially Finland, Sweden, and the United States. Over time, I had amassed ten folders—a full file box—of NGO materials.

One booklet that I received during a meeting with the municipal NGO incubator memorialized a Republic-wide seminar hosted in 2009, organized by an NGO run by parent advocates. The seminar was funded by a grant from the Karelian Republc, with materials for the seminar developed through a project funded by a federal grant (while the organization was also partially supported by foreign grants). The participants included members of different government bodies, centers of social service, and public organizations as well as youth with disabilities, parents, and teachers. The seminar covered forms of support available to young people with developmental and emotional disorders, the types of support activities, an interdisciplinary approach to the system of support, and fundraising to support developmental activities. The organizations sought to influence how the regional government responded to the needs of people with disabilities and their families and to demonstrate the need for further services. The report asserts, "At the basis of life activity of young people between 18–35 lies the need for work (*trud*) as the means for financial wellness and self-realization. The studies of inclusive education conducted by [the hosting NGO] in 2007 among young *invalidy*, showed that almost all participants seek to achieve an independent life. To realize this goal, it is necessary to have a profession and a job as a means to independence" (Osobaia Sem'ia 2009, 8). Overall, the seminar stressed establishing and strengthening partnerships among various government institutions and organizations.

"In the end, all actions from government bodies, municipalities, and society have to lead to the main goal—return of people with disabilities to active life, destroying of a reformed understanding of people with disabilities as dependents (*izhdiventsy*), disposable people" (Osobaia Sem'ia 2009, 27). The booklet creates an extensive comparison between European Union (EU) countries and Russia, suggesting that the Russian state should become more like EU countries in furthering state-NGO partnerships to further the provision of social services supporting social inclusion.

A 2011–2012 pamphlet for the Weekend School, put out in association with partner NGOs that also supported parents of children with disabilities and a rehabilitation center, drew on the same phrasing that Felix had used in a presentation to foreign funders in 2010. It described the space as an "Inclusive Educational Center for Children" that "creates conditions for including children with limited health abilities in collective educational and cultural life." This formulation emphasized inclusion, significant in that the predominant model for special education supported by the state was either segregated "specialized" schools or at-home education. The pamphlet features the phrase "I Can Do Everything Myself" as a motto for the school. The center is described as bringing together youth leaders with disabilities, volunteer students, and "specialized social workers" for activities. The activities of the center are described as broadening the socialization of children with limited abilities and their families; mutual adaptation of society and family with children with limited abilities; social-pedagogic rehabilitation of children through creative and leisure activity; and development of creative abilities of children.

Pamphlets for other organizations from 2012 onward, however, took a rather different tone. Although they exhibited the same interchangeability of translated foreign terminology and existing Russophone phrasing, in contrast to the foreign-funded projects that mentioned and oriented themselves to shifting society, subsequent projects focused only on disabled children, people, and their families. Any mention of the need to alter society, or social attitudes of the broader population, had been abandoned in favor of services for disabled people, which were presented in terms of social rehabilitation using phrasing drawn from social work concepts that apply psychological discourse to social problems. These projects, funded by state actors—municipal and regional government agencies—were therefore distinct from the civic-minded projects from 2010 and earlier that emphasized the need to change *society*.

Although there was very little overt discussion of the foreign-agent law during my fieldwork, its effects reverberated through the landscape of how disability services professionals oriented their labor. As I conducted fieldwork, I interviewed numerous leaders of disability organizations throughout the fall of 2012 reckoning with this change and wondering if they would find themselves closing their doors, having existed for a decade on funds from USAID, United Nations Children's Fund (UNICEF), Soros, and other international donors.

In my archive of brochures and documents, as well as in my experience in the field, there was a sudden surge in 2012 of art therapy projects—or projects for people with disabilities described as *art-terapiia* (a new paradigm for the community). This initiative was supported, in part, by an earlier project to provide exchange between Finnish and Swedish NGOs and Petrozavodsk groups. Art therapy was described as an important tool for "overcoming social deprivation" experienced by disabled children and adults. Several articles based on nearly a decade of cooperation were published in a locally distributed brochure in 2011, and numerous projects appeared in this model in 2012, including one that I attended for a few sessions for mothers of children with disabilities. During this weekly project, the participants simply made small craft projects and chatted with other mothers. Most of these programs, however, were hosted by social service agencies, rather than NGOs.[3] Another such project, hosted by an organization otherwise not involved in disability advocacy, created a theater project. A pamphlet describing the project asserted that art therapy was needed for children with disabilities and their parents because they were physically isolated as a result of "disability barriers" (*bar'ery invalidnosti*). This mistranslation of the concept of barriers to social inclusion reattributes social barriers to the disabled people, thereby reinscribing disability as a property of disabled bodies. This mistranslation also demonstrates how local incentives to create art therapy projects become drivers of global access friction, with ideas about disability inclusion at once proliferating and taking on different inflections and meanings.

The shift is otherwise seen in the transformation of partnerships with Finnish donors from partnerships with independent NGOS to partnerships with state agencies. For instance, a 2012 document describing an event dubbed as a "Learning Lab" for accessibility in the built environment indicated that the lab was supported by several Karelian and Finnish Universities, as well as by Saint Petersburg Region state rehabilitation groups. The project was targeted at building long-term partnerships with Finnish organizations and companies to improve accessibility, comfort, and quality in the built environment through the use of "accessibility solutions and technologies." In this new iteration, these partnerships were not being formed between foreign funders and community nonprofits, but rather between foreign funders and state agencies. Although the project targeted accessibility in the built environment, it was not focused on building awareness and power among disabled self-advocates. Instead, it focused on building competency in a domain of international standards—accessibility in the built environment—among professionals and practitioners. In this way, professionalization of disability services was relocated to the domain of state agencies and accessibility was appropriated not as the purview of grassroots advocacy (e.g., Sarah Phillips's work in Ukraine in the early 2000s), but as the business of the state.

The New Generation: From NGO to Municipal Project

This shifting array of services for people with disabilities in the city since the 1990s was well understood by professionals working in disability services in Petrozavodsk in 2012. In an interview with Nastya, a psychologist and assistant director of a municipal early intervention center that I call *Elements*, she helped me to conceptualize these changes. Elements started out as an informal parent organization, then became an official nonprofit, and finally, was a municipal agency. Throughout this time, it provided a similar array of services for children with disabilities and their parents, with a consistent staff and leadership. Nastya described the shifts in attitudes toward disability in the city between the 1990s and 2012:

> Little by little the awareness of the parents and the understanding that they have to accept such a child, and not be ashamed, but usher him into life, to give him as much as possible whatever services are available, so that he would develop and could be integrated into society. The active (*aktivnye*) parents of such children got together and mounted a lawsuit so that their children should go to kindergarten, but while it was being deliberated, the children already outgrew the pre-school age, and they went to school. That is these parents appeared who decided to move forward and assert their rights. And now, today, when parents come to us, it seems to me that their mindset (*psikhologiia*), and their understanding of the situation has changed a little. And having worked here for so many years, I can see that there are already a lot more children who you can catch sight of in the sandbox or out for a walk in their strollers/wheelchairs. But before that kind of thing happened very rarely, that is they [the parents] really felt ashamed and were isolated. Now parents are really actively involved with these kind of children, they understand that a child needs to live and to be integrated. The paradigm has changed.

In this sense, for Nastya, this shift to a more municipal- and state-run array of services was a natural progression of building a new paradigm in the post-Soviet era and a legitimate process of professionalization of disability services as a sphere.

The shift to municipal services from more independent family-based nonprofit organizing also came up in interviews with parents of disabled children engaged in advocacy in the city. One important indicator and result of the changing NGO landscapes appeared in the form of a conflict between two generations of NGO parents. The generation who had children in the 1990s preferred independent NGOs that carry out projects based on limited-term grants from international organizations. These parents (that is, mothers) all fell into a group that social scientists have categorized as "professional NGO workers" (Hemment 2007). Younger parents, with children now in elementary school, had a different focus: Instead of relying on foreign grants, they shifted their attention to taking on as much power as possible in government organizations.

Lena was from the older generation of parents. Throughout the 1990s and early 2000, she was the director of a small, independent nonprofit serving families of children with disabilities in Petrozavodsk and around Karelia. Indeed, Lena was having difficulty finding funding following USAID's exit from the city. She felt frustrated that a younger generation of parents, rather than joining her group, had taken on other modes of advocacy, which, in a sense, was related to the competition for funds. Lena's son was now grown up, and her practice of receiving funding to carry out projects or support international actors had dwindled since 2008. A large project on inclusive education resulted in the publication of a professionally researched policy volume in 2007, yet in 2012, her organization was without a major project. They still maintained their two-room office space with desks, computers, and files, and continued to serve those families that had worked with them for years, but they had no grant funding for programming.

In contrast, younger parents, observing this shift, had begun to take a different strategy: to import models of inclusion from abroad and to fund their implementation through Russian state agencies. Considering the trajectory of the Elements NGO, now an office of the city's department of education, this seemed to be a sound strategy. For instance, recall Katya, the organizer whose daughter had severe DTsP. Leaving behind her earlier strategy of working informally with other parents to organize and pursue legal court cases, Katya shifted her strategy to obtain a position within a state institution that she might then help shape in the future. Katya worked to insert herself into the work of the state office for labor rehabilitation, another center in the city, which had long languished under a disinterested director. When that director finally left, Katya and another colleague were appointed to take over the functioning of the center. Although they had little money, and the building was badly in disrepair, the position of the center as a state agency afforded Katya a degree of security in building programming that she felt would be safe from intervention and stable over the long term. Because Katya's daughter will likely rely on adult day services to lead a full life after high school, the stakes of what kinds of programming this languishing state office can provide were high. By investing the caliber of state services, Katya was laying the groundwork for a program that she hoped would be in effect when her daughter became an adult.

I was privy to a degree of tension between Lena and Katya, who, if I spoke about either one to the other, would respond with an air of frustration. Mutual miscommunications seemed to be the status quo; each seemed to think the other was missing something crucial in her approach to the problem of how to work toward creating the best possible services for children with disabilities in the city. Lena, in particular, was distressed by what she perceived to be the younger parent-advocates' insouciance: Katya and her ilk seemed oblivious to the level of work that Lena felt she was able to conduct with international funding. Moreover, they did not look to Lena as a mentor, but instead they struck out in different directions, as if starting from scratch. Katya was aware of this dynamic, but she unsure of how to smooth things over. During our interviews in 2012, Lena reacted to any mention of Katya and her projects with timbre of someone whose feelings were hurt by a professional rebuff. This standoff may partially have been the result of a difference of opinion or framework about how to coordinate services between informal parents groups, internationally funded NGOs, and state agencies. Lena had long sustained her NGO on foreign grants that supported an array of short- and long-term projects. Therefore, she considered the institution of the NGO and the freedom and flexibility and independence it provided to hold great value. This approach was shaped by the conditions of the second phase of post-Soviet NGO culture. Meanwhile, Katya's orientation was based on an assessment of what could be possible in this third-wave NGO culture, in which, under Putin's foreign agent law, it was nearly impossible to receive consistent foreign grant funding, as it had been throughout the second half of the 1990s and the early 2000s. But how did the disabled children who came of age during these transition years—the Weekend School generation—understand these conflicts and shifts?

Always a Guinea Pig: The First Post-Soviet Generation's Experience

For my research participants who included children with disabilities growing up in Petrozavodsk in the 1990s, this turn to art therapy and similar paradigms, and the appearance of new practitioners of this new method in the disability services scene, was not surprising. For this core group of interlocutors, the one constant in their experiences of disability services was persistent change and instability. Projects started and stopped on the whims of foreign funders, the energy of NGO professionals, and the caprices of relationships among the various actors.

When telling stories about their childhoods, this cohort rarely reflected on inaccess. Rather, they reflected on the shifting paradigms of disability services built on different models of social inclusion. Each model of social inclusion suggested a different set of stakes for disability access. In this way, the inaccess stories of childhood were stories about the instability and precarity of institutions providing disability services, and the lack of continuity that this provided. At the same time, these stories functioned in the course of interviews with my interlocutors as coming-of-age narratives in which my interlocutors shared their personal histories of coming to disability politics.

Sergei's cohort was part of the first generation of children to attend a pre-school program for children with disabilities. They spent their childhoods attending a special education school in a remote region of the city. Mainstream education would not be introduced to Petrozavodsk until 2006; in the early 1990s, however, changes were unfolding in the way that Petrozavodsk social attitudes and social services infrastructure related to people with disabilities. Sergei recalled:

> S: So it was, right away—after I finished kindergarten, which was also a special program for children with disabilities, so—um, that kindergarten, I was in the first class that we had. And I, in general, I feel like throughout my whole life, we've been doing experiments on me—I am always surviving experiments!
>
> C: (laughs) Ahh, you're from the very first group that went to the kindergarten?!
>
> S: Yes, yes. So this kindergarten—this kindergarten had just opened, the special education one. So. I—I went there. And when the special kindergarten had a graduating class, it graduated the children to the specialized school. So. To the *internat*. [. . .] everyone from the kindergarten was designated [by the PMPK (the Psychologo-Medical-Pedagogical Commission, the official entity responsible for evaluation of disability status)] to go to the *internat*. So. Then there was the first nonprofit organization (*obshchestvennaia organizatsiia*) also, not long after it was started. So, it was ongoing. Everywhere everyone was doing experiments on me.

Sergei attended an *internat*, a boarding school for children with motor impairments in Petrozavodsk. Because he was from one of the "city" families, he was able to go home each afternoon, a fifteen-minute bus ride from his house, whereas those children whose parents lived outside of the city often saw their families only at holiday recess.

> C: So, were there ever moments during your childhood when you asked, why do I go to the *internat*? As in, "the neighbors go to the neighborhood school, but, I go to the *internat*." Did you ask about it?
>
> S: (immediately) No. I mean, there somehow wasn't—there wasn't [not sure how to put it]—it was just considered normal [laughs, a little embarrassed]. Actually, it was the opposite—I thought it was good that I got to go to school. And so what if I go to the *internat*, it's still a school!

Sergei's mom perceived the possibility to attend school at all as a positive opportunity, and she instilled this understanding in Sergei as well. Although the *internat* was a segregated educational setting for disabled children, it was a new option in the 1990s, distinct from total institutions that preceded it.

Although Sergei was happy as a student at the *internat*, other interlocutors, especially those whose families lived far from Petrozavodsk, disliked it and wondered why they were not allowed to attend their neighborhood schools. Policy toward the education of children with disabilities continued to evolve throughout the 1990s, and by the early 2000s, a new push by parent activists began to pave the way for mainstream schooling.

Because of the changing landscape of disability services and the resulting difference in experiences and social identity as *invalidy,* subsequent generations (and even people just a few years younger) have had vastly different experiences than my core cohort who were in their early thirties when I was conducting my fieldwork. Sergei explained:

> If before, there was a tendency, if you had *invalidnost'*, then you go to the *internat,* like everyone else with *invalidnost'*. Because before, the thinking was that it would be difficult for such people to adapt to a general school environment, because they are not *like* everyone else. So that's what they thought previously. And so they sent everyone right to the *internat,* so that there wouldn't be any questions or problems. But now—it's come around to a situation where, if you communicate well (*khorosho razgovarivaesh'*), regardless of whether or not you have difficulty getting around (*plokho peredvigaesh'sia*), the important thing is that you can hold a conversation (*obshchat'sia*) and get on with people. Then, in that case, you can attend the general education school. And those kinds of kids—now they're assigning to the regular schools.
>
> And so the *internat,* then is left for those kids who, due to their illness/affliction (*zabolevanie*), can't communicate, and don't understand, for example, if you try asking them a question. These kids are the ones that have started going to the *internat.* Of course—everything's different. Everything's totally changed.

Note that Sergei was also trying out a new grammatical construction—that is, a person *s invalidnost'iu,* which translates to a person "with a disability." Although this usage had started circulating in the activist literature, it was still unfamiliar to him. Sergei articulated the changing paradigm in this way:

> There are different opinions. Because some people think that it's good when a person with special needs (*s osobennostiami*), um, well, with

invalidnost', yes with *invalidnost'*, when they send him to the mainstream school. And then he more or less adapts. It might be hard for
him, or, maybe—well, he has to adapt somehow. And then there are
those people who really take that perspective. But then some parents
really are of the opinion that—what for? Because they think that, here
in Russia (*u nas*), with our government (*gosudarstvo*), um . . . people
have hardly seen people with *invalidnost'*, right? In our time it was
even embarrassing to talk about it (*stydno*) [literally: stigmatic, shame-
ful]. Um, they more or less didn't talk about it. So, for that reason, well,
parents have different opinions.

For himself, he felt most comfortable in these protected environments.

A person *s invalidnost'iu*—so say they take him in the mainstream
school, right? And at that point, maybe they're not even thinking
about the fact that it might be really hard for him there. Um, because *u
nas*, we, in the first place—well, we don't hate people *s invalidnost'iu*,
they don't *hate* them, but they are somehow hidden away from society.
So, because of that, it will only be with difficulty that they accept him
at the . . . mainstream school.

[At the *internat*] there was a sense of stability. Yeah. . . . It didn't
seem like—for us it was joyful, life was interesting. We celebrated New
Years together, and—um, there were holidays—creative projects,
crafts, different kinds of concerts, dancing. Everything. We really had
a full and satisfying life.

Sergei recalled his childhood at the *internat* fondly. He felt conflicted about
the changing landscape of educational inclusion practices in Petrozavodsk. On
the one hand, he recognized that his segregated school experience led him to
identify as an *invalid*, separate from his broader peer group, but he could not
imagine another way. On the other hand, in spite of all of the experimental
programming, he had not succeeded in finding work as an adult, and he still
lived with his parents with no plans to leave or marry.

Following high school, both Sergei and Alina participated in the first class of
students to enroll in a charter initiative to establish the first inclusive course for
people with disabilities at the local teacher's college. Sergei recalled:

And now, after high school, in 2007, right, in college they also organized
an experimental group—of people with disabilities who participated in
the coursework at Petrozavodsk Pedagogical College. And I ended up
there, again, as part of the very first group, and it turned out that once
again, it was an experimental situation, "What happens if people with
disabilities get higher education?" And then after I graduated, the whole

program was free for me, only of course, without the grant money, without the support for the project, of some kind. Because, [pause] in the college, the classroom was renovated for us, Schnitz, right, I think, a philanthropic something or other, from Germany, I think. So, they renovated, and then, from that point on, it just continued, only without support. There was—the college had invited specialized workers, they invited social workers, and—individual professionals who work in that sphere, with *invalidy*. And . . . they still work there. So, we still meet up, even after finishing college. We meet up every now and then, like three times a year. [. . .] So . . . I went three years full time to college.

Sergei, Alina, and a few others in their group again took on the role of experimental subjects. The international support was provided by a Swiss grant-making organization that made it possible to renovate the first floor of the school and launch the program, which appeared to be a prestigious and progressive opportunity. For the students who went to the college as the first class of *invalidy*, however, the experience was challenging, socially strenuous, and offered mediocre results. Sergei's description, in particular, emphasizes the ways in which the move to offer degrees to people with disabilities was one of mandated desegregation. Sergei recalled the timbre of social interactions with peers as being stressful.

I asked Sergei about his thoughts regarding mainstreaming. He had talked with me previously about his conflicted feelings about the changes to the education system since he was in high school. Today, students with disabilities like his might go to a mainstream school, or more likely, complete high school through a distance learning program. Sergei's thoughts about attending a mainstream school were colored by the expectation that he would have been socially excluded if he had done so. He presented this information as a matter of fact, rather than as supposition, or as a reason for pity or self-pity. His perception was informed not only by dominant narratives but also largely by his experience attending college with nondisabled peers.

> S: I haven't had that experience, of going to the mainstream school, of getting tossed into the crowd (*vlivat'sia v kollektiv*). The only example I have is that in college, we had our cohort, and—I went to class with a group that—besides me, there were, I think three people s *invalidnost'iu*, and all the rest—we had thirty people—all the rest were *zdorovye* (normal/healthy).
>
> So . . . I wouldn't say that we had a *friendly* relationship. With these people. But, you could say that we were *neutral* in our attitudes towards one another. That is, people weren't cruel, there wasn't a sense of cruelty,

there wasn't really anything, and it also wasn't friendly. It was just like a *meeting*. [. . .] Maybe it's just that people when—I was already old enough to know what was going on, that you don't necessarily have to have friendship, or else some kind of really close relationship. For me, what's really important is that—we are fine with one another (*my adekvatno drug k drugu*) . . . like, maybe we asked one another for advice on something, or once or twice called each other on New Years. Wished each other a happy holiday. But all the same, if it's nothing more than that, it's not the end of the world. Or—or else maybe it was just that all we had was three years together, and so, maybe if we had gone to school together for twelve years, then maybe, of course— wee-e-e would have gotten to know each other better. But this, just three years, it didn't work out that way. But it's not too bad. The main thing is that—everyone acted more or less fine towards me.

C: [sad laugh]

S: Yeah. . . . And then, not everyone will be nice, you know? As much as they put up with you, it's pretty much certain that *someone* won't like you for some reason. . . . so. But going to school [at the *internat*], I have good memories of that.

After university, Sergei took part in yet another experimental program with the Bureau of Employment. Incentives were offered to employers willing to take on an employee with a disability for a new position for a period of six months. The position was subsidized, so that the disabled worker was paid, at no expense to the hosting organization. Sergei did two such placements, and still has continued to work occasionally from home on projects for one of those organizations. He described the project:

I—I, well, like I said already, I am a subject for experiments. They're doing experiments on me all the time. [laughs] So, this time, I ended up in this program. That at first I was with the employment agency (*sluzhba zaniatosti*), after I went to my studies at the college, the employment bureau ran a project (*provodila aktsiiu*), "Finding work for qualified young people" (*trudoustroistvo dlia molodykh spetsialistov*). After finishing my degree, for the period of a year, I think it was, I was supposed to find a job. During this time the employment bureau paid your wages. So [. . .] the money came from the employment bureau, to that employer, and then to you. [. . .] they were thinking about it in the sense that the employers would, after that first half year, start to pay your salary themselves. You see? After half a year they would begin to pay the *invalidy* money themselves. But—well, as it worked out, it didn't work.

This project offered interesting possibilities. It allowed a government agency to subsidize NGOs and for-profit institutions if they applied to host a disabled worker. It helped Sergei and others gain valuable work experience. It failed, however, to result in meaningful employment: Although Sergei continued to do piecemeal work from home for one employer, he has not been employed full time or been able to work on site. Sergei asserted that he was glad he participated in the program; however, he was also clear that the program had not delivered all that it promised.

Sergei's narrative tell us several things. First, the segregated approach to primary and secondary education that this group, unlike younger generations, experienced has resulted in a situation in which they are unprepared to build friendships with their nondisabled peers, or their nondisabled peers are unprepared to build friendships with them. Second, the continually shifting profile of social services and climate of NGO culture left this group feeling like guinea pigs. The programming and practitioners were temporary, and efforts to create innovative programming in a shifting cultural field resulted in promises that never materialized. That is, the segregation of people with disabilities in school and in the workplace has continued to result in discriminatory practice.

These narratives also reveal important stories about the on-the-ground consequences of this third wave of post-Soviet NGO culture, characterized by the Russian government's crackdown on civil society and its reconsolidation of authority under the auspices of the state. How have and how will the efforts of the Russian government to limit the influence of foreign funders (specifically in democratization efforts) change the ways that people with disabilities receive services? NGOs across Russia have developed since the 1990s to support the civic needs and provision of social services to Russians with disabilities. As Meri Kulmala (2011) has observed, the boundaries between nonprofit and governmental projects in these kinds of local-level organizations have always been thin. Now, however, with less international funding available, nonprofits may be faced with fewer options other than merging or joining forces with government services.

When I met this group of interlocutors in 2012, they were taking part in a municipal art therapy group run by social workers. Unlike Felix's foreign-funded programs, the social workers tasked with running the art therapy group were not acquainted with independence discourse that placed primacy on doing simple tasks for oneself: As mentioned in the introduction, I was once even tut-tutted for suggesting that Vakas could take off his coat and mittens by himself. Instead, social workers were focused on encouraging the group participants to develop self-actualization (*samorealizatsiia*) and socially appropriate behavior (*kul'turnost'*), psychological markers of self-confidence and individual agency.[4] This approach was based on sociologist Svetlana's findings that many young adults with disabilities were isolated and therefore lacked social interaction because of disability stigma. Svetlana had advocated for the city to take up programming to encourage social rehabilitation.

Sustaining Disability Politics Amidst Authoritarian Reconsolidation

The history of disability services during the immediate post-Soviet era created a particular kind of disability consciousness among the young people who frequented the Weekend School and their age-mates in Petrozavodsk. The framework of civil democracy and skills for self-advocacy proffered by internationally funded NGO projects in the early 2000s was coming to an end at the time of fieldwork for this book in the 2010s. Even as Putin's reconsolidation reshaped the landscape of disability services in Russian Karelia, the social imaginary of disabled interlocutors in the first post-Soviet generation was still being profoundly shaped by the frameworks of the earlier era.

As Sergei's narrative use of "guinea pig" or "subject of experiments" so vividly captures, the actual effect of the NGO culture in the 1990s and 2000s, while dynamic, in some ways resulted in instability. Sergei, Alina, Aina, and Vakas are part of a generation that came of age on the vanguard of the democratization and civil society wave. Thus, they often were offered the chance to be the first to utilize a given service or participate in a new program, which frequently were funded by and inspired by international organizations and models. In one sense, this put them in a privileged position—they were afforded opportunities to participate in society, to have active social lives, and to move through the city and attend college in ways that previous generations were not. Conversely, it also put them in a position that many other Russians would recognize from this period—that is, they were constantly participating in programs that then closed as funding dried up or they were promised results that failed to materialize as pilot project worked out the kinks. Frequently, when discussing the problems facing people with disabilities, my interlocutors, including people with disabilities as well as parents, social workers, and advocates, wished above all for a different kind of government.

As Sergei put it, when discussing a documentary he had seen about government support for jobs for adults with disabilities in the United States: "The [US] government has made that possible. And I had to sort of come to terms with that, that in principle, if people like that are able to hold a job, then I realized that to an extent I could [. . . but,] I'd have to find my way to a different government, because there I certainly would be able to find work. According to my strengths."

At that moment in 2012, some interlocutors felt cautiously optimistic about the move on the part of the Russian government toward reconsolidation, imagining the strengthening of state social services as a legitimate response to a call from the citizens for a more functional government. This view was starkly different from standard Western readings of reconsolidation as a geopolitical power grab, and from diasporic leftist Russophone critiques of the so-called verticalization of power (variations on the phrase *vertical' vlasti* is a widely popular way to refer in Russian to Putin's hierarchical centralization of power). Not all of my interlocutors experienced the 2012 changes hopefully. Putin's reconsolidation resulted in yet another shift in disability service provision and in the underlying politics of disability politics. As new state institutions launched art therapy pilot programs premised on the concept of social rehabilitation, Sergei and his cohort once again found themselves in this position as guinea pigs, this time at the mercy of the social workers instead of the NGO workers running disability programming. Civil rights and independence discourses were supplanted with self-confidence and self-actualization rhetoric, training disabled citizens to make personal psychological change rather than public political claims. In this way, the notion of what, precisely, disabled young people should understand from the phrase "I can do it myself" was reinterpreted: Rather than imagining themselves as democratic citizens making minority claims, they became neoliberal citizens, working on themselves.

Concepts of disability inclusion discourse moved into Petrozavodsk in the immediate post-Soviet period through democratization development projects, and it subsequently collided with the verticalization of Putin's reconsolidation of power. There was another important legacy of the Soviet era shaping the way that my interlocutors experienced daily life in the 2010s: the enduring infrastructure of the built environment and the codes and policies that shaped them. In the next two chapters, I turn to the inaccess stories that my interlocutors shared about public space and private homes.

In chapter 2, I explore the downtown center of Petrozavodsk as a built environment through the lived experience of disabled interlocutors and local civil engineers. For people with mobility impairments, especially wheelchair users, access to public space has been a major concern. Access ramps, with a gentle slope and handles, symbolize and facilitate wheelchair access. I consider how wheelchair ramps, as an architectural design element, move in friction as a global technology.

INACCESSIBLE ACCESSIBILITY

Ramps in Global Friction

In the fall of 2012, not long after arriving in Petrozavodsk, I befriended a journalist.[1] He was about my age—late twenties at the time—and a distinctive personality around the small city for both his dark red hair (an unusual color) and his gleeful enthusiasm for investigative human-interest journalism and the trappings of a vibrant public sphere he imagined it might offer. This was a political moment at the start of Putin's reconsolidation of power, when the Russian foreign agent laws had just come into place and were squeezing the myriad local nonprofits that had professionalized in the first two decades of the post-Soviet period, returning civic life to the provenance of state organs proper. Although some so-called foreign political discourses, especially feminism and LGBTQ rights (e.g., the Pussy Riot affair), were under fire in Russian public discourse that fall, I observed that disability access did not seem to attract the same degree of controversy (see Borodina 2021). Despite moments of political crackdown, the journalist, unlike many other young people I met in the city, was still optimistic, and although we did not meet often, he sometimes invited me to interesting public events (such as an event series in which another young journalist interviewed public figures). I sometimes wrote him direct messages on social media or via text to inquire about the general popular opinion held on an issue.

I had come to know of the journalist through one of his investigative pieces, when a friend sent me a link. The link led me to a video investigation produced by the journalist and his colleague, a news camera operator. In the video, they follow a tip from local disability advocates that the provincial theater building in the city center, a historical building that had recently been renovated, was still exceedingly difficult to navigate. They observed how difficult it was to get to the theater in a wheelchair using public transportation. When I met the journalist for coffee, he explained that he was aiming for a web 2.0 style of entertainment news. Rather than produce another story simply interviewing disabled citizens (other journalists had produced several such pieces over the past few years following a lawsuit related to inclusive education), the journalist decided to obtain a wheelchair and try to access the theater himself.

In the clip, he sat in a borrowed wheelchair and attempted to get from a small vehicle parked nearby, up the curb, up the front entrance ramp, and into the theater. The piece is problematic from the perspective of disability studies in that the journalist possessed none of the lived experience, arm strength, and expertise that comes from navigating in a wheelchair regularly. Thus, his repeated failures to navigate barriers in the built environment came as no surprise. Charming as he was, the piece still managed to be entertaining, and, at the end of the clip, he moved on from the theater to try to gain entry to a city bus. In this clip, the ableist barriers of the transit system are more apparent, as one bus driver simply drove off when he asked for help getting on board, and then another is shown struggling to help him through the door.

When I interviewed the journalist, he admitted that he knew very little about disability issues in the city. He had decided to make the clip because he thought it would produce good content and because the issue of barriers was a good example of a bigger problem—that is, the lack of follow-through on the part of the city, provincial, and federal government. These agencies claimed to be attending to disability access issues (not only by renovating the theater but also by ratifying the United Nations Convention on the Rights of Persons with Disabilities), but they obviously did so without concern for the end result in terms of convenience and usability for actual citizens. At the time, and later as I started writing what would become this book, I was puzzled by this interview. I couldn't quite fit it into the story I had imagined that I wanted to tell. How could I write an ethnography of disability advocacy that completely left out disabled people? What could I make of the way that the journalist mobilized barriers to disability access in the built environment as a sort of metaphor or vehicle to make a larger point? Later, as I developed this book, I understood that the journalist's video was one example of the second type of inaccess story that I kept stumbling on in Russian public discourse— that is, inaccess stories that use disability access as a metaphor for the broader failures of the state to make good on the promises of public infrastructure to deliver a degree of ease and convenience for every day (nondisabled) people.

The journalist's reportage made me curious to ask disabled people in the city about their experiences of inaccess in the built environment. As I started to collect stories, many of them homed in on the irony of inaccessibility even while accessible design elements were present. The journalist's project also reminded me of the 2010 interview (discussed in the introduction) that I recorded with Nina Anatolievna, a schoolteacher whose daughter, twenty-two at the time of the interview, had cerebral palsy and used a wheelchair. Describing for me the kinds of frustration that she and her daughter had faced over the years, Nina recalled only being able to enter a theater through a service entrance in the back, which she referred to using the memorable phrase *chiornyi vkhod,* black or dark entrance, before the renovation that the journalist reported on. Subsequently, another parent, Katya, remembered having to run around looking for a janitor to request that the newly renovated accessible washroom be unlocked—it was apparently kept locked because it was understood to be for special occasions—invalidating the ease of use the notion of accessibility implied. Like the ramp at the corner store near Galya's house described in the introduction, Nina's description of the corner store near her apartment was a memorable example of another case in which an accessibility ramp did not actually function to provide access.

> In a lot of cases it's just for the check mark (*galochka*). Is there a ramp?! [mimes checking something off on a list] It's like, this nearby store, where they also *built a ramp* [sarcastic emphasis].
> So Sveta says, "Oh!! They built a *ramp!*"
> And I say, "Sveta, you know, you can go up the ramp but that's it—you'll stop right there!"
> Because she can't go into the store itself. Because there's—it's only about [shows the width of the door with her hands]. That's it! You get it? She can't even go through the aisles at all. Oh, there's a ramp—a ramp. So something here is *equipped* [sarcastic emphasis] (*oborudovano*).

In this example, Nina sarcastically emphasized the word *equipped*, stressing the contradiction between the purported intent of access and reality of a retrofitted environment that, while "equipped" with a ramp, was not actually accessible. This observation drew attention to the ways in which elements of the built environment in Russia, recognizably designated as objects intended to provide access, or, *disability things,* failed to actually facilitate access to public space for people with mobility impairments.[2] Nina's commentary fits into broader Russian narratives about the material results of economic and moral corruption in Russian public life, specifically, that the government and wealthy business owners—those performing "official" functions (whom she refers to *en masse*, as is common in Russian, using the third–person pronoun)—cannot be relied on to carry out their tasks in such a way as to actually benefit the intended recipients (e.g., Rivkin-Fish 2005b, 6–9).

Ramps as symbols of accessible design suggest that a space is designed well. "Good" design communicates a kind of arrival in a desired modernity. Critical studies of design across global contexts suggest that not just designed objects but also the valuation of design thinking as a discursive formation, have become desirable markers of status across global locations. For instance, Lilly Irani argues that objects like sharpie markers and social formations like hackathons, artifacts of Silicon Valley design culture, circulate in India's capital city of Delhi as a modality by which entrepreneurs configure themselves as producers of value and arbiters of India's modern future (Irani 2010, 2019). According to this logic, "design thinking" has a global center, a core of innovation and start-up capital, from which the very concept of design as expertise flows. As Sasha Welland writes, "A well-designed thing structures what is perceived as proper social functioning" (2018). Therefore, the idea of accessible design becomes an object of desire, circulating beyond disability-advocacy communities. An access ramp communicates an idea of access, proffering a symbolic meaning that suggests a certain kind of modernist imaginary is within reach.

After revisiting this interview, I came to think of these inaccessible accessibility ramps as "checkmark ramps," following Nina's assertion that "it's just for the check mark." According to Nina, the inaccessible ramps came into being when someone tasked with building a ramp did so merely to fulfill minimum requirements without attending to the ramp's functionality. I wondered: What were the reasons that someone might build such a ramp? What checklist? Who was enforcing it? If these ramps were not working for people with mobility impairments, for whom were they working?

In this chapter, I consider the urban infrastructure of public space in Petrozavodsk as a space in which inaccess stories unfold. I consider also the Russophone internet as an additional sphere in which the meaning of accessible design is forged and travels in friction. I argue that in Russia in 2012, the symbolic function of a ramp was decoupled from the actual function of a ramp—to provide access for wheelchair users and others with mobility impairments. To do so, I consider the "work" that ramps and images of ramps do in the social world. First, I attend to inaccess stories about inaccessible ramps told by my research participants. I observe that in these inaccess stories, the symbolic function of an access ramp as an architectural form may have more to do with performances of professionalism and Europeanness than with a desire for an inclusive public sphere and that the design and construction of ramps plays out through the logic of checklists, a modernist technology that replaces the concern for function of a given form with a list of decontextualized norms. Second, as the concept of "accessible design" circulates globally,

FIGURE 5. A view of a central bus stop in downtown Petrozavodsk, near the university's main building. A small ramp is visible on the left side of the image, where two stone steps separate a sidewalk from a park walkway. The ramp has a steep slope and no handrails, visually marking it as not "for" disability access; it was probably installed with deliveries to nearby businesses and pedestrians with baby carriages in mind. The park's fountain, partially visible, is aging and modestly maintained and reflects an abstract constructivist style. Photo by Cassandra Hartblay, 2014.

the accessibility ramp becomes an object that exists in global friction, taking up different, but interlocking, local meanings. Because we understand the category of disability to be culturally, historically, and spatially and materially contingent, we cannot assume that *dostupnost'* as a conceptual category in Russia is reproduced in the same way that *barrier-free access* is reproduced in Britain (Gleeson 1999; Shakespeare 2006) or that *canji* mobility is reproduced in China (Kohrman 2005). Observing how disability appears through and with the local material conditions is part of a broader global critical interpretive disability studies.

By attending to the friction surrounding disability access in contemporary Russia, I contribute to a rich body of literature in anthropology chronicling the ways in which discourses making claims for social and political inclusion of minority groups, such as feminism, LGBT activism, and so on, take on different meanings and spark different debates in the post-Soviet context (Phillips 2008; Rivkin-Fish 2005a; Hemment 2004; Kay 1999, 2007; Sperling 1999; Essig 1999). By unpacking the ways in which accessibility ramps move as objects or disability things, and accessible design moves as a conceptual category and technology of modernity, I also attends to tensions between universal categories or norms as a strategy for institutionalizing access.

Access in the Russian Built Environment

The Russian built environment is strikingly inaccessible. Russian sociologists working to document the social politics of disability conducted a survey among citizens of the cities of Saratov and surrounding regions in 2004. They found that public roadways and sidewalks were particularly inaccessible, and other public spaces were only slightly better (Romanov and Iarskaia-Smirnova 2006, 109–110). According to their study, although private spaces might be renovated or retrofitted by users, businesses or government offices had made only a few gestures toward accessible design.

Similarly, Human Rights Watch and the Russian disability advocacy non-governmental organization (NGO) Perspektiva documented the egregious degree to which the so-called social marginalization of people with disabilities is related to material elements of the built environment. International NGOs play important and varied roles in translating international human rights discourses about disability into Russian, in disseminating these ideas to Russian advocates, and in advocating for elements of the international concepts of disability access (such as accessible buses, inclusive public education, and social service programming beyond monthly pensions) to be adopted by the Russian federal government.

In Petrozavodsk, accessibility ramps began to appear in new shopping centers built in the 2000s; shiny mall-like facilities, these new spaces also had large, Western-style elevators, escalators, indoor atriums and food courts. These elements were unusual in the centrally planned, utilitarian logic of Soviet architecture. Most apartment buildings, shops, grocery stores, schools, offices, and public parks had no elements of accessible architecture—most visibly represented by the ramp. Some walkways had outdated ramps designed for delivering freight or pedestrians with baby strollers (e.g., without the railings, slope considerations, and other elements of design that enable disability access). Private citizens and disability NGOs installed makeshift ramps in homes and office spaces. Hospitals lacked even accessible bathrooms, but sometimes they had ramps at a main entrance or had elevators.

The Physics of Friction: The Ramp in Global Motion

To most North American readers *the ramp*, as an architectural feature, has a particular meaning: it is a "disability thing" (Ott 2014). That is, a ramp as an architectural feature is already linked to the thing that we call "disability." A ramp abutting an entranceway in a building or near a short flight of stairs is an object that, at a glance, is immediately legible as serving a specific purpose: It facilitates access for people with disabilities. Unlike stairs, a ramp can be navigated by a person in a wheelchair; it can also be a preferable route for people with an unsteady gait, poor balance, or an injured or lesser-functioning leg (stairs require balancing on one leg to lift the other). Although steps assume that people are a certain height, a well-proportioned ramp can make mounting a vertical divide more hospitable for people with short legs. Along with people with a broad range of disabilities, children and elderly people often prefer ramps to stairs; in this sense, it is nondisabled adults who prefer stairs.

This meaning of the ramp has not always been evident. In fact, the ramp as a tool for accessibility in public space emerged as part of the Universal Design (UD) or Accessible Design (AD) movement. Certain elements of UD were incorporated as minimum standards in the Americans with Disabilities Act of 1990. In turn, they became elements of the legal infrastructure of the US building code. Like feminist design theory that preceded it, accessibility by design starts from the premise that "design is never ideologically neutral. Whether explicitly or implicitly, built environments always reference and imagine bodies and spatial inhabitants. . . . both the presumed body *and* the marginalized body are always implied in, structurally incorporated into, or actively excluded from, physical environments" (Hamraie 2013). Aimi Hamraie argues that the look or visual vocabulary of an architectural mode, called *parti*, can be at once both aesthetic, and imply use by particular kinds of bodies using particular kinds of technological assistance (2013). In this sense, although ramps at the entrances to buildings or between floors or levels can serve all members of an urban population, the accessibility ramp is often imagined as being "for" a wheelchair user—perhaps the white stick figure of the international "handicap" sign.

This evokes what Martha Lampland and Susan Leigh Star have described as the "slippage between a standard and its realization in action" (2009, 15). Presumably, whoever ordered the ramp built might check off the word "ramp" on some checklist of items required for renovations; or, they might want a ramp in front of their store to convey some quality that a ramp evoked. That is, an accessibility ramp might have multiple uses beyond its titular intention. This idea echoed a theme that is familiar both in stories about Russia and in ethnography—that is, a gap between intended and actual use or meaning, the emic and the etic. In the Russian case, the concept of "Potemkin villages" offers a shorthand for something that appears to exist, but turns out only to be a facade (e.g., Bernstein 2013, 42–66).

But what is a *ramp* actually? A ramp is a machine. In fact, a ramp, called an *inclined plane* in physics, is one of the five simple machines that make up the basic building blocks of mechanical engineering (Hendren 2017 (originally published by Hendren on her then website, slopeintercept.org, in 2012). Along with the wheel and axle, the screw, the lever, and the pulley, the ramp is one of the five basic mechanical tools. Each of these simple machines redirects energy or force in a particular way; designers and engineers put them together and in combination to form the tools that make up our world (Asimov 1966, 88). In a classic popular physics book, physicist Isaac Asimov describes how a ramp "works" with the example how one might use a ramp to aide in loading a barrel onto a truck; the ramp "dilutes" the amount of force used to raise the barrel to the height of the truck bed, in proportion to the slope and length of the ramp (a longer ramp will dilute the force more, but require transporting the barrel across a longer distance) (1966, 91–92). In introductory physics, to consider this relationship of slope, length, and force, students are often instructed to discount friction. Physicists consider friction to be an "imperfection" in the environment, which inhibits the flow of kinetic energy (Asimov 1966-98). But *friction* is also a factor in allowing for passage up and down an incline—only by calculating the friction can a physicist or engineer know how difficult it will really be to move an object up and down a ramp. In the real world, not the imagined world of physical modeling, humans *need* a certain amount of friction to move up and down an incline plane without slipping and simply sliding to the bottom.

Extending Anna Tsing's concept of friction by combining it with the physics of ramps might point ethnology in an interesting direction. In many ways, the ramp as a design element or architectural feature has moved through multiple cultural or ontological spheres to arrive on the streets of Petrozavodsk and in pixelated images on my internet browser. What are the tensions and incongruences of meaning and interpretation that have aided the accessibility ramp in spreading and replicating across multiple global contexts? At what points are students of access or purveyors of human rights instructed, like physics students, to "ignore friction"?

Friction in Function and Form

In the spring of 2013, I recorded an interview with Anya, a psychologist and a power wheelchair user. Anya was a compelling person to interview. Not only did she frequently talk for long stretches at a time with only minimal prompting, but she was also a keen observer, had sharp sense of humor, and was highly entertaining. She often deployed her sarcastic wit to drive home the absurdity of a particularly element of inaccessibility—a tactic that many disability activists in the West will find a familiar element of telling inaccess stories.

> For some reason they are trying to make the buildings of certain social services, or medical facilities, or the town hall and mayor's office, accessible. Like, they did something with the grounds of the pension office, and then something else. But how useful is building a ramp to the town hall, if I can't get down the stairs from my apartment?! [laughing] How am I supposed to use a ramp to the town hall? I think that in the first place, they need to adapt the entranceways (pod"ezdy) of the buildings where people with disabilities live. To start from there and work on out. To make public transportation accessible! . . . Like in Finland—I showed up, I stood at the bus stop, a bus came, laid down a ramp, I got on, the doors closed, and we were off. What's so bad about that?! . . . I don't need a ramp at the pharmacy if I can't get out of my house!
> . . . if we *do* have a ramp, it's covered in snow and no one shovels it!
> But who ever said life would be easy? No one promised an easy life! [pause; then, sarcastically, thinking of how hard it is to get around in the winter] It's our little way of doing rehab!"

In this quote, Anya observed that recent construction in the city had seemed to prioritize making accessible particular buildings that had some official function related to the state—the post office, the courthouse, or the town hall and mayor's office. These isolated islands of accessible passages remained disconnected from the broader network of transportation and passageways. Without the broader grid of the city undergoing similar renovations, a ramp to the town hall, to Anya, seemed to be an empty gesture, a cruel joke.

Anya imagined an alternate universe in which people-centered design would consider her home space, which she had adapted herself, as ground zero, and work out from there. Instead, accessibility started at points of state power, as a symbolic expression of the Russian Federation's compliance with the minimum standards of international norms of access. Anya drove home this point by drawing a comparison between her own city and cities in neighboring Finland.

Anya's monologue illustrated that for an accessibility ramp to function, a person must have already arrived at the bottom (or top) of the ramp. If a wheelchair-user could not get out of her house, or across town on public transportation, she would not be able to make use of a perfectly executed design element in the new shopping mall downtown. Ramps as tools to facilitate access to public space in Russia, even if perfectly executed as discrete architectural elements,

FIGURE 6. Pedestrians navigate a snowy sidewalk and courtyard driveway in a residential neighborhood of Petrozavodsk. Apartment buildings in the late-Soviet style surround the courtyard and the entrance to a neighborhood grocery. The ground is covered with compacted snow and appears to be slippery and hard. One family pushes a child in a stroller that has sleigh runners in place of wheels, a popular option for navigating the city in winter with toddlers. Photo by Cassandra Hartblay, 2013.

often did not function fully, as a ramp presumed certain other technological minimums, which may not have been met. As part of a heterogeneous network of sociotechnological actors (Callon 1991), such ramps may or may not find convergence with other elements.

That is, a ramp alone is only an indicator of access; the ramp requires numerous other elements of the infrastructure to converge to actually function for access. Ideally, a ramp functions as an enabling device or technology, allowing for what Moser and Law (1999) have called "good passage," a sense of smoothness, where otherwise social boundaries might need to be broken, such as requests for help getting over a threshold or up a set of steps.[3] As Anya's narrative illustrates, however, there are multiple ways in which the diverse elements or sociotechnological actors in the infrastructure may not align to promote the function of the ramp. In these cases, the form of the ramp, and its symbolic function as a "disability thing" and element of global design culture remain, but its active function as a technology of access is lost.[4]

Consider another example: for wheelchair users, the usefulness of a ramp presupposes a wheelchair. If there are no wheelchairs, or if wheelchairs are broken, a ramp is not a useful tool (of course, a well-built ramp can still be a preferable option to stairs for ambulatory people with chronic fatigue or impaired mobility). An unevenness in the distribution of wheelchair technology is a significant problem for access both in Petrozavodsk and in the former Soviet Union more broadly. Sarah Phillips (2011) has documented the ways in which wheelchair users in post-Soviet Ukraine worked to form complex alliances to convince business owners and government agencies to support the manufacture, purchase, and distribution of well-designed wheelchairs in the 1990s and early 2000s. Wheelchairs are expensive, usually manufactured abroad, and difficult to obtain. Because the supply and distribution of wheelchairs is slow and unreliable, if a part breaks or wears out, they can be difficult to fix.

In Petrozavodsk, Anya complained that the frequently encountered rail ramp design (a ramp that is not a flat incline plane but rather two rails installed over a staircase into which the wheels must fit) tended to wear out the treads on her automatic chair's tires as they rubbed the sides of the railings. This caused additional problems, because the tires were expensive and a hassle to replace.

Alina from the art therapy group waited six months of 2012 for the replacement part for her broken manual wheelchair. She was able to borrow another chair to get around in, although it did not fit her as well. We laughed when I came to visit, because the broken wheelchair took up so much space in her room that she had taken to using it as a desk chair while she waited for a replacement part. In another interview, she told me that when she was taking courses at a community college three miles from home, she would often "walk" (her mother Valya pushing her chair), because it was too difficult to get lifted on and off of the city bus. Like Anya's complaint, this situation illustrated the ways in which particular elements of the sociotechnological infrastructure of Petrozavodsk were inaccessible. This led wheelchair users to create alternative networks or pathways that facilitated smooth passages.

These objects—wheelchairs, ramps, and other design elements (or their absence)—can be understood as part of a sociotechnological network, in that they are always embedded in social relations. It is not only an object that facilitates access but also social attitudes that foster or dismiss the implementation of design elements for their intended use. As geographers of access have argued (Church and Marston 2003, 84–85), whether or not access is provided in an absolute or a checkmark sense does little to explain the complex spatial and temporal experiences of partial, limited, and occasional access that people with mobility impairments tend to encounter in navigating the built environment. In this way, the nuanced definition of access as a globally circulating concept related to disability rights always hinges on the relationship between *a given person* and the social, cultural, and material environment around them.

When ramps, wheelchairs, and other technologies of access and elements of accessible design move into post-Soviet spaces unevenly, their function is compromised by gaps in the network of sociotechnological actors. This means that whether or not a ramp is a checkmark ramp, or visibly nonadherent to the formal design principles that facilitate good passages, from the perspective of the wheelchair user, the ramp may not be fully functional.

Checklists as Smooth Passage

The checklist, as well as the ramp, is a particular kind of technology. Bowker and Star discuss the *list* as a particular tool of modern bureaucracy and civilization (1999, 137). Foucault (1970), they argue, conceptualizes *the list* as key to the development of modern science—for example, the elaboration of *kinds of* animals or plants in the elevation of biology from a rich man's hobby to a science. Latour (1987) also considers lists—as physical objects that can be shuffled and compared, moved across space, and held as proof of protocol by a bureaucrat. In this way, Bowker and Star note, list making is "foundational for coordinating activity distributed in time and space" (1999, 138). It attempts to streamline, coordinate, or make congruent a decision-making process that occurs across space and time. The list also produces a certain expectation of reality, in that it presupposes a bureaucratic action that might be applied "in response to a recurrent situation" (Bowker and Star 1999, 138).

In this sense, list-making technology becomes an important tool in the execution of the infrastructure of modernity. As particular ideas, forms, or norms are disseminated through a geographic territory, lists serve to normalize and standardize practices of design and implementation. As power has taken different forms, so too has the reach of the list and its norms. Now, as the flows of global capital distribute ideas and technologies across uneven cultural settings, lists and norms attempting to reproduce infrastructures of modernity are taken up and implemented in a diversity of cultural settings in which the meanings of the products they presuppose are heterogeneous and contested. That is, precisely because lists attempt to standardize across time and space, they operate as a system for managing the heterogeneity and disagreements of global friction (Bowker and Star 1999, 139).

A suspicion of norms, and of modernity's obsession with the mean or average body, is central to disability studies (Canguilhem 1989; Davis 2006; McRuer 2006). Yet, disability rights activists working in global contexts rely on norms or standards as central technologies of list-making to disseminate the principles of accessible design to diverse global contexts (Djumagulova 2004; Kohrman 2005; Abilis Foundation 2014). Concerns with material and environmental inaccessibility as bound up in the social exclusion of people with disabilities are central to both the theoretical debates unfolding in disability studies (Imrie 1996; Charlton 2010) and international development and human rights discourses. Standardized modes of constructing accessible infrastructure, characterized by specific norms in the form of measurements and materials—the architectural building codes that make up accessible design—are considered to offer potentially universal solutions (even as many disability scholars and activists rebuke the very idea of "universal"). In this way building standards, or norms, already occupy a place of tension in relation to accessible infrastructures. Even as disability studies is wary of norms, or norming, when it comes to disseminating elements of the built environment, disability advocates may opt to "ignore friction." Even as list-making is a tool to smooth difference, and therefore checklists always function in friction, individual components of the list (e.g., the aesthetic look of a ramp, the check mark itself) may become fetishized and sought after as ends in themselves.

What happens when we apply these problems to the checkmark list and ramp-building habits in Petrozavodsk? If we consider checklists as universal standards that are developed in relation to international building code standards, a checklist could be a functional tool used to implement accessible design principles in Petrozavodsk. If, however, checklists are haphazardly implemented, or the details are not upheld, something that "looks like" a ramp may come to stand in for an actual tool for accessibility. By exploring some of the anecdotes and tensions on the ground in Petrozavodsk, we can see how these frictions play out in the logic of checkmark ramps.

Minimum Requirements and the Logic of Checklists

The first time I visited Anya, she told me to come over for tea, and gave a date and time and an address. Soon enough, I found myself in the back of a worse-for-wear taxi (in the way of the region, a used sedan with a little plastic taxi marker on top, and the phone number of the dispatching company plastered across the windshield and passenger window with vinyl numbers), explaining to the driver that, in fact, I did not know where in the sprawling complex the particular set of buildings I was looking for was located, because it was my first time going there. I kept checking my phone, because I realized that as we drove in and out of court-yard driveways looking for building numbers posted by various entranceways, I was possibly going to be late. I zoomed in and out on the Yandex map app in vain. In 2012, the app had not yet added enough detail to find specific addresses in apartment complexes in the city. I tried the Google maps app, knowing it was even less helpful. Finally, the cab driver found what seemed to be the correct *pod"ezd* (or entranceway), according to the number on a small enamel plaque on the side of the building. I hastily paid in paper rubles and thanked him and hopped out of the cab onto the frozen-but-not-yet-snowy ground, the last yellow leaves of autumn gathering and turning brown in corners of the courtyard.

When I found the right doorway, I called Anya, and she told me her mother would buzz me up. The stairwell to the sixth-floor apartment was shabby but warm and dry, and there were not many belongings clustered on the landings as in some shared entranceways. A late-middle-age woman was standing at the door, holding it open, when I turned onto the sixth floor landing. She waved me in, and did not say much, just a brief hello, and then pointed to where I should put my bag and hang my coat, and a quiet declaration, *tapochki!*, pointing at a pair of house slippers reserved for guests. I shuffled after her, my phone in hand and bag on my shoulder, and she led me down a hallway nicely renovated with light-col-ored wood furniture and laminate flooring, and pointed to a doorway where Anya sat in an electric wheelchair, smiling and waiting. Her mother turned and rushed off to another room, and Anya explained something about her brother's children, then, calling over her shoulder as she turned, led me into her small bed-room with a neatly made bed, dresser, and desk, and pointed to a desk chair. I felt flustered and breathless after the dizzying cab ride through the potholed court-yards, and my climb up the stairs. But Anya wasted no time, diving right in to getting acquainted. I was impressed by her quick wit, sharp intellect, and know-ing sarcasm. Anya had attended university and completed a master's degree in psychology at the city's university. When we met, she was working as a psycholo-gist in a program outside of the city relying on her mother to transport her the long drive in each direction; she later was hired at a new municipal center for adults with disabilities, closer to her home. She had a critical, analytical style of thinking and a way of sharing a point of view in a manner that invited the lis-tener into a conspiratorial insider perspective. Anya soon became the interlocu-tor that I turned to when I found myself looking for a grounded perspective.

Anya was also a master of the inaccess story as a genre. During one interview, I asked Anya to tell me what she thought about the concept of accessibility in the built environment. I used the phrase *bezbar'ernaia sreda* (literally, a barrier-free area or surrounding environment), a conceptual and linguistic translation from international disability activism. Disability activists in Petrozavodsk used this term when talking to the media about accessibility in the downtown area, drawing on examples from ongoing activism in Moscow (facilitated by internationally connected disability rights organizations), which they followed online. In this sense, Anya's response to my question was to immediately situate *bezbar'ernaia sreda* in the Russian context, as a traveling term that had to be distinguished from the Western contexts from which it had been adapted.

> Accessible space—*bezbar'ernaia sreda*? It's a painful question. The law on accessible space, well . . . last year they rewrote it several times, so that in the end they could implement it. I was following one particular point in the law. [. . .] there's this word, "minimum conditions of a barrier-free environment." I thought about that and realized that the word *minimum* is the key word. That someone could just argue that *this* word—*here* is the standard. I'd be saying, "You understand, that we have a right, as everywhere else, to the minimum standards of a barrier-free environment." And they'd answer, "Sure, our ramp is set at the wrong angle of incline—that's nothing, because the main thing is that a ramp is there! So, take a look, here are your minimum conditions." And I'd say that this is wrong, but I can't prove that it's wrong. There's no way to beat it. So, in this sense, I guess you could say that [the law] is written exactly how they wanted it.

In this discussion, Anya expressed the sense of frustration that she felt about the notion of accessible public space. Although the phrase for the concept (*bezbariarnaia sreda*) is now standardized in Russian, the real-world work of implementing the concept, through a system of legal rights, seems to her to apply to some *other* place and to have been adopted in Russia only symbolically. *Bezbariarnaia sreda* as a concept traveled in friction. Anya's inaccess story is laden with multiple layers of meaning. This is evident in her example: "Sure, our ramp is set at the wrong angle of incline—that's nothing, because the main thing is that a ramp is there!" On the one hand, Anya is making a joke: In Russia, she implied, we define things (like accessibility) to wiggle around them. On the other hand, she was speaking seriously. As a power wheelchair user, whose mobility device was too heavy to be easily lifted, she very much counted on ramps to be able to get in and out of buildings. She had personally overseen the installation of a ramp outside her apartment building and of several installations at a previous place of employment—never without significant hassle (a story that will be familiar to power chair users both in Russia and elsewhere). Although this latter experience could be part of a litany of complaints from a wheelchair user anywhere in the world, the particular cadence of her interpellation of legal code as difficult to enforce aligned with broader Russian conversations about government accountability and paying lip service to rather than integrity in implementation.

In Anya's experience, a "minimum requirement" was the requirement that *might* have a chance of being met (but only after a long process of complaint, threats, and incorrect or unacceptable half-hearted stop-gap measures). Anything above and beyond a minimum requirement simply would not be considered, she insinuated. In her description of these *minimum standards*, Anya used the common Russian construction of assigning actions to an unnamed "they"—that is, the faceless mass of government bureaucracy or the powers that be. Who, I wondered, were "they"? Who was actually responsible for designing, building, and assessing the implementation of accessibility ramps?

The question of responsibility was a natural consideration in the course of inaccess stories, particularly inaccess stories about ramps or places that purported to provide access but did not. In the spring of 2013 Anya tried to get a ramp built in the entranceway to her new apartment, having moved a few doors down from the apartment that she previously shared with her parents. Unfortunately, no one from the building management knew what she was talking about, and no one was convinced that it was their job to build such a ramp. In Anya's telling, she left several messages for her building manager over the course of two months; she joked that they began simply answering the phone and hanging up to get rid of her when they saw her number on the caller ID. Finally, she announced that she was calling the local media to do a story on the fact that no one was responding to her request; a handyman showed up shortly, and in Anya's estimation, spent about fifteen minutes laying an asphalt wedge along half of the single step in front of her apartment building entrance. The work was not great, but it allowed her to get on and off the stoop daily on her way to work and back without ruining her tires. Haphazard, off-the-cuff ramps like this were frequently built onto storefronts and homes as afterthoughts, by workers who had little or no training and paid little attention to building codes. The proliferation of "bad" access ramps that failed to provide access suggested the inextricable link between access and the precarious labor conditions of those whose work was intended to provide that access. This reality of access labor in neoliberal conditions—or "crip times" as McRuer (2018) has put it—can be demoralizing. Anya explained:

> The worst [part of talking with other people with disabilities] is when you run into this question: "What's the point of it all? All the same nothing changes. . . . " You understand that if everyone talked like this, that nothing changes, then really nothing would change. So, I start from the beginning, explaining to everyone, so they don't decide it for

everyone. . . . It's a drop in the bucket. Take your little contribution and make it useful for something, and your little tiny drop in the bucket helps a stranger and then something changes. But if everyone will go around saying that nothing changes, then oops, nothing changes.

Why should the state be thinking about how to make it easier for us to live? [incredulous] The state doesn't need to think about anyone and it doesn't have to do anything for anyone. If you don't take care of yourself, no one else is going to take care of you. . . . Why should you get used to the idea that someone should be looking out for you, if you have your own head to work from and you can look out for yourself? . . . and then help someone, and look out for someone else . . . look out for someone who needs your help, or protection or support.

Every drop in the bucket counts, if each person will make their own little contribution. The laws are written, and if there are strange and not very honest people driving the bus, then you and your crew have to do something so that the laws work in your favor. And if you came and met with resistance and you say, "Oh, I'm not doing that any-more," . . . then it ends up that that side won and that's it. I understand that it doesn't have to be this way, but that's how it worked out and we can change it only with our own power.

Anya suggested that a moral person is obligated to continue to work toward access justice, even when justice remains elusive. She argued that advocates had to work together and persevere, especially because accessibility policy in Russia was continually undermined by the notorious gap between Russia's written laws and their implementation in Russian society.

Wheelchair user and multimedia-artist Rudak offered another perspective. I met Rudak through a mutual friend at a concert in a popular basement venue in the center of the city where his band was playing. His bandmate who was a friend of a friend introduced us before the show, and after a brief interview, Rudak invited me to message him to talk more in the future. Then his bandmates lifted him and his manual wheelchair on stage to start tuning up for the show. A few weeks later, at his mother's apartment on the east side of the city, he showed me the band's YouTube page and his documentary and feature film work at the desk-top computer in a combination sitting room–bedroom (typical for Russian apart-ments), and then acquiesced to a general interview over tea at the kitchen table. When I asked Rudak about how inaccessible ramps came to be, he responded:

Why are they cropping up (*voznikaiut*)? Because, first of all, the people building these ramps are doing it so that the ramp *exists*. So if some-one asks them, "Do you have a ramp?" Not a person with a disability, but a person, let's say, from some kind of committee or something like that asks. Someone or other comes with a clipboard and whatever documents, and puts down a check mark (*galochka*), like "That's it! Access for the disabled is accounted for (*obespechen*)!"

Rudak's description stressed that business owners build ramps merely to satisfy "some kind of committee, or something like that," with little regard for promoting accessibility for people with mobility impairments. Like Nina, he summed up this theory with the idea that the builders will put a check mark on some imagined document or form, with the check mark rhetorically glossing an inferred hierarchy of accountability and politics of implementation (Lampland and Star 2009). Rudak was vague about which committee, precisely, was responsible for access—he was not sure. Yet he had extensive embodied knowledge about when and how he did experience access.

In another scenario, Anya and Rudak, along with another local activist, worked to find out who in the town administration was responsible for enforcing building codes. The train station in the center of town was scheduled to be renovated, and they wanted to ensure that the renovation would include ramps and elevators to facilitate wheelchair access to the platforms (currently accessible only by stairway). Having narrowed down responsibility to one of two possible offices, they were curtly informed by bureaucratic workers in each department that the question of enforcing building codes was out of their respective jurisdictions. The activists then obtained a letter from a federal agency, which stated that, according to federal law, an office in the city administration must accept responsibility for this role. But, having obtained this letter, and presented it to the same offices to no avail, the activists were stumped. Aside from the state, they could think of no organization with the authority to enforce the building codes. After Rudak first shared this story in 2013, I made a habit of asking him if there were any major developments; in 2014, he remarked that he would not be surprised if it never happened. In the end, it was a historian colleague working abroad who happened to read the Petrozavodsk news and share a news clip documenting the installation of an elevator in the train station at long last.

In this sense, my interlocutors who are wheelchair users had a fairly good sense of how these unstudied ramps get built at apartment buildings, and they also had limited ideas about how to enforce a standard of access. This made other type of ramps that existed in the city—the architecturally designed, professionally built ramps that could be found in front of government buildings or in shopping malls—somewhat of a mystery. I asked Rudak how he thought that these ramps came to be built according to standards of accessible design, and he suggested that the reason that these well-designed ramps could be found only in such buildings is that shopping malls were simply built according to existing modular plans adapted from European cities, and the ramps happened to come along with the design. That is, in his estimation, a well-designed and well-executed accessibility ramp, by definition was not Russian, and could not have originated in a Russian context. The details of how ramps traveled in friction into designs for new construction in Petrozavodsk turned out to be somewhat different.

Checklists, Norms, and Standards: Technologies for Distributing Expertise

I brought my questions about architecture and accessibility to a nondisabled friend, Olya, who worked as an assistant in a Petrozavodsk architectural firm. At that time she already had completed most of a four-year degree in civil engineering, and she was preparing to take the licensing exams. We had known each other for several years, and she knew that my research was on how disabled people—*invalidy*—lived in the city.

Thinking of the checkmark ramps, I asked Olya to record a proper interview, repeating for my digital recorder what she had explained to me in a casual conversation as we sat in a grassy city park eating chips out of a bag while other friends played frisbee nearby. Later, sitting in my apartment, suddenly and uncharacteristically shy in the presence of the recorder, Olya explained that using checklists to ensure that draft plans for new buildings were in agreement with building codes (*normy* in Russian) was a key element of her job.

> O: I work in a company that does contracting for residential buildings, public buildings, sports complexes, and so on. And, I work in the architectural division. And—mostly our work is to see to it that all the building codes are fulfilled. And, included in those are norms for—[pausing to emphasize or recall the official term] accommodations for low-mobility groups in the population.
>
> C: What are some of the other codes?
>
> O: Other codes? Well, for example, mmm. There are codes to make sure that there is good natural lighting in a room. [. . .] There are codes, for example, so that the toilet in your apartment isn't next to the living room of a neighboring apartment. That's against regulations. Because it would be bad if there were a leak—it wouldn't be very pleasant! There are lots of codes, in general. Really a lot. You have to set the thickness of the walls, the thickness of roofing, so that people will be warm, and—so that it will be comfortable, and you won't hear your neighbors, and so on. So, among all of those, now these last few years, they've really been actively following up with implementing codes for people with limited mobility

(*malomobil'nykh grupp*) . . . in the population. That is—this goes for wheelchair users (*invalidy-koliasochniki*), and, also for pregnant women, women with strollers, mothers . . . like, there are a lot of these people.

Olya went on to explain to me that her work was made up of verifying numerous, seemingly unrelated measurable elements of a building plan with established norms. Although she intellectually recognized that each norm was based on a particular corresponding function (e.g., thick walls and roofs so that people could stay warm), her job was not to establish the norms, or work out the norms, but rather to verify that the architects who laid out the plans met the existing norms. In her telling, she made sure to demonstrate to me that the work of meeting standards regarding access was not set apart from the other elements of her job, but rather was included in the same manner and importance as light, heat, and sound. She emphasized repeatedly that there were "a lot of norms—really a lot!" Later in the interview, she elaborated: "It's an interesting job, of course, but sometimes it can be—tedious to work out. Like, when you're like, [adopts a sarcastically delighted voice] 'I'll come in! I will draw a building! I'll add staircases! Oh, it's so pretty!!' [returning to her normal voice and cadence] But, in reality, you are sitting there with all these building codes (*normy*). And you spend a lot of time on it."

Olya contrasted her vision of architecture as a romanticized, exciting career and a chance to change her environment by building her world, with the much more mundane reality of checking figures. *This*, she emphasized, was the actual content of her work: endless verification. Checking that the elements of a given design met the standards established for accessibility for "people with limited mobility" in Olya's telling was not an afterthought or chore, but rather was a routinized element of her work, seamlessly integrated with others.

I asked Olya how it was that the norms for groups with limited mobility came to be instituted.

> O: I don't know exactly what year it started. But, when I started with this work, the first job, well, it was like four years about. And—it was already, like—well, they were trying. To implement it. Lately, they're *really* strict that we follow up on this.
>
> C: What does *strict* mean?
>
> O: That—it means that—we *have to* do it, so that there's a *ramp*, with the right incline. So that we can't just—you know, how a lot are done, like lean some kind of board up against something, and say, so there it is—a ramp. We are obligated to do it so that it has a comfortable incline [—] so that a person can get in and out. We are obligated, like I said, to make a nice big bathroom stall. An elevator. Et cetera.

In this exchange, Olya contrasted the work of using checklists with nonexpert vernacular design, like the ramp outside of Anya's apartment, which she implied was haphazard and unprofessional. In Olya's estimation, it seemed that part of the utility of a strict building code was a more beautiful and well-executed public space. Without professional norms and standards to follow, ramps and other elements of the built environment might be poorly executed. In other conversations, Olya, like Anya, described the jolt of jealousy she felt every time she crossed the border of the Russian Federation into Europe. Immediately, she said, the roads were smoother. The sidewalks were not only well designed but also well executed, and the bus stop shelters were new. I often heard her joke with friends about how poorly the infrastructure of the city stacked up to other cities they had visited abroad. Although Olya was busily making plans to continue to live in Petrozavodsk—she recently had married and bought an apartment—she wanted to live in a Petrozavodsk that looked more like Helsinki or Stockholm.

Olya's "obligation" to ensure that her bosses' drawings met building code standards was therefore, for her, not only busy work, but actually linked to a real-world outcome: a built environment to be proud of, that functioned well, and that expressed her professional expertise. She went on to explain how the building code was enforced.

> O: [. . .] So, it's not *just* that we have to follow up on all of this. There's a regulating body (*kontroliruiushchaia organizatsiia*) that then checks over all the projects, and says, well, *orders* corrections on mistakes. And, then we fix them. It's not only—it's not just about accommodating the movements of people with limited mobilities. It's also about all the other regulations in general, too.

> [. . . then,] when we finish a project we give it to the expert review panel—[it's called] *ekspertiza*. It's made up of educated people, who sit on the panel and look out for everyone. For compliance with all the regulations (*za sobliudeniem vsekh norm*). When they say, yes, you have it all correct, *theoretically*, only then can work start on the project. Like, construction on the project can go ahead and begin. But, more *often* (laughs), construction is already underway while the plan is still being worked out (both laugh). So then it's going on in parallel sort of, so the work is coordinating it all, and moreover, then to make it all match up, to finish building peacefully, and so on. So, like, in order to not have to throw out the final construction, we'll start to build the building. [The project financer] could, at any moment, on his judgment, take his resources and leave.

Olya's description of the role of checklists in ensuring accessibility standards revealed a Russian design expert culture that was concerned with executing their work according to the highest European professional standards. In Olya's perception, civil engineering in Petrozavodsk ought to be considered in relation to that in geographically comparable international cities, rather than only in relation to the Russian domestic sphere.

In contrast to Rudak's supposition that ramps in Petrozavodsk shopping malls came about because the building plan was copied from a European shopping mall, in Olya's telling, each building and each renovation was carefully designed by trained Russian professionals. As professionals, she and her colleagues executed the elements of design laid out in checklists, including the checklist for *malomobil'nye gruppy*. According to Olya's perspective, it was not at the architectural stage that plans for accessibility standards broke down, but rather in the hands of the building contractor. This was not about Soviet bureaucracy, but rather about the precarity of public–private negotiations of capital in neoliberalism. Olya retold a story that she had shared before. She recalled it, in particular, because it represented a moment of ethical conflict. She had recognized it as a point when the execution of accessibility norms broke down.

> There was this big building (*dom*). It was divided into two floors. And, they needed to make some kind of way to get to the second floor. They made this giant, enormous ramp. It was for cars and people and everything else. And, along the edge of the ramp, they made a handrail. There were high ones—according to the regulations they have to be [something like] 100 centimeters—and a lower one. It could be for children, or for wheelchair users (*invalidov-koliasochnikov*). That is, we do all of this. We drafted everything. When these railings or handrails went—to the people who—well, who make them, from metal, they calculated the cost, and they sent it to our boss, and said, *That's expensive. Take out the handrail for invalidy (invalidov).* So [the project underwriter] took it upon himself and just got rid of it. I don't know, how it all happened—[but in the end when I visited the building, there was only one railing].

When I asked her to elaborate, Olya explained that the project foreman proposed some changes to cut costs. When the revised plans were presented to her, she refused to sign off on changes that did not meet the building code. But, she shrugged, embarrassed, someone else must have signed off.

In these tellings, both the architect and the ramp users failed to imagine one another as individuals and disregarded each other's expertise. Olya's story suggested that the architects would point fingers at the builders for being at fault in moments when norms were not upheld. They would not think to reach out to ramp users to raise a fuss about an oversight in execution. In Olya's telling, wheelchair users were the recipients of a built environment, not the codesigners. As a mere employee, Olya, and the sanctity of her checklists, were ineffectual in the face of a bottom line. In an economy of capitalism, scarcity, and every-person-for-themself, if the one footing the bill wanted to take out a handrail, that was his or her gamble to make, regardless of how well Olya's drawing executed the elements of the checklist.

Anya also described a scenario in which building norms were subverted at the hands of builders. In her case, however, it was not the boss overriding a well-designed plan, but rather, day laborers following orders and guessing what a ramp should look like.

> At the Martial Springs retreat center (*Martsial'niye Vody*) they made a ramp, so that you could get [from the main building] down to the spring. The springs with the healing waters are down the hill and leading down to them is a long staircase. And last year, the good people [sarcasm] decided to build a ramp down to the springs.[5] And it ended up, that at the same time that they were doing the renovation work, my mom happened to be driving in to the resort. She saw what they were up to and stopped and asked, "What are we doing?" and they answered her, "We're making a ramp." And mom says, "You're not building a ramp, because I can already see that a wheelchair won't be able to get through there." They started to wave some documents around, they go, "we have the regulations (*normy*), we have the standards (*standarty*)!" And so, Mama says, "I don't need your standards, I am talking to you as a person who has spent 35 years of my life with an *invalid*, and I am saying that a wheelchair won't be able to get through here.
>
> So, what do you think happened? They erected the ramp all the same. And . . . so then it ended up that I started to bug them to redo the ramp. I chipped away at them and in the end they redid it.

In this telling, the fault for an inaccessible accessibility ramp fell on the day laborers tasked with building it. Again, a barrier of class or identity separated the executor of the ramp design from the user. The user's perspective was subverted to the laborer's informal checklist: Use the materials they were given, build something that looked like something else they had seen, follow the instructions they were given, get paid, and go home. These black-and-white norms and instructions overrode Anya's mother's lived experience as a source of expertise. Operating in conditions of scarcity, and as laborers, the workers had instructions to follow that aligned with hierarchies of command, and they could not be interrupted by horizontal avenues of advice from a passerby. In these cases, the purpose of the ramp and its meaning existed in friction between each set of parties involved. Inaccess stories told by wheelchair users revealed the gaps that existed between their disability expertise about what made an infrastructure accessible and the failure of legal, technical, and capitalist systems to implement access.

On the Circulation of Images and the Aesthetics of Access

The inaccess stories that my interlocutors told based on their disability expertise were one kind of story that I heard about inaccessible accessibility ramps. The images of ramps and stories about inaccess—like the one that the journalist recorded at the theater building in Petrozavodsk in July 2012—circulated independently of disability expertise. Not only bad ramps, but also images of bad ramps, images of access, and images of disability circulated in popular culture, not through crip counterpublics but as part of the second type of inaccess story—that is, a critique of how things are, as a metonym for social breakdown.

One afternoon in the fall of 2012, I was sitting in my fourth-floor walk-up apartment in Petrozavodsk, editing fieldnotes on my laptop. A Facebook alert pinged. A colleague from the United States, halfway across Russia conducting his own fieldwork, had sent me a link. I clicked. The link led to an Imgur thread—an image gallery of seventeen photos, all showing inaccessible accessibility ramps.[6] Here was one ramp in which the railing to the adjoining steps actually cut off access between the stoop and the ramp. Here was another—in my experience ubiquitous in Saint Petersburg and Moscow metro entrances—which consisted of nothing more than a pair of inch-and-a-half wide metal rails, screwed into the granite steps, and descending at the same steep angle. The spaces pictured in the image gallery are marked as Russian by Cyrillic signs in the background and by architectural vernacular. Another version of the same meme had circulated first on the Russian-speaking internet. In this case, the images were presented on a blog as an amassed body of evidence that the Russian authorities had failed to provide an accessible environment for its citizens with disabilities. A popular subject with Russian journalists interested in uncovering government incompetence, a Russian-language Google image search for further images of inaccessible ramps (*nedostupnyi pandus*) produced numerous examples. On the Anglophone internet, the meme circulated as an example of irony (inaccessible accessibility!) and Russian incompetence.

How do images of inaccessible accessible design work as social critique? Design as a practice is an exercise in world-making. As Kim Kullman has put it, "recognizing the world-making capacities of design methods necessitates attending to the very 'designing of design,' or the ways in which the processes and sites of design are themselves designed, as these shape what design can become" (Kullman 2016, 74; Fry 1999, 5). In the case of the way that mediascapes of disability access "things" circulate and garner symbolic value in contemporary Russia, we might invert the paradigm. Here, accessible design becomes something quite different than its intended technological usage in design process had foretold. Images of accessible design technologies in Russia operate as symbolic vessels for broader cultural critiques of social and political infrastructure and affective valences of comfort and discomfiture.

The Imgur thread, as a meme, quickly replicated on the English-language internet. Web analytics show that the image has been successively shared at a steady rate since it was posted in September 2012, with a slight surge around the time when I first viewed it, again shortly after, and again around the time of the Sochi Olympic Games, when a similar meme (#SochiProblems) highlighting shoddy construction in the Olympic Village also circulated.

In the fall of 2012, the gear-up for the Sochi Olympics of 2014 had just begun in Russia. The Olympic committee had promised to make the Olympic village "the most accessible ever." This goal came up short, however, according to disability activists (Andrea Mazzarino, personal communication). But the inaccessibility of the Olympic Village infrastructure became a footnote in a much larger story about infrastructure and inaccess: In the week before the games, foreign journalists arrived to find a barely finished, slap-dash infrastructure rife with awkward mistakes and indications of rushed, haphazard construction. The news media around the globe tweeted and blogged about half-finished sidewalks, oddly installed bathroom fixtures, and faulty hotel doorknobs. As the Olympics opened (even though one ring did not) the Russian predilection for constructing subpar infrastructure was paraded as a touchstone in both Western and Russian comedy. When the Paralympics opened several weeks later, the media in both Russia and the West largely overlooked the immense changes in the ways that Russian official discourse has recognized disability issues since the collapse of the Soviet Union. As Sarah Phillips has documented, the last time the Olympics were held in Russia, in 1980, the official statement about Paralympic athletes was quite different: "A Western journalist inquired whether the Soviet Union would participate in the first Paralympic games, scheduled to take place in Great Britain later that year. The reply from a Soviet representative was swift, firm, and puzzling: 'There are no invalids in the USSR!'" (Fefelov 1986, cited in Phillips 2009, 1).

By 2014, not only did Russia host the Paralympics, support Paralympic teams, and pay lip service to infrastructural accessibility in the Olympic village, but the country also ratified the UN Convention on the Rights of Persons with Disabilities.[7] Putin met with a group of select Paralympic athletes in the lead up to the games, and children with disabilities across Russia had the opportunity to participate in adaptive sports. In this way, adults with disabilities in Russia, having seen enormous change in the course of their lifetimes in terms of the state's relationship to disability and the public visibility of access, now had the dubious distinction of being able to join in and share with the rest of Russia a collective embarrassment over the gap between what was promised and what the government and its contractors actually delivered.

The hashtag #SochiProblems, which became popular on Twitter in the weeks leading up to the games, and continued to circulate thereafter, harnessed a register of complaint familiar to Russians and Westerners: complaints about the problem of failed infrastructure. The hashtag indicated and made memetic and searchable a genre of images cataloging infrastructural failures in and around the Olympic village. Here, inaccess stories, spliced with a fail-blog ethos, became an international joke du jour. Complaints about infrastructural failure in the Olympic Village fit into a familiar pattern of critique: Russia's failure to manifest Euroamerican modernity. In many iterations, this failure signified corruption: the contractors, landholders, and officials each scraping something off the top, leaving a reduced budget for the actual implementation of the planned infrastructure. In this way, the #SochiProblems meme suggested a fail-blog-style critique of Russian cripwashing, and the popular recognition of cripwashing as a technique of power in the Russian Federation. These critiques came from both an orientation of disability expertise—for example, one year after the Sochi Olympics, a disability advocacy blog reported that none of the wheelchair lifts installed along public stairwells in preparation for the Olympics remained in working order (neinvalid.ru 2015)—and from the general public.

Complaints about infrastructural failure and disability in Western conversations tend to assume that disabled people, encountering barriers in the built environment, are a minority group facing hurdles that majority groups need not reckon with. In contrast, in Russia, inaccess stories—although frequently about ableism—are also frequently about corruption leading to broader infrastructural failure. In this way, inaccess stories in Russia, like the interspersing of disability access with other infrastructural problems in the #SochiProblems meme, act as assimilationist rhetoric rather than special-minority group discrimination built on liberal democratic legal principles. At the same time, elements of material design that are intended to facilitate disability access sometimes circulate in Russia independent of disabled people's own advocacy.

Forness: Generating Inaccessible Accessibility

The #SochiProblems example drives home a question that kept coming up as I considered the inaccess stories that I heard in Petrozavodsk: *What is a ramp for?* As Sarah Ahmed (2019) asserts in her treatise on the concept of use and usefulness, the very being of an object in relation to humans suggest a question of *what it might be used for*, a purpose, which she glosses as *forness* (the forness of an object).[8] Ahmed explains: "In treating usability as communication, we would be thinking not only of whether it is obvious how to use something but who can use something" (2019, 59). The semantic address of the ramp as an architectural form communicates something to passersby, a digital representation communicates something to the viewer (or ALT text reader). Moving in friction, the notion of inclusion is abstracted into attributes of liberal modernity. The forness of a ramp at a building's entrance suggests that the ramp ought to be a purveyor of access. The meaning of the access and inclusion, however, and the material coming-to-be of ramps in the built environment move in friction. The friction between these two kinds of forness, function (access) and form (semantic address), generates a proliferation of both images of inaccess and actual in inaccess. The journalist's video feature appeared to be "about" injustice for disabled people, and yet, it did not incorporate any disability expertise, and it imagined a nondisabled public audience, mobilizing the semantic meaning of inaccess to suggest a broader political critique.

The nonfunctional ramp fails as a tool *for* accessibility for wheelchair users or other members of the *malomobil'nye gruppy* (those with strollers, children, the elderly and others with poor balance or compromised mobility). It is functional, however, as a symbolic element of the visual public sphere. The ramp, as a cultural icon, references access and social democracy as well as aesthetics of European society. A ramp is not just a requirement of meeting building standards (after all, with the right kind of bribes and lack of oversight, these might be overlooked altogether): it is a vessel for a particular kind of cultural flagging. This is a place of modernity that the ramp is imagined to indicate. A ramp carries with it the mark of modernity, a standardization of the built environment, that, through the logic of checklists and norms, bit by bit, overtakes local vernaculars.

Checkmark ramps continue to spring up, as they are implemented by architectural firms in new constructions or executed by workers following orders. Anya's insight that by establishing a norm, a process also establishes a de facto minimum level of satisfactory execution, begins to circulate in interesting ways, as we watch the manipulation of "minimum" come into negotiation between different parties with different interests. A norm operates as a necessary and useful tool of modernity—offering the possibility of sharing potential measurements for a well-functioning ramp between different locales. Yet, the establishment of a norm also creates a fundamental situation of friction by decoupling the design process from function. From the perspective of centralized planning, the shortcut of creating a checklist or instructions prevents the kind of mistakes that vernacular architecture might make, or the replication of a costly design process through trial and error, assessing the properties of various materials and measurements. By centralizing expertise, however, the checklist prevents fellow citizens from recognizing that knowledge of what counts as a working accessibility ramp can be found in the ramp users. The check mark reveals itself as fundamentally belonging to systems of centralized, hierarchical design and planning. Materials and energy may actually be wasted when checklists are incorrectly interpreted, elements are left off to save on costs, or design elements are added without integrating them fully with the overall environment. The checkmark ramp appears where universal design travels in friction. The form of the ramp implies the invisible presence of the checklist, and the power relations facilitate the execution of the checklist's guidelines.

In this way, we might return to Rudak's (ultimately untrue) comment that ramps most likely came to Russia not as individual elements, but rather as part of plans for shopping malls that were imported wholesale from Europe. The logic of this statement underscores his certainty that accessibility ramps, as an element of material design, were patently not Russian in origin. That is, the concept was one that had been imported, and moreover, the import of the accessibility ramp was something that traveled into Russian infrastructures not as an independent unit, or as a design element actually intended to facilitate the access of minority populations, but rather *as part of a larger imported infrastructure.*

Instead of being part of the plans for a specific building, the concept of the accessibility ramp is continually being imported to Russia through distributed professional expertise and as an semantic concept that conveys a longed-for modernity. The ramp as a technology, and the checklist of architectural accommodations for *malomobil'nye gruppy*, travels within Russia as part of an infrastructure of illiberal democracy, which, on the one hand, reconsolidates centralized power of in an autocratic, modernist state, and on the other hand, privileges profit-making and economic growth in private industry as an end to itself, as the social good from which other social goods might follow. In this mode of logic, ramps are built in the most symbolically important government buildings as a way to play lip service to internationally disseminated democratic principles of human rights and minority inclusion: In this incarnation, the ramp symbolizes the egalitarian access to the tools of governance that charac-terizes democracy in the global imaginary. In shopping malls, the ramps play into an aesthetic of access that has to do with luxury, comfort, and ease, with technology and Europeanness. That is, these ramps are tied up in a global poli-tics of development, wherein a symbolic inclusion of minority groups is not an end in itself, but rather is leverage toward entrance or membership in Western systems of governance that privilege minority inclusion as a precept of moder-nity. The aesthetic work of the ramp as evidence of dissemination of these var-ied value systems appeals to a heterogeneous array of stakeholders—most of whom are not members of the *malomobil'nye*. This pattern of proliferation works in friction with the purported forness of accessible design, and the actual needs of actually disabled people.

Tracing Inaccessible Accessibility Ramps in Global Friction

When worlds are built and rebuilt, when norms travel, power and exclusion are built in. Power relations do not operate as nested binaries of exclusion or domi-nation: Russia/West, able/disabled. Rather, valences of power move through, across, and with one another, producing frictions that propel unexpected rela-tionships or objects, such as the inaccessible accessibility ramp, into existence and prominence. Standards and norms—elements of design or infrastructure, and their implementation—are always already engaged in an ontological pre-supposition about what kinds of human bodies count.

In this chapter, I picked up the story of an inaccessible built environment in the public spaces of the city of Petrozavodsk outlined in the introduction to this book. I explored how ramps and stories about ramps—narrative and visual—proliferate in friction. Inaccess stories based in disability expertise as well as inaccess stories that mobilize the concept of the failures of accessible design to raise broader political critique without input from disabled people both contribute to this generative friction. In the next chapter, thinking with Anya's observation that public buildings are renovated for access before dis-abled peoples' homes, we turn to a consideration of access and inaccess in domestic spaces.

HOUSING FATES

Negotiating Homespace Barriers in the Material
Afterlife of Soviet Socialism

In 2016, a few years after the main period of fieldwork for this project, I returned
to Petrozavodsk to workshop an engaged element of the project with some of
my interlocutors. Early on in that trip, I visited my collaborator and research
participant, the filmmaker and musician Vladimir (Vova) Rudak (a wheelchair
user with lower-limb paralysis). He lived with his partner Larissa in a new
apartment in a newly constructed building in the northeast part of the city.
I was excited to see their apartment; when we had last met in 2014, Vova was
still living in his mother's apartment in a walk-up building with no elevator
from the 1960s. The move to a new building with an elevator meant greater
ease of ingress and egress for daily errands, a fact that Vova explained, grin-
ning, by describing the novelty of running down to the corner store to pick up
a pack of chips and a soda on a whim (previously impossible for him without
two friends to carry him down a couple flights of stairs). Even though he was
now many floors up, the elevator enabled a whole new orientation to movement
in and out of the home, and thereby, access to the rest of the city.

The new apartment had a view of the lake, which Vova and Larissa pointed
out before giving me a tour of the bathroom that they had redesigned and renovated to be large and accessible, making wry comments about how they had
acquired the tile for the *evroremont* (renovation in the European style, sometimes, as here, delivered ironically) in little piles over several months whenever
they could spare the funds. I recalled that according to the building code, newly
constructed apartment buildings were required to include one or two accessible
apartments (determined by an arbitrary ratio related to the total number of

units), and asked whether this had been a factor in choosing the apartment. In fact, they told me, those accessible apartments were always on the ground floor, and thus understood to be more accessible, but they preferred an apartment with a view, and after all, there was an elevator.

Of course, a few months later, they already had a story of the elevator breaking. Larissa had to carry Vova down eight flights of stairs on her back, and then run back up to get the wheelchair. This anecdote was made funnier by the fact that Larissa's outstanding physical fitness and part-time job as a physical trainer at a local sports complex had prepared her well for this spousal duty.

The trade-offs and shenanigans in the couple's description of their new living space suggested a complexity lost in the official designations of "accessible apartments" (as opposed to "normal" apartments) and the circumstances that allowed this couple to move into a newly constructed building. Their enthusiasm to share their renovated bathroom and disdain for the officially designated apartments for *invalidi* revealed a mismatch between the kind of accessibility they valued, personally, and the kind of access that was legally codified. The tour of the renovated bathroom enacted a kind of inaccess story that I often heard during fieldwork: one based around the complex social and material relations of the domestic living space afforded by Petrozavodsk's postsocialist infrastructure. These inaccess stories lay bare the limitations of a binary concept of access or inaccess. In this chapter, I consider this category of inaccess stories and the deeply inequitable fates of interlocutors navigating housing with different social and family circumstances.

As we have seen in previous chapters, accessibility in the built environment is coemergent with constantly contested and continuously changing social assemblages. Accessibility is not a static state—maintenance, use, and technological and social context shift, and so too does accessibility. Moreover, as the very authors of universal design have observed, access for one person may mean inaccess for another. Access is contingent, temporary, incomplete, and relational.

In this chapter, I shift focus from the city center to the family apartment. How do adults with mobility disabilities in Petrozavodsk navigate the need for accessible egress and ingress in aging, multistory apartment buildings? What kinds of apartments are desirable, and why? How do interlocutors with different social positions weigh and navigate the options available to them? I argue that the family apartment as a material structure both enables and disables interlocutors, and that it does so in specific ways that are shaped by the material history of infrastructure. Housing infrastructure in Petrozavodsk is neither purely disabling nor potentially enabling, but rather is a changing material configuration, shaped by Soviet and post-Soviet political economy, that residents must continuously negotiate. Disability appears, and inaccess stories are narrated, in relation to the material conditions of leaving and returning to domestic space.

In this chapter, I argue that desire for access—not as a discrete object—but as an experience of ease—animates considerations about domestic space and living arrangements. These stories of desiring access belong to interlocutors who are members of families with widely varied socioeconomic resources. I find that the in/accessibility of a given family apartment depends *not* on the variegation of mobility capacities of my interlocuters, nor only on the barriers in their specific apartment building, but on the intersectional identities and systems of oppression they navigated. Mobility—in the home and movement in and out of the home—was a privilege differentially available.

In this chapter, I focus on interlocutors' narrative performances of desiring access in, to, and from their family apartment. In so doing, I attend to the myriad factors facilitating or preventing access to the world beyond the home for my interlocutors. Thus, apartment stories are one way that my interlocutors perform inaccess stories, and these stories of in/accessible housing are an important domain in which their theories of access are mobilized. A commonality across interlocutors was the enduring impact of the Soviet-era housing infrastructure on daily life. In this way, I argue that the material afterlife of state socialism in the infrastructure of the built environment remained a significant factor in daily life in Petrozavodsk in the early 2010s. These ethnographic accounts are inflected through the continuously developing scholarly debates about Soviet citizens' claimed agency as creative actors in the context of Soviet centralized and top-down decision-making, richly manifest in the history of Soviet architecture (Zubovich 2021; Varga-Harris 2015; Reid 2006, 2018; Smith 2010; Buchli 1997) and contemporary sociology and postsocialism studies (Zavisca 2012; Fehérváry 2013).

I explore this experience of the post-Soviet apartment building through the stories that my interlocutors shared about their housing situations. To do so, I first consider how my interlocutors described stories of egress and ingress. I then consider the question of what kinds of apartments were imagined as desirable in this context and turn to considering how the question of which floor one lived on became a central factor of discussion. I then nuance the question of desirability by examining how my interlocutors sought to mitigate the impact of barriers and negotiate more favorable apartments in the context of a stark housing shortage, characterized by illiquidity and prohibitively expensive market prices, and given the wide range of familial socioeconomic resources.

The Ubiquitous Soviet Apartment Building

Each New Year's Eve in Russia, a 1976 romantic comedy titled *The Irony of Fate, or, Enjoy your Bath!* (*S Legkim Parom ili Ironiya Sud'by*; Ryazanov 2002) streams into living rooms across the country. The film, a sort of Russian *It's a Wonderful Life* in the sense of holiday season nostalgic ubiquity, hinges on a peculiarly Soviet plot point: Across the Soviet Union, not only did many city centers have streets with the same names as one another, but block after block of apartment buildings were constructed using the same design.[1] Moreover, the centrally planned economy and limited availability of domestic goods meant consumers had very little choice when it came to furniture design. The film's protagonist, drunk after a particularly adventurous New Year's Eve, fails to notice that his friend has dragged him from Moscow to Leningrad. Finding his way home, he locates his street, his apartment building, and his apartment number; enters the apartment; and falls asleep on the couch. He awakens not much later to find the true owner of the doppelganger apartment (albeit in Leningrad instead of Moscow) in a state of panic about the strange man sleeping on her couch. Hijinks ensue, and whether or not you have seen the film, the ending comes as no surprise—the two falling in love, succumbing to the irony of fate.

The premise of the film hinges on a nuance of the architecture of Soviet life, which has since become the architecture of post-Soviet life: the ubiquitous design of the Soviet apartment building. This premise is evident in the opening credits of the film, an animated illustration of Soviet architecture's collision with the kind of central planning that led to all-Soviet designs for domestic residences. The credit sequence begins with a parade of anthropomorphized rectangular Soviet apartment buildings marching forth on iron legs to plant themselves in various unsuspecting landscapes. The cartoon concrete buildings stride confidently into warm beach towns (representing southwestern Russia), peaceful snowy landscapes (of the north), and desert steppes (Central Asia). The animated scene shifts to a sketch of the globe, a single apartment building taking it over, multiplying, and then becoming ubiquitous and manifold. The opening animation sequence is quickly followed by a wide-angle scan surveying the apartment blocks of 1970s outer Moscow, where building after building melts into a repetitive pattern of concrete cubes. At once a jovial illustration of socialist progress—the buildings are multiplying!—and a tongue-in-cheek critique of that ubiquitous Soviet discourse, the animated opening of the film stands as an example of late Soviet *stiob*, skirting the line between promoting an official narrative and critiquing it.[2] This short cartoon illustrates a different kind of universal design from that declared by disability advocates in the West several decades later: The socialist economy of scale and centralized optimization of living needs and standards, combined with a historic housing crisis after World War II, led to the construction of so many apartments based on the same plan in different cities.[3]

Far from the miserable automatons that inhabited US Cold War depictions of Soviet citizens, the characters (and, indeed, the authors) of *The Irony of Fate* are colorful, endowed with a sense of humor and fully human. They just happen to live in a social environment that has been engineered in a strikingly unvarying manner. *The Irony of Fate* revels in the implausible absurdity of the vast geographic expanse of the Soviet Union being populated with nearly identical apartment blocks. Despite this observation, the characters find lightness, life, and complexity in an architecture of uniformity.

It would be easy to imagine the Soviet apartment building as a cultural object that eschewed originality in favor of mass-produced design that valued function but not form, an infrastructure of repression. In US popular culture (or propaganda) in the second half of the twentieth century, Soviet-era uniformity was frequently represented as a repression of individuality. Soviet citizens were imagined as victims, and the uniformity of centralized planning represented a lack of freedom of choice. Binary logics of oppressed versus free led to a totalizing narrative in which Soviet citizens were deprived of choice and thereby of human self-expression (Yurchak 2006). From this vantage point, American consumers were understood to exercise choice in domestic consumer decisions, facilitating a consumer-connoisseurship as mark of cultural sophistication, an experience that it seemed from afar that Soviet citizens lacked and wished for (Fehérváry 2009). Post-Soviet apartment life, however, was neither purely limiting nor enabling. Instead, we can eschew the binary logics of Soviet citizens' agency (or lack thereof) in favor of a more nuanced view that reimagines the Soviet and post-Soviet Russian citizen as a bricoleur, making do and deploying creative, but culturally rooted, solutions to the problems presented by the postsocialist-built environment.[4] This argument follows on from this critique of binary perception of passive versus active citizens. It suggests that we might apply a similar skepticism to the widely recited refrain that *Russia is so inaccessible*, a sentiment frequently expressed by my Russian interlocutors and by foreigners who have visited Russia. As historians have shown, Soviet and post-Soviet Russians are neither captives of an inaccessible regime, nor passive recipients of Western disability advocacy, but rather, they are creative and agentive self-advocates drawing on domestic and global discourses to craft rhetorical approaches and advocacy strategies (e.g., Shaw 2017; Galmarini-Kabala 2024; Bernstein 2024).

FIGURE 7.   A Khrushchev-era apartment building in Petrozavodsk. The style of nine-story buildings can be found in many cities; yet, the detailing on the building, from the customization of windows added to insulate the balcony, the addition of curtains, and the choice of interior paint mark the specificity of each family apartment. Melting snow and tufts of grass around the building suggest that it is early spring. Photo by Cassandra Hartblay, 2013.

Life in Four Walls

A common refrain in interviews with and about people with disabilities in Petrozavodsk was the phrase *zhizn' v chetrikh stenakh,* life in four walls. In this idiom, "four walls" refers to the walls of one's room or apartment, and the expression denotes the sort of mundane lack of stimuli that someone who spends most of their days at home experiences. The same colloquial expression came up, for example, in conversations about the quarantine during the early days of the COVID-19 pandemic.

"Life in four walls" was a shorthand to describe the experience of not being able to access the world outside of one's apartment. Svetlana, the sociologist, found that young adults with mobility impairments in Karelia were deeply in need of social experiences outside of the home (Driakhlitsina 2009), and her dissertation led her to advocate for more city programming to support the social needs of unemployed adults with disabilities, resulting in the creation of social rehabilitation groups, like the one where I first met several of my interlocutors. Other scholarly accounts note the centrality of the problem of getting in and out of one's family apartment as essential to and significant in the lived experience of disability in Russia (Kikkas 2001; Phillips 2011; Romanov and Iarskaia-Smirnova 2006). A 2013 Human Rights Watch report, based on interviews with activists and people with disabilities in Russia, suggests that physical confinement to homes is the primary barrier that Russians with disabilities face in their environment, ahead of, if compounded by, inaccessible sidewalks and street crossings, public transportation, and entrances to public spaces, businesses, and government buildings (2013a 20–32). An advocacy campaign started on Twitter during the COVID-19 pandemic (several years after my fieldwork ended) used the hashtag #ButWeAreAlwaysAtHome to raise awareness of the inaccessibility of going in and out of the Soviet-era apartment buildings where most Russians live to those complaining about life in four walls during quarantine (Mullins 2021). This issue raised the question of whether or not an interlocutor with mobility impairments could leave the family home easily, or only with significant organizational labor and physical effort.

During my fieldwork, I often traveled across town to meet Alina, who was in her early thirties and a wheelchair user with cerebral palsy (or *DTsP* in Russian). We would meet at Alina's apartment, where I would be buzzed in by her mother, Valya, who then greeted me at the apartment door on the second floor. Valya would usher me into the vestibule to take off my coat and then lead me down a dim interior hallway to the sitting room in their family's section of the shared apartment. Whereas most other families I visited would bring me to the kitchen and serve me tea, because Alina and Valya shared their kitchen with another family, I saw it only briefly passing by. Instead, I would sit on the worn sofa in their sitting room, sometimes moving to the table for tea and sweets, or we would meet in Alina's computer room, with Alina shooing off her mother so that we could talk as age-mates.

My interviews with Alina and Valya took place in their apartment, and I rarely saw them elsewhere. As I got to know them better, I realized that they rarely left their neighborhood, and Alina rarely left the apartment. I started to understand the way this played out in terms of class and architecture one afternoon over tea at the round table in the sitting room, when Valya recalled a time when Alina was still a child. Caring for her daughter, who needed assistance to go to the bathroom, made it difficult for Valya to work.

> Valya: A lot of the parents didn't work, but I worked. [. . .] So I would lock
> her in the apartment and walk to work [as a janitor] for three hours. . . .
> After a year and a half I was going into the city to [work at] the medical clinic. I would leave keys with the neighbors, and they would feed
> her, change her, and sometimes they brought her over to their place—
> that was when we were renting an apartment in a house. But when we
> moved here [to a bigger apartment building], I would lock her in . . .
> they didn't give me medical leave, even when she was in a cast after an
> operation . . . I walked to work, and locked her in . . .
>
> C: [to Alina, with empathy] You must have been lonely in a cast and not
> able to move . . .
>
> Alina: You didn't say it right, I was never alone, I always had a lot of people
> around . . . there were always people around me.
>
> Valya: I would leave the keys and the neighbors would come, it was simpler
> then.
>
> Alina: I would play with the kids and no one picked on me. It was only
> when they grew up a little that they realized that I couldn't get around
> . . . Even now, everyone in the building can't believe that I go places,
> that I do things.[5]

In Valya's account, the moral dilemma that she faced as a mother who both had to work and care for a child with intense physical needs weighed on her. She portrayed her decision to work as one that required her to leave Alina alone in the family's rooms of their communal apartment. Alina, in this exchange, challenged this perspective. She did not want her mother to present a story of her childhood that would induce pity. "I always had lots of people around me," she countered, asserting her capabilities and an array of experiences outside of the apartment. In Alina's perception, an *invalid* who stayed alone in an apartment was truly disabled, in that that person had no social value. Alina asserted her own social worth and diversity of experiences. In fact, although she spent many days in her apartment, she often had visitors and had relationships with neighborhood children, neighbors, and peers. During periods when programs with accessible transport like the art therapy group were running, she participated in weekly meetings with disabled peers.

Alina asserted that her social world reached beyond the walls of her family apartment and contrasted that fact with the culturally expected situation for people with severe physical disabilities like hers. "Even now," she said, "everyone in the building can't believe that I go places, that I do things." In her conversation with her mother, Alina contested this dominant perspective that to be an *invalid* and to stay at home rendered her socially isolated, or "needed by nobody."[6] Instead, she suggested that her social relationships were both fulfilling and cast her as a friend and peer to others. In this way, Alina navigated the reality of "life in four walls" asserting that despite perceptions, living in an inaccessible apartment did not diminish her social personhood, even as she wished for a new apartment to become available.

Vera: Trading Up to the First Floor

Most families in the city, whether or not they had a disabled family member, had elaborate stories to share about the locally specific logics of what constituted a good apartment. A good apartment could be an apartment with proximity to the downtown city center, where one could easily walk to museums, premiere businesses, the university, a variety of grocery and consumer stores, and the lakefront. For another friend, a good apartment might be one that was separate from, but in the same neighborhood as, extended family (even if that meant taking a bus or *marshrutka* to work or the city center). Others valued new construction over older buildings; the solid stone prewar Stalin-era apartments in the city center were considered to be prestigious. The worst housing was widely understood to be the old wooden buildings, which were notorious for poor heat, frozen pipes, and the many design flaws of their slapdash construction (built when Petrozavodsk was a frontier town funneling lumber from Karelian forests to other regions in the new Soviet Union), and the temporary barracks, which were constructed after the city's occupation during World War II. In all cases, questions of convenience and ease permeated considerations of whether or not a particular apartment might support an imagined good life. This good life was imagined in terms of standards of comfortable modernity.

Many families had complicated stories of negotiating available housing resources to support the best outcome in an illiquid housing market with insufficient housing stock. One family rented out a large three-room apartment near the city center to earn extra income, while living for two generations in a smaller apartment elsewhere in the city. A young couple shared a room in a student dormitory, preparing food in an electric hot pot. A twenty-something moved out of his family apartment shared with parents and a younger sister in a neighborhood twenty minutes outside the city center to share a small apartment with his grandmother that afforded him a five-minute walk to work.

A musician friend worked as a real estate agent on the side to earn money to buy his family a better apartment, because he realized the two rooms would be difficult as his two daughters grew up. That is, the "two-room" apartment had an entryway for coats and boots, a small kitchen with a small table, a washroom (shower/tub and sink) and toilet, and two other rooms – one adjoining the kitchen with a foldout sofa bed, and one bedroom where the children slept. This layout was quite typical. Following the logic of Soviet housing planning, apartment size is described in terms of the total number of rooms aside from hallways, kitchen, and bathroom facilities, therefore including living room/sitting room/dining rooms (e.g. unlike in the US and Canada, where bedrooms are counted but living rooms are not (e.g. a two-bedroom apartment typically also has some common room). Soviet designers imagined the room closest to the kitchen as a multifunctional living/dining/sleeping/socializing/tv room, in contrast to what they understood as petit-bourgeois backwardness inherent in monofunctional room design of early twentieth century Europe; they designed modular and multi-purpose furniture to meet this plan (Buchli 1997). But, in my experience, by the 2010s, the Soviet political commitment to multifunctional living had given way for a different imaginary: the *evroremont* and desire for monofunctional sleeping quarters depicted in film and television. Still, most of the housing stock in Petrozavodsk had been built in the Soviet period. New constructions offered some opportunity for large open-plan kitchen-living room spaces. But constructing a new, stand-alone house (or *kottezh*, in local parlance) required a good deal of capital, both financial, to purchase the land and supplies, and social, to ensure security and avoid swindle, in the course of the construction. In general, the cost of renting apartments was high compared with local wages; those whose families had managed to take ownership of apartments during privatization of the housing stock in the 1990s were better off and engaged in complex strategizing to negotiate the most livable space for themselves and their families.

For my interlocutors with mobility impairments, the relative accessibility of one's living space was an important part of the equation when it came to what constituted good housing. This was a common topic in interviews with adults with mobility impairments and parents of children with disabilities in Petrozavodsk. One trade-off that people often made was leaving behind a smaller apartment for a larger one. For some interlocutors with disabilities, first-floor apartments were also desirable (although not for Vova and Larissa, as previously described).

The notion of trading up for a first-floor apartment came up in an interview with Vera, a bright, social, outgoing woman who lived at the time of our interview in a three-room apartment with her parents, her husband, and her two young children. Vera told me the story of her family's journey to their current living situation.

> V: So where we live. . . . When I first became disabled (*poluchila invalidnostu*), we were living in a dormitory. And after that, my parents waited in line for a long time until . . . I think they even wrote a request. So. They got a two-room apartment. But, a two room apartment in a regular building, a five-story building, on the second floor, that's what we had. As long as I was little, and my parents could still carry me up the stairs well enough, because there wasn't an elevator . . . so. But, when I got a little bigger and became a teenager, like up to seventeen years old, I got heavier, and at the same time my parents were getting older. So, we moved to a different apartment on the first floor, but there wasn't a ramp there either, so it was a long time, um, that we were petitioning our administration with the ministry of health and human services, so that they would build a ramp for us. So, they finally did it all, it took probably seven years to get it together. But—it worked out, I mean, I have my own ramp at home, and inside we remodeled so that, because the passageways were really narrow everywhere, there were really narrow doors.
>
> So, then, we thought everything was really set up. I can get through the doors without a problem, I can get outside on my own. I mean, the problem that most people in wheelchairs have is that they can't get out of their house, and, thankfully, I don't have that problem.
>
> C: Yes, a lot of people can't get out of their homes.
>
> V: Yes, REALLY a lot of people.

Vera was glad that the apartment her parents had, through years of work and organizing, obtained for their family offered her the possibility to come and go using a ramp.[7]

Vera's valuation of her family's first-floor apartment as accessible was part of a broader pattern ensconced in history of the desirable first-floor apartment in Soviet disability advocacy and law. She was not the only interlocutor to consider similar perspectives. Anya, the psychologist, moved to a new apartment during my fieldwork, noting that she jumped at the chance to spend her savings and buy when a first-floor apartment in her neighborhood became available. In spite of the fact that Anya used a power chair, she required assistance to get in and out of the front door, given a short half-flight of stairs between the building entryway and the landing to her first-floor apartment. Still, Anya considered that apartment to be more accessible, in that she did not need to rely on an elevator, and she imagined a possible future opportunity to build a separate ramped entrance to her apartment, as Vera had (see Hartblay 2020).

The idea of the first-floor apartment as a more accessible apartment than an apartment on a higher floor is a curious artifact of post-Soviet housing code, which also circulates in popular logic. On one hand, first-floor apartments are much closer to the street exit, and it is sometimes possible (if expensive) to build a private entrance with a ramp into the apartment, thus creating a fully wheelchair accessible passage to and from the street. On the other hand, first-floor apartments in Russia are not actually built at ground level, but half a story, or a flight of six steps plus a one- or two-step door stoop, from the street. Moreover, as Vova and Larissa pointed out, once you are inside an elevator building, any floor is wheelchair accessible.

Yet, several interlocutors noted the existing provision in legal code that those with mobility impairments should be entitled to a first-floor apartment. This observation was usually conveyed without a clear reference to the actual statue, and a raised eyebrows as if to say, but look how far that provision has gotten us, with our government as it is. In fact, evidence of the first-floor apartment idea can be found in Soviet newspapers dating back to the mid-twentieth century, when war-wounded veterans of the Great Patriotic War held a special status, and thus the moral standing to demand better housing (Tchueva 2008). While the word accessible (*dostupnyi*) was not used in Russian in reference to disability until the 1980s, a review of the digitized archives of several major all-Soviet newspapers demonstrates repeated claims made by veterans with mobility impairments for better housing, one characteristic of which was apartments that were more convenient to enter and exit (i.e., fewer stairs, not on a hill, and close to transit and shops).[8] Certainly for five-story walk-up buildings, the first floor was indeed more accessible, and by the 1970s, entitlements were introduced, if rarely successfully enacted.[9] This policy was documented in one 1972 article in the newspaper *Pravda* about infrastructural developments to make shopping districts more convenient for consumers.[10] The concept of the first-floor apartment as the "apartment for invalids" gained new life in post-Soviet construction (ironically, including in elevator buildings like the one where Vova and Larissa live). Building codes introduced requirements to include at least one *dostupnaia* apartment in a new construction (more depending on the number of units), which typically was understood to be accessible in terms of having an accessible toilet and being located on the first floor. In this way, the notion that the first-floor apartment is "for" those with mobility impairments (whether war veterans, elderly, or otherwise) has been codified; at the same time, it is unclear whether adults with mobility impairments actually find these apartments desirable, or if they are even successful in acquiring them. Of all my interlocutors, not one had acquired such an apartment in a newly constructed building.

Stairwell Stories

The concept of the first-floor apartment as more convenient for mobility impaired Soviet and now-Russian citizens is rooted in a recognition, promoted by disabled veterans, that stairs are disabling infrastructure. As Vera pointed out, a central concern for *invalidi* with mobility impairments was how they would be able to get in and out of their family apartments. The architectural design of the entryway or shared staircase that led to the individual

FIGURE 8.   An interior apartment building staircase in Petrozavodsk; these stairwells are the location for numerous comings and goings and various scenes of daily life. Seven steps separate each landing, with flights in alternating directions and one landing with a window between each floor. A person who is holding a large bunch of multicolor balloons with ribbons, as if for a party or event, descends the stairs. The stairs are worn concrete, with metal hand railings that are bent in some places and painted with a glossy finish. The walls are painted with the same color up to about five feet from the floor, and then are whitewashed to the ceiling. A large window casts light onto a tiled landing, backlighting the balloons and reflecting off of the glossy walls. No elevator is visible. Photo by Cassandra Hartblay, 2013.

apartment doors in all of the various Soviet-designed apartment complexes were patently inaccessible. Most residents in Petrozavodsk in the early 2010s lived in apartment buildings, and the specific dynamics of getting into and out of those buildings were a major consideration when I asked interlocutors about their experiences of daily life with a mobility impairment. Interviews frequently turned to the subject the proximity of one's home apartment to the exit to the street.

Ethnographers have documented the peculiar nature of the stairways in post-Soviet buildings: They occupy a certain kind of spatial category that is neither public nor private in the US sense (Utekhin et al. 2008). When the buildings were privatized in the 1990s, the staircases remained *obschestvenniye*, although the apartments became private property. As a result, apartments were renovated internally, and even doors to apartments look different within the same staircase, as apartment owners purchased their own security doors in several different styles. The space of the stairway also became a particular kind of place—some frequented by smokers who ash into coffee cans or empty jars while avoiding smoking in their own apartments; others filled by a neighbor's well-tended houseplants; children's tricycles or sleds might be stored in one stairwell; another stairwell might be clean but empty; and still another might reek of urine and vodka.

This shared nature of parts of the building create hassles when it comes time to make renovations. This could be particularly frustrating for people with disabilities who want to renovate entranceways for accessibility purposes. Alina and Valya described one such occurrence:

V: Did you see how they redid the roof above our entranceway?

C: I didn't notice.

V: They put the announcements up, but didn't take them down . . .

A: The neighbors around here aren't all happy with the renovation . . .

V: Well, I say to them, "Say thank you that they did anything at all!" So that the awning wouldn't be crumbling down on anyone who was going in and out . . . how many kids does it have to kill before they fix it . . .?

C: It's good they redid them.

V: People are so dissatisfied around here. [impersonating a dissatisfied neighbor] "They didn't do it right!" Well, I say: "Then you do it better!" The neighbor's son was asking me [mocking voice]: "Are you satisfied with how they did the new entranceway roofing?" And I told him that I'm satisfied with everything. And he goes to me, "Well what for, you're not signing any documents." And I say that I'll sign whatever, and if he doesn't like it, he can go and fix it himself.

They're saying that they spent the money for nothing, but I say, they're not just doing the awnings, soon they'll do the driveway as well. And of course this comes out of the general housing fund. Soon they're going to fix the second driveway.

Generally, some arrangement exists in which a resident acts as the custodian of all the stairwells for a block, collecting money from residents to keep the stairwells swept and washed, to repair the outdoor stoops, keep light bulbs changed, and to clear ice and snow from the doorway. As with anything, however, there are variable levels of functionality, often erring toward mismanagement.

The negotiating of coming and going, and the problem of how to escape life in four walls was particularly felt by my interlocutor Vakas. Although Vakas was ambulatory, his balance was off, and because of his brain injury, he tended to fall a lot. (He liked to regal me with stories of particularly nasty falls, pointing to the front tooth he had knocked out, which his mother had paid to have replaced at a private dental clinic). Although his family apartment was cozy and nicely renovated, his mother worked hard to support a family of four, and he often grew bored during the day. He and his father both spent most days at home, and according to Vakas, they often fell into conflict with one another, or retreated to their respective bedrooms to stay apart. Vakas would have liked to go outdoors, to sit in the courtyard, or walk around the neighborhood, but after repeated falls, and the problems that he sometimes ran into with strangers misunderstanding his slow speech (assuming he was slurring from alcohol) and often unusual ideas (the result of spending his days socializing only online without a peer group to let him know when he had gone down a rabbit hole), his mother forbid him from going out without a chaperone. As a result, Vakas was the most trapped in four walls of all my interlocutors. He frequently plotted escapes, and fantasized about living alone without his parents (even going so far as to make entreaties to a social worker to help him work out what such a move would take while keeping these deliberations secret from his parents, whom he was sure would forbid such a thing). Visiting Vakas, I sometimes made my way across his apartment building courtyard, buzzed in, took an elevator and a flight of stairs (for some reason I always forgot if the family's apartment was on the seventh, eighth, or ninth floor, and then had to walk a few more flights of stairs to find the right landing), and took off my coat and boots in the threshold, only for him to insist that I rebundle so that we could go back downstairs and sit outdoors for a time. Vakas made it clear to me that the barriers keeping him from leaving his apartment were not physical or material but social: The fights and emotional toll of upsetting his parents if he left against their wishes—scared as they were that he would fall or encounter some sort of trouble if he went out alone—were what kept him inside. For Vakas the stair-well, elevator, and courtyard were already "outside," and to his consternation, were beyond the interior of the family apartment that his parents understood as the only place he might be totally safe.

Desiring Normal Life: Intersectional Strategies for Obtaining Better Housing

As anywhere, in Petrozavodsk, some apartments are more desirable and present fewer barriers than others. But how does one come to inhabit a particular apartment or acquire a different one? Typically, among my interlocutors with mobility impairments, stories about one's home included not only a description of what it took to go in and out of one's apartment but also a history of the family's journey to their current apartment that entailed a variety of trade-offs. The work of obtaining a new domestic residence was entangled with locally specific economies and systems of exchange, and post-Soviet logics of entitlements.

FIGURE 9. A view of a Petrozavodsk neighborhood. Snowy dirt driveways run between apartment buildings, garages, and houses under a winter afternoon sky. Photo by Cassandra Hartblay, 2013.

Some interlocutors without other financial prospects held out hope that their disability status entitled them to a socially distributed apartment. Alina and her mother Valya explained the waiting list for a government apartment to me during one visit to their shared apartment, while eating sweets and drinking tea in their living room. Their building was located in a factory region with only the minimum of local amenities—a small convenience and grocery shop, an elementary school, and a bus stop, and a fifteen-minute walk to a nearby factory.

Alina and Valya's experience of apartment destiny was perhaps the most starkly distressing—or at least, they were the most forthcoming of my interlocutors with their complaints. Unlike other families that I knew, they had no breadwinner. Alina received a monthly disability pension, and her mother received a monthly retirement pension. Alina's brother, in his early twenties, was not in a position to contribute much to the household, and he showed up only occasionally to eat and sleep. They had moved into the current apartment when Alina was a small child. They had opted for this far-from-the-center apartment instead of the previous apartment they had in the center of the city, which was too small for a family of four (her father was alive then) and located in one of the poorly heated old wooden houses that dotted the city in small clusters. The apartment that they were granted after moving up the waitlist of people entitled to housing based on social need was a communal apartment. Their family had three rooms, and they shared a bathroom and kitchen and entrance way with whomever was living in the other room. I had not realized the apartment was so divided; I assumed that the family had chosen to rent out a room for extra income. "Oh, no no no!" Valya told me, with the particular gleam in her eye reserved for moments to reveal injustice. "It might be technically illegal, officially communal apartments no longer exist, but WE live in one!" For the past seventeen years, they asserted, the family had been on a waitlist to receive a new apartment. When Valya scurried off to find the latest letter that they had received stating their place in the queue, Alina waived her hand in an expression of disgust: "It's barely moved in seventeen years!" Without the financial resources to rent an apartment at market rate, and frustrated that the Soviet system of distributing housing seemed to still exist in the form of the waitlist, but without an actual apartment forthcoming, Alina and Valya seemed resigned yet indignant, and expected that they would be living in their communal apartment for some time (they just hoped for "socially adequate" neighbors to be assigned to the other room, as over the years, certain assigned apartment mates had sometimes caused problems or behaved in ways that offended Alina and Valya (e.g., drinking and drugs).

Marina: Living Normally in an Inherited Apartment

During research for this project in 2012–2016, in spite of a period of relative economic stability in Russia (compared with the 1990s and early 2000s) and relative market flexibility compared with the Soviet period, housing scarcity remained a key factor influencing how residents of Petrozavodsk experienced their desire for what they imagined to be a normal living space. Scholars argue that since mid-century onward in the Soviet Union, the desire for *svoi* (one's own, that is, a single family's) apartment emerged as a primary element of what Soviet citizens imagined as the basic standard of living that ought to be acheivable (*zhit' normal'no*) (in contrast to the early Soviet configuration of communal apartments) (Zavisca 2012). Yet, throughout the twentieth century and the following decades, the availability and cost of actual housing has remained illiquid, and most young Russian families in the 2010s did not have enough living space to *zhit' normal'no*, live normally, nor the financial resources to acquire more spacious housing in a market with insufficient supply. Furthermore, the scarcity of housing made families hesitant to give up apartments that they do not need. This contributed to illiquidity, in that rather than selling unused apartments, instead, families prefered to maintain ownership, renting the apartment or unofficially offering it to family members who "officially" live elsewhere (Zavisca 2012). This strategy makes sense given that real estate was one of the only assets that remained valuable and in family's control through the upheaval and uncertainty of the post-Soviet economic transition (although many families did lose ownership of homes during this time). Housing market illiquidity makes it harder to move, which reduces the capacity to move to a more accessible apartment if a family member is experiencing disabling barriers in the current space. My interlocutors in Petrozavodsk who were not able to move apartments were more persistently disabled by their environment than their peers who had the financial resources or social capital to move in a competitive housing market. Also, moving was not always a sign of success, but sometimes a retreat to an older or less modern family apartment where one did not have to pay rent.

Marina and her ten-year-old son lived with her boyfriend in her inherited family apartment. For some time, they lived in one apartment, but they moved during the time that I was doing research, so that I visited them in one apartment in October 2012 and in a different apartment the following winter. The apartment, in a rundown building, was a long bus ride from the center of the city and had not been updated for many years.

Marina's son, who has *DTsP* (Cerebral Palsy), attended the specialized school for children with disabilities. He received a vigorous course of physical therapy at school, supplemented by Marina's implementation of various elements of physical therapy at home gleaned from internet research or talking with other parents. She managed, even living on a meager pension, to acquire a "home gym" for her son, a sort of indoor gymnastics apparatus. On occasions when I visited the family in the evening, I found her enforcing a daily regime of "standing" for her son. Although he was ten years old, he looked quite a bit younger and was small for his age. Propped up between the kitchen table and the wall, he was made to stand for forty minutes at a time, although he much preferred to sit. The family held on to hope that with continued physical therapy, his constricted muscles could be trained into the capacity to walk. In the meantime, family members carried him up and down the four flights of steps, under an arm, like a much younger child of four or five. He was just on the cusp of being too big to be carried. His tricycle and wheelchairs were stored on the staircase landing just outside of the apartment, for safekeeping, which therefore required a second trip, or two adults, to take him outside or to school.

Although the apartment was, on the surface, undesirable given its aging infrastructure and the distance from the city center, Marina explained how meaningful the apartment was to her in her childhood. She told me the story as she prepared tea in the kitchen on my first visit after the family had moved. During her early childhood, she explained, her family had lived in a barracks—emergency housing the Soviet government constructed in the immediate postwar period. With families clustered around bedding areas in undivided warehouses, outdoor toilets, and shared kerosene stoves, these barracks were very much stop-gap measures. Their family, she told me, really could not wait and was ecstatic to get this three-room apartment with a kitchen and indoor plumbing.

The apartment that her family eventually received was a top-floor walk-up in a four-story building in the Kliuchareva region of the city. Far from the center, the area was developed around two factories—a bread factory and a shipbuilding factory. Although the factories no longer operated at the same capacity now that they were privatized and food supply chains in the city had diversified, and although the region was far from the city center, the apparatus of residential life (most important, including public transportation) still served the region, making it a livable option. Today, numerous new housing projects are being built in this area, and the amenities and available apartments have attracted young families. The gas stove lines and indoor plumbing, which once were cutting-edge amenities, now (sixty years later) were markers of outdated modernity. As Marina lit the pilot, she recalled fondly:

"This stove was the best thing we had ever seen when we moved into this apartment." At the same time, the financial possibility that this apartment afforded a family surviving on a low income was an enabling factor that made living there preferable to other options.

These anecdotes illustrate the way in which the local personal histories of housing and inheritance have shaped the life opportunities of young people with disabilities in Petrozavodsk. Indeed, Marina inherited the family apartment, but ironically, with a son who had a mobility impairment, that apartment was on the top floor of an elevator-less building. As a working-class and sometimes single-parent family, Marina was largely priced out of the housing market in much of the city. For Marina and her son, as for many residents, opportunities to choose where one might live were few and far between.

Housing Fates and Normal Life

The logics by which interlocutors in Russia valued and desired particular living spaces have continued to be shaped by personal and political histories. When interlocutors talked about domestic living spaces, their stories were shaped by considerations of what elements of the material housing infrastructure were particularly disabling for them. Disabling barriers in the built environment of the home were material in two ways: (1) the infrastructure that presented barriers, and (2) poverty and access to social capital. Interlocutors occupied different relationships to an imagined normal, middle-class ideal of housing and domestic materiality, glossed as normal life. This imagined normal life for residents of Petrozavodsk in the 2010s—as for other Soviet and post-Soviet families— implicitly indexed ideas about Western European and North American middle-class life (Fehérváry 2013; Zavisca 2012). The concepts of "normal" were often understood in relation to images depicted in films and music videos from the West; at the same time, they were embedded in historically rooted understandings of norms for domestic life.

The stories that interlocutors told about disabling design were inflected with everyday logics of historical materialism inherited from Soviet rhetorical patterns for making claims about justice and about infrastructure, patterns of thinking about justice materially that endured as a legacy of socialist design ideology. Disabling structures in domestic residential buildings presented real challenges to social and political participation for interlocutors. The specific cultural history of the Soviet-built apartment building continued to structure how residents of Petrozavodsk in the early 2010s narrated housing stories: from communal stairwells and elevators, to advocating for or ignoring statutes that promised better access in first-floor apartments, the material conditions of daily life echoed with history.

For my interlocutors, the irony of fate is to wake up each day in a material space that was designed according to an ideology that sought to create a more equitable society through the design and distribution of space. However, the question of stairs as a disabling design element was not considered in Soviet architecture, and minor capitulations to veteran demands were rarely enforced. Examples of inaccessible infrastructure in apartment buildings circulated and continue to appear in popular mythology about the failures of the state to provide what is needed to live a normal life. The material afterlife of Soviet design ideology continues to shape social experience in a time when the rules formulating pathways to social equity have changed: when it comes to renovating, moving, or renegotiating domestic living spaces, the playing field is unequal. Intersectional familial considerations profoundly shape the possible egress futures that my interlocutors imagine and bring into being.

Inaccess Stories and the Material Afterlife of Soviet Dwellings

What is specific about the inaccess stories that these interlocutors in Petrozavodsk tell? What distinguishes them from the inaccess stories about places of residence that disabled people in other regions of Russia or in other parts of the worlds might tell? As we have seen in the case studies in this chapter, each of the interlocutors has continued to negotiate the material afterlives of Soviet design and centralized architectural planning in the ways in which they navigate the variable accessibility and accessibility of their home space.

The culturally specific character of Soviet and post-Soviet apartment buildings has shaped the considerations, strategies, concerns, hopes, and desires interlocutors have about their homes. Vera and Anya imagined how first-floor apartments might become accessible, in part thanks to advocacy of disabled people during the Soviet era. Alina and her mother made sense of what it meant to desire a different apartment while living on a limited income in Petrozavodsk. Soviet designers imagined the room closest to the kitchen as a multifunctional living/dining/sleeping/socializing/tv room, in contrast to what they understood as petit-bourgeois backwardness inherent in monofunctional room design of early 20th century Europe; they designed and modular and multipurpose furniture to meet this plan (Buchli 1997). Some of these inaccess stories shared a familiar congruence with inaccess stories of urban middle-class families in other regions. The inaccess stories about family homes shared by my interlocuters, however, were inflected by the material conditions of post-Soviet life that were deeply specific to this context.

In my broader consideration of inaccess stories that interlocutors with mobility impairments and their family members in Petrozavodsk told, apartment stories became a genre of consideration. The family apartment, Anya argued (in her discussion of accessible public space in chapter 2), played a central role in the capacity of each interlocutor to access the rest of the city. Accessible pathways, from a user's point of view, as she pointed out, started at your front door and went out from there. Getting onto the street from one's front door was a major point of consideration, as the apartment inaccess stories in this chapter demonstrate. Conditions of illiquidity, avoidance of market tactics to obtain housing (usually because markets were prohibitively expensive), an overall scarcity of housing, aging and inaccessible Soviet architecture, and a history of communal systems that made accessibility renovations to common areas difficult all combined to make the typical apartment in Petrozavodsk a disabling structure.

In this way, inaccess has emerged through a particular historical configuration of material objects, and socially coordinated infrastructure design and planning. The post-Soviet Russian patterns of dwellings and the manner in which housing is distributed has created a particular infrastructure of ableism. Interlocutors navigate this infrastructure, working with vastly different resources, managing their living quarters to their minimum disadvantage. These tales of how to navigate the ableist infrastructure of the Petrozavodsk housing stock offer important insight into the kinds of in/access stories that my interlocutors told. In chapter 4, I further examine Petrozavodsk access stories by considering the attributes of accessibility that my interlocutors valued and the specific vocabulary my interlocutors used to describe experiences of access. I contextualize the attributes of this access in relation to the ways in which access has continued to circulate as a metaphor and commodified abstraction in popular Russian culture.

NORMAL, CONVENIENT, COMFORTABLE

Lexicons of Access in Urban Modernity

Sitting in my rented apartment in Petrozavodsk at a small kitchen table, yellow autumn leaves fluttering on birch branches outside the window, I asked my friend Olya, a civil engineer, to elaborate on her work for the architectural firm in the city, as described in chapter 2. I was curious to elicit as much description as possible about the work of designing an accessible building. I asked open-ended questions and encouraged Olya to talk at length on her own terms, hoping to better understand the categories that she used to make sense of her world. Later, after my fieldwork had ended, I returned to the transcripts of this interview while sitting at a desk overlooking a university green. I was curious to identify the words Olya had used to describe *access* in Russian: I wanted to understand how she talked about access beyond the formal direct translation. While I had a general sense of the vocabulary of accessibility in Russia, I wondered if there might be vernacular nuances that a sustained investigation might reveal. I set out to analyze transcripts from interviews with Olya and others to amass a Russophone lexicon of access, and, in doing so, to consider what synonyms and attributes of access circulated beyond a direct translation of the word access (*dostupnost'* or *bezbar'ernost'*).

At one point in the interview, I asked Olya to describe the kinds of tasks and considerations she might undertake in relation to the checklist of accessible design elements she was charged with reviewing.

> Well—look. So—in general. In general in, for example, a public building, we have to work it out so that, for example, there are two floors in

the building. On each of the floors there has to be toilet facilities for *invalidy*. An *invalid* should be able to get from the first floor to the second floor. In some way. So, this could be a ramp. Or, it could be an elevator. . . . He—the person in a wheelchair, or in general a person with limited mobility—he should be able to easily/peacefully (*spokoino*) enter any office that he needs to go to. That is, he needs to be able to take care of himself. So, it follows that there are two considerations. For, like, you have to figure out the turning radius of a wheelchair. That is, we can't make the bathroom facilities too narrow, because a person has to be able to go in, turn around however he needs to . . . [quieter] like, so that it would be comfortable/convenient (*komfortno*) for him.

Olya is a nondisabled architect's assistant, a design worker who considers accessible design to be part of her professional area of responsibility. In this telling, she thoughtfully outlined in general terms the kinds of considerations that might come up in relation to the category of low-mobility groups in the population, the official designation of those entitled to accessible design according to Russian legal code and architectural professional standards. Proposing an imaginary wheelchair user, Olya described the essence of what she understood accessible design was meant to provide—that is, the capacity for a wheelchair user to move easily (literally, peacefully, *spokoino*), to look after oneself and move independently (to be responsible for oneself, *sam sledit'*), and ultimately, to be comfortable during the experience or find it convenient (*komfortno*) to move through the space. On the one hand, Olya's description suggested that she exercised professional competence to express the transnational definition of the purpose and function of good accessible design and its implementation. On the other hand, Olya used an array of specific vocabulary to talk about access in this passage, while never saying the word itself (*dostupnost'*). Considering Olya's descriptive vocabulary, and the ways that other interlocutors described experiences of access and inaccess, I started to notice that certain Russophone words kept coming up. This friction in vernacular terminology of access between English and Russian led me to consider how the globalization of accessible design exposes cultural mismatches between political imaginaries and social histories in anglophone and Russophone political claims. In this chapter, I turn to a close examination of how interlocutors in Petrozavodsk described and theorized *access* as a concept. I argue that in these vernacular usages, *access* indexes both transnational disability advocacy discourse, and historically rooted Russophone rhetorical strategies for raising political claims and complaints.

In the previous chapters, I explored how disability politics and claims about social inclusion unfolded in Petrozavodsk in the 2010s, and described the kinds of inaccess stories about public infrastructure and domestic space that circulated among my interlocutors and in Russophone public discourse online. In this chapter, I turn to the specific Russophone vocabularies that appear in conversations about disability access, and in political complaints about failures of public infrastructure more broadly. Which words do people with disabilities in Petrozavodsk use to talk about inaccessible infrastructures? How do their discursive strategies align with and fit into broader Russian performative practices of citizenship? What lexicons of disability access circulate in global friction in Petrozavodsk? How do those lexicons align or overlap with other conversations about mobility in the built environment?

I argue that local imaginaries of inaccessible infrastructure offer new ways to theorize accessible design as a technology for disability inclusion. That is, the Anglophone term *access* always already indexes infrastructure, which carries with it sentiments about development, modernity, and governance. In examining the specifically Russophone cases presented here, I observe (1) that the constitutive meaning of an inaccess stories (the literal story) is complemented by a performative meaning, in which the speaker may build affinity with the listener or index other, complex ideas, and (2) that the Russophone lexicon of access indexes Soviet arguments about everyday convenience as part of the state's responsibility to provide material conditions conducive to building socialist consciousness. Specifically, this leads me to consider the relationship between in/access and in/convenience. What kind of political claim is a complaint about inaccess? What kind of a political claim is a complaint about inconvenience? What work did these terms do in Petrozavodsk's linguistic and political context in the 2010s? In this chapter, I examine inaccess stories—both about and not about disability—as political speech acts in historical context.

In this chapter, I consider how interlocutors in Petrozavodsk and other regions of Russia referred to the transnational concept of disability access, or *dostupnost'* or *bezbar'ernost'*, in Russian. I examine the attributes of the concept, that is, the qualities that the concept of access described, according to my interlocutors. This approach crips the primacy of the term *access* connoting a universalized concept of experiences of good passage for people with mobility impairments (as well as other forms of access beyond the scope of this study) by considering a comparative etymology of access in contrast to other potential near synonyms in Russian. In particular, I explore how the Russian word *udobstvo* (convenience) carries a political history related to state infrastructure that makes it synonymous with access, even in cases in which its anglophone counterpart might have produced problems for political advocacy in North America. To think expansively about how the performance of political complaints about infrastructure work, I compare inaccess stories about disability/mobility with a genre of complaint common in Petrozavodsk during my fieldwork about poorly maintained roadways, which I sum up as "pothole talk." Situating this talk in relation to Russophone patterns of political complaint and interlocutor inaccess stories, I argue that, in Petrozavodsk in the 2010s, the vocabulary of disability access was propelled in part by friction with other genres of political complaint about infrastructure and the imagined good life.

How Do You Say "Accessible" in Russian?

Since the collapse of the Soviet Union and the entrance of transnational actors into the Russian and the Russophone public sphere, the use of translated Anglophone phrases to describe services, goods, and habits have become a common part of daily Russian life. Russians read and write emails on *mobil'niki* (mobile phones) or *noutbuki* (notebook computers), aspire to live not in apartments but in *kottezhi* (cottages or single-family homes), discuss the merits of a particular *pi-er* (PR or public relations) strategy, meet friends for *sushi*, and are likely to *postavit' laik* (like) a friend's social media post. As in many languages, in some cases, the Russian word for an imported object or novel concept is a simple cognate, adjusted to Russian pronunciation; in other cases, transnational political, social, and manufacturing concepts appear as technical direct translations of a foreign term. For instance, Russian language terms exist for weapons of mass destruction (*oruzhie massovogo porazheniia*) and domestic violence (*domashnee nasilie*). While accessible design falls into the latter category—a concept that is discernibly not endemic to Russia and Russian but adapted and mobilized in Russian social and political contexts—the phrase *dostupnyi dizain*, a direct translation of accessible design, does not circulate as a distinct concept. Instead, the concept of barrier-free environment is more widely used, translated as *bezbar'ernaia sreda*.

The Russian translation of the word accessible, *dostupnyi*, does not necessarily index disability access, although it may. While disability advocates and advocacy organizations use this word to describe disability access, its conceptual domain in general discourse is less readily related to disability than its English counterpart. The English language use of access in relation to disability access is a relatively recent development. The Oxford English Dictionary (OED 2014) includes an entry under *accessible* (adjective) that relates to design and disability, which specifies this usage as originating in the United States, and states, "Capable of being conveniently used or accessed by people with disabilities; of or designating goods, services, or facilities designed to meet the needs of the disabled." The general definition of accessible is "Capable of being entered or approached; easy of access; readily reached or got hold of," deriving from the Latin *accedere*, to approach. The Oxford English Dictionary entry for *barrier* (noun) does not have specific mention of disability, but it may be an obstruction, material or immaterial, something that stops an advance. In this sense, "barrier-free" and "accessible" function as synonyms in contemporary popular discourse in English, although disability advocates and scholars might distinguish the two in terms of theoretical underpinnings and regional derivations.[1]

The middling association between the word *dostupnyi*, the direct translation of "accessible", and disability or accessible design, is also evident in the way the word is used in Russophone mass media discourse. A search of the Universal Database of Russian Central Newspapers shows that most uses of the words *dostupno* and *dostupnyi* (adverb and adjectival forms of all genders and cases) in print news stories still refer not to disability but rather to the affordability of goods and services or to the capacity of average citizens to obtain said goods or services. It is a common word, with 116,575 entries between 1980 and 2015—including, for example, a sentence in relation to health care for women and children, *A glavnoe, chto eto dostupno vsem* (The main thing is that it be accessible [available] to everyone). The database searches as far back as 1980, and by date, the majority of instances of words with the root *dostup* relate to this concept of availability or practical capacity to obtain to a resource. The use of *dostupnost'* in relation to disability is much more scarce. In fact, the relationship of the Russian *dostupnost'* to space and infrastructure is less central to the usage than the English *access*. In this way, the concept of access as a subdefinition of the general definition that specifically relates to barriers affecting people with disabilities seems to have a limited circulation in journalistic discourse. That is, most Russian-speakers would understand the concept of *dostupnost'* for *invalidov* not as a conceptual domain in and of itself, but rather as an appropriate extension of the general meaning of the word *dostupnost'*, although disability advocates would recognize the phrase *dostupnaia sreda* (accessible built environment).

I heard a similar phrase, *bezbar'ernaia sreda* (barrier-free environment), from disability advocates in various regions of Russia. It was used by the Moscow-based disability advocacy organization Perspektiva to describe material conditions that facilitate access. Svetlana, my colleague and interlocutor who wrote her dissertation (2009) on the socialization of young adults with disabilities in Karelia, also used this phrase in her academic work. Having heard Svetlana use this term to describe advocacy efforts in Petrozavodsk in September 2012, I subsequently used it in my conversations and interviews with my interlocutors. However, reading my transcribed interviews, I noted that while my interlocutors sometimes used the phrase in direct response to a question that I asked using the phrase, they rarely used it on their own accord.

Reflecting on the register of this translated term, I wondered how legal disability rights advocates in Russia might think of it. In 2014, I wrote to a disability advocate I know, Galina Gorbatykh, who lives in a different region of Russia. Galina received her master's degree in Francophone Canada in the 1990s, and is a lawyer and a local politician (as well as a wheelchair-user). Given this background, I was curious how Galina understood the term *bezbar'ernaia sreda* as one that had moved into Russian discourse from abroad, as I suspected that the derivation was a technical one related to legal provisions or architectural standards. In response to a short private message that I sent online (in polite but colloquial Russian), Galina sent back a long response, in which she cited numerous laws and provisions in which the phrase had appeared, frequently slipping into the highly technical jargon of official or legal Russian. While she may have copied and pasted some segments of this response from some of the advocacy materials she uses in her work, it is also possible that, given her professional area of expertise, this is simply the register of language in which she describes the question of accessibility.

For instance, she opened her response with a definition of the term as it operates in Russian, and then immediately situated this usage in relation to transnational disability advocacy concerns.

> The term *dostupnaia* or *bezbar'ernaia sreda* is called up on many legal acts in the Russian Federation and in various sources has different shades of meaning. In most contexts, the term '*dostupnaia sreda*' can appear in the sense of: a barrier free environment (*bezbar'ernaia sreda*)—that is, those elements of the surroundings (*okruzhaiushchie sredy*) through which people can enter and move freely and which people with physical, sensory or intellectual impairments can use.
>
> A setting (*sreda*) for the activities of daily living, that is accessible (*dostupnaia*) for the disabled is usually an environment (*sreda*) that has been renovated (*oborudovannaia*) with consideration for the needs that arise in connection with disability (*invalidnost'iu*), and that in using, the disabled may carry out an independent way of life.

Galina confirmed that both the phrases *dostupnaia* or *bezbar'ernaia sreda* are primarily used in legal discourse, entering the Russian language through legal doctrine beginning in the 1990s.[2] In this sense, we can understand the derivation of the terms as located in an official register of speech related to Russian legal doctrine. Galina also specified that the origin of the terms is related to a global context in which accessibility in public space for people with a disability is a concern that circulates transnationally. She wrote:

> Creating accessible environments (*sozdaniia dostupnoi sredy*) for all is also a worldwide problem. Addressing and solving the issue of eliminating barriers begins first of all with architecture. Starting from the end of the 1950s, steps have been taken to create accessible environments for all, beginning with proposals from disabled people's organizations in the countries of Western Europe and North America including practical recommendations for city planners and designers and architects.

Galina's experience studying disability transnationally, and her role as a leading advocate and authority in her region, was clear in her tone and the way that she situated disability access as a shared struggle worldwide. She oriented her understanding of the origin of the concept of accessible built environments to narratives emerging from North America.

Galina's language was pitched toward legal advocacy. It had the forceful tone of someone accustomed to writing to enforce the weight of the law. The terminology of accessibility—that is, the direct translations of the terms *access* and *barrier-free environment* that circulate globally—in Russian remain tied to formal registers of language. My interlocutors—in the inaccess stories they shared in interviews and in general conversations—tended to use more colloquial endemic Russophone terms to describe qualities of good passage.

Interlocutor Inaccess Stories: Colloquial Vocabularies and Attributes of Access

Through a colleague at a local university, I was introduced by email to Artyom, a university student with cerebral palsy (CP). We met on an early spring day in 2013 when there was still drifted snow along the sidewalks, the sky a low gray, at a café not far from the city's eternal flame monument. We had a cup of tea and a pastry and talked, and Artyom suggested a walk, moving along the sidewalk using aluminum crutches with plastic arm braces. Later, I returned to this interview when I searched my ethnographic archive for terms that I noticed were often used alongside the word *dostupno* or *dostupnost'* (accessible or access). At one point in my interview with Artyom, he explained that when he is walking in the city or boarding a bus, "I need to consider every act, and consider the possibilities, consider how [I go about things so that it] will be more convenient (*udobnee*) for me." He was responding to a question about access in his family's apartment, which he explained was a fifth-floor walk-up. The staircase was particularly difficult during the long process of gaining strength following a procedure that left his leg in a cast. It was in the context of this longer inaccess story that he considered convenience.

> After the cast came off, you can imagine, it was difficult. For half a month my legs wouldn't flex, because they had been in the cast, and then you start to work them . . . basically, physical therapy, pain, a whole lot of tears, and then it gets better. [. . .] at first you won't be able to do anything at all, then you'll have worked out something about your system and you start to walk, and then it starts to come to you more quickly. [. . .] Then you can go downstairs only holding on with one hand, but you can always put down a crutch. Before it was only sideways, holding on with two hands and going pretty slowly. [. . .] Now I can go down either with or without a railing, just with my legs and my crutches. [. . .] Then the next phase is public transit—trolleybus, bus . . . not many people understand, but for me, I need to consider every act, and consider the possibilities, how will it be **more convenient** (***udobnee***) for me. [. . .] Before, in the winter—on crutches and without help—I wasn't able to go anywhere—it was hard, and if it was slippery it was even scarier [. . .] The past two years I have been getting around **normally** (***normal'no***) in the winter, even when it's all snowy I can come and go, wherever I need to.

In this interview segment, Artyom described the progress that he made in terms of a growing ability to move independently through the city as he gained strength and skill walking with a metal crutch following his surgery, a journey that began with small movements in his family apartment, and slowly expanded to include the stairwell, then the street, and finally the city's old, difficult-to-enter-and-exit, and often-bumpy-to-ride buses and trolleybuses. The structure of the built environment, particularly the fact that his family's apartment was on the fifth floor created a disabling structure. Reflecting on his experience working up to riding public transportation on his own (essential for attending university in the city), he described the degree to which a particular manner of doing something (*sposob*) would be convenient (*udobnee*) for him. In this construction, convenience approached a semantic conceptual realm similar to that of disability access. Artyom could have used the word *dostupnyi* (the direct translation of "accessible" but derived from the translation of the transnational concept into Russian) as an adjective to describe a given experience; however,

TABLE 1. Mobility access terminology observed in the Russian lexicon, 2010–2016

CONCEPTUAL DOMAIN	TRANSLITERATED RUSSIAN TERMS	ENGLISH TRANSLATION
Accessibility in the built environment	*dostupnyi*	accessible
	oborudovan	renovated, equipped
	bezbar'ernaia sreda	barrier-free environment

the comparative adjective (*dostupnee*) is a bit awkward and unwieldy, and he opted for the more colloquial *udobnee*. Interestingly, *sposob* shares a root with *sposobnost'*, a noun meaning ability or capacity, which is frequently used in translations of disability terminology (e.g., a person with limited abilities). But here, the short form remains squarely within Russophone morphology, not straying into formal phrasing that allude to translational concepts; the tone is deeply personal and self-reflexive. Similarly, Artyom used the adjective *normal'no*, colloquially a turn of phrase like the English "just fine," to assess his present capabilities in getting around in public space in the winter. Artyom's use of these phrasings were echoed with other interviewees in Petrozavodsk, adults in their twenties and thirties with mobility impairments, who often used both the formal lexicon of disability advocacy and more colloquial terms to describe moving through their daily lives.

Artyom's use of synonyms and attributes to *dostupnyi/ee* was part of a wider pattern of discursive engagement with the idea of disability access observed across interviews with several interlocutors in Petrozavodsk. In addition to *udobno*, my interlocutors with mobility impairments used other attributes of access—including *normal'no*, *komfortno*, and *spokoino*—to discuss experiences of (in)access (see table 1 and table 2). Furthermore, in Artyom's use of the comparative adjective, and other interlocutors' frequent reference to experiences that are more or less accessible, accessibility functioned as a relative concept, established by way of comparison. When asked about their experiences navigating daily life, interlocutors with disabilities made use of this lexicon to draw

TABLE 2. Attributes of mobility access, 2010–2016

CONCEPTUAL DOMAIN	TRANSLITERATED RUSSIAN TERMS	ENGLISH TRANSLATION
Experiences of mobility access (attributes of *dostupnost'*), according to people with mobility impairments	*udobno*	convenient
	komfortno	comfortable
	spokoino	peaceful, smooth
	normal'no	normal, fine, not bad, of a European standard

comparisons between different kinds of experiences and express approval or disapproval for elements of the urban built environment in their city and elsewhere.

One example of this lexicon of access emerged in an interview with Vera, who lived in a first floor apartment, as described in the previous chapter. Vera had used a wheelchair since childhood as a result of a spinal cord injury, and at the time of our interview, was in her thirties. She had two small children, and lived with her parents, husband, and children in the apartment that her parents had obtained, and which she had worked to make accessible. Describing the apartment's accessibility, she commented:

> So—it's like halfway passable, we have, I mean at my house there is a separate ramp, and the apartment has been remodeled so that, well, because the hallways were really narrow everywhere, and the doorways were narrow. So, now everything is like, they planned it out so that it's just fine (*absoliutno normal'no*). I can move without a problem (*spokoino*) through the doors, I can get out to the street by myself. The thing is that, the problem that most people in a wheelchair have is— umm, that they can't get out of the house, but, thankfully, I don't have that [issue].

Normal'no is a highly generalizable word that can be deployed in a wide variety of conversational contexts, either wholeheartedly or sarcastically to mean, "not bad at all" or "the same as usual" (which, given the implication, could mean quite bad indeed). As others have argued, the concept of *normal'no* or normal living conditions in late-Soviet and post-Soviet life often references a longed-for vision of European modernity, which was understood to be out of reach in socialist eastern Europe and (post-)Soviet Russia (Fehérváry 2013; Zavisca 2012). In this example from Vera's description of her apartment, the term suggests an adequate level of accessible design execution.

Another word used to refer obliquely to access in interviews was *komfortno*. Similar to *udobno* in terms of denoting convenience and comfort, the term *komfortno* is also similar to *normal'no* in terms of indexing a European middle-class standard of modern urban amenities. For instance, Tania, a woman with dwarfism (or, a little person, as many in anglophone society prefer) in her thirties, used this term when describing how accessible design and attitudes of social inclusion coincided in her experiences visiting neighboring Finland, which she characterized as more accessible and more inclusive of disabled people than Russian Karelia. Sitting together one sunny winter afternoon in a quiet room, the sociable and vibrant Tania pushed her blond-highlighted bangs to the side, her large blue-green eyes flicking from the upholstery pattern on the bed where she sat to me and back again. Unpretentious and earnest, but with a sense of humor, Tania reflected,

> I go to Finland often, because it's close, and then also because I have a good friend there. [. . .] Well, almost every year [. . .] I get there somehow or other . . . [. . .] they have these really little cute houses, there, and I don't know, green lawns, it's all so nice, right? [. . .] In general it's a totally different feeling. [. . .] And there isn't litter all over the road. Everything is done so nicely, the asphalt is good quality, smooth (*gladkii*), when you're driving in the car. So, it's *komfortno* there.

In this excerpt from a longer quotation in which Tania described her experiences as a woman with dwarfism in Finland, she collapsed and intentionally drew parallels between ease of movement, the built environment, and social attitudes. While she did not use a mobility device, she did rely on transit to get around, and she appreciated the smoothness of driving in Finland as reflecting an urban modernity that was convenient and inclusive. As I read the interview transcripts, in Tania's description, I found a persistent slippage or metonymic association between the structure and maintenance of the built environment and the experience of moving through public space as someone marked by difference and hindered by access barriers.

In these examples, disabled interlocutors make use of a variety of Russophone terms in conversations about disability access. The attributes of access described by my interlocutors at once echoed Soviet logics of comfort, ease, and convenience and were interlaced with demands for a normal standard of living, that suggest a dissatisfaction with the Russian state. I argue that this dissatisfaction points to the second, metaphorical way, that access moves in friction. I argue that the metonymic association between the design and maintenance of accessible infrastructure and the idea of a normal life or the good life were deeply linked for my interlocutors: practically (in the sense that access really is convenient), rhetorically (because aligning calls for access with popular critiques of the state is strategic), and historically (because Russophone concepts of public infrastructure are deeply inflected with Soviet communist claims about the relationship between the material and the political). It is to this last valence that I now turn for further analysis.

Inconvenience as a Soviet Political Claim

As I considered the taxonomy of attributes of *dostupnost'*, however, I began to suspect that the attributes that adhere to these near-synonyms of access in

English and *dostupnost'* in Russian might diverge. That is, the historical lexicon of terms related to disabling barriers in the built environment evidently developed somewhat separately, and therefore the overlapping semantic domains of the various terms would not match up across the two languages over time. In order to think through this relationship, I conducted a brief etymological survey of Russian dictionaries and English-Russian and Russian-English dictionaries published over the course of the twentieth century.[3]

I found that in Russian usage in the mid-20th century, the anglophone perception that convenience is somehow apolitical was in fact inverted in the post-Soviet Russian usage of *udobnost'* and its various forms. In Russian etymology, the term *udobstvo* is particularly connected to concepts of desirable living spaces with modern accommodations. In Soviet terms, this often meant public heating, hot water, indoor plumbing and toilets, a slew of services that at mid-twentieth century and onward was referred to as *blagoustroistvo*, literally, well-appointed constructions, colloquially, modern domestic quarters. These are spaces that are equipped for the necessities of the everyday (*byt*). Meanwhile, this connotation of public infrastructure was, for most of the Soviet period in the dictionaries I consulted, absent from definitions or cross-definitions of the word *dostupnost'* (access). That is, the attribute of referencing the politics of infrastructure in the built environment appeared in usage as closer to *udobstvo* (convenience), as compared with *dostupnost'* (access).

While it seems an anglophone perspective that access is invariably a more political concept than convenience, a historical consideration of the Russo-phone concepts of *udobstvo* and *dostupnost'* suggests that perhaps the opposite may be true in the post-Soviet context. If so, we may find that inconvenience is the politically coded complaint that mobilizes the second type of inaccess stories that circulate in Russian public discourse independent of lived experience of disability. To examine this possibility, it is necessary to explore further how convenience appears in Russophone political complaint.

Citizen complaint as a genre of political speech is a topic of substantial scholarly attention in Russian area studies. In her ethnographic account of what she calls the "unravelling" of professional journalism in Russia in the 1990s and early 2000s, Natalia Roudakova (2017) studied how working journalists conducted and understood their work in the newsrooms of regional Russian newspapers. She demonstrates that their sense of duty to offer voice to public sentiment was rooted in a Soviet journalistic ethos that also sought to represent a vox populi—so much as was possible in an era of pervasive censorship, and then through the opening of *glasnost'*. In her chapter on the ethics and politics of Soviet journalism, Roudakova devotes substantial attention to the genre of the letter to the editor. She argues that in spite of the pervasive censorship that made direct consideration of certain topics impossible, an ethic (in the sense of unfolding practices) of truth-telling and truth-seeking guided journalistic practice in the late-Soviet period. Moreover, Roudakova argues that in the beginning of the Soviet era, Bolsheviks placed an important emphasis on soliciting citizen complaints, grievances, and suggestions, as "popular control from below." This drew on the practice of complaint that peasants brought to regional authorities in imperial times (Muravyeva 2014). In spite of pervasive perceptions in the West that Soviet citizens had little capacity to affect social change and make political claims on the state, scholars of Soviet and post-Soviet Russia tell a different story. For instance, historian Sheila Fitzpatrick argues that complaints about misuse of funds, abuse of power, and so on were widespread throughout the Stalinist period (2000, 28–29). Moreover, the Soviet press played an important official role in whistle-blowing at the regional level, Roudakova argues, and Soviet journalists had a duty and obligation to participate in governing by airing complaints that served as surveillance from below (2017, 30). She asserts that while much of the Soviet press was indeed devoid of the capacity to speak truth to power, "in the back pages of newspapers, particularly in *ocherki* (long form commentary essays), as well as in reviews of readers' letters, the courage of the writer pushing the limits of the sayable could come across" (2017, 48).

In this light, my journalist friend's video exposé on the lack of access at the purportedly accessible regional theater building (described in chapter 2) looks less like pandering to "global" *globalniye*—a gentle way of saying "*innostran-nye*" or foreign—interests by invoking terminology of disability access, and more like a genre of reportage that takes seriously a duty to air the pervasive issue of Potemkin villages, false facades, and unfulfilled promises. Roudakova gives numerous examples of these genres in the late-Soviet period and the truth-seeking effect they held.

In our own study of major Soviet newspapers *Izvestiia* and *Pravda* digitized archives (1945–1989), Gyuzel Kamalova and I found numerous examples of oblique references to physical disability in relation to the design, construction, or maintenance of infrastructure and the built environment (Novopolianskii 1975, 1977). From assertions that veterans needed adapted showers in the public baths in Saint Petersburg, to calls for war-wounded veterans to be first in line to receive newly built apartments with proper modern conveniences, commentary typically used the politically speakable category of war veteran or elderly to address these considerations (in our assessment, there was almost no mention of physical disability outside of the paradigm of war injury, for young people and almost no mention of disabled children in spite of pension changes in the wake of the polio epidemic, which also went unmentioned). In one example, a veteran wondered why he was allotted housing on a hill, as it was inconvenient for someone like him with difficulty walking to get to a bus stop. In the examples we reviewed, convenience was connected to the question of building socialism, either implicitly or explicitly. This emerged in two ways: First, the idea that because *bytie opredelaet soznanie* (or being) determines consciousness, insufficient infrastructure is emblematic of a society that does not strive to improve or build a political consciousness that allows citizens to imagine a better future. Second, it reflects the notion that a public complaint about inconvenience is a kind of duty that should be aired. Therefore, in this example, claims about disability access constitute claims about a state's failure to produce minimum standards of infrastructure for normal life, convenience, and thereby the establishment of an imagined political sphere of society that draws on these long-standing ethical norms.

Therefore, the concept of *udobstvo* is significantly related to the anglophone concept of accessible design as a domain of political complaint, although the direct translation of *access* would be *dostupnost'*. There are a few specific concerns with the suggestion that the Russian words *dostopnost'* (accessibly) and *udobno* (conveniently) might be understood as semantically overlapping. On the surface, in English, although the practical usage of convenient and accessible overlap, only *accessible* has been designated as the term that applies to political advocacy concerning the attributes of the built environment to prevent or enable the social and political participation of disabled people. Moreover, in English, the word *convenience* tends toward the trivial or inconsequential. When we speak of convenience in North American English, we refer to quotidian concerns: errands, whether to get out of the car at the bank or use a drive-through ATM machine; whether to take another route on a commute that requires fewer transfers or turns but takes five minutes longer; if a movie theater has long wait times or not; if excess energy will be expended on hassle, bureaucracy, distance, or waiting. Indeed, the definition of convenient in English includes the idiomatic usage "convenient to" meaning close to, or within easy distance of. This suggests a possible affinity between convenience and the notion of crip time. We often ask, "whose access is prioritized?" in English when we are considering design bias for nondisabled users. But, we might also ask, "whose convenience is prioritized?" a question that also gets at assumptions of privilege. In short, while access makes something possible that would not otherwise be possible for a disabled person, convenience makes something a little bit easier[4]; therefore, in English, convenience is not related to ableism, while access describes a politics of rectifying ableist structures.

If, and this is the main problem, we contrast *access* with *convenience* in English, it presents a possible—and possibly troubling—slippage for disability advocacy. Because *access* is the term mobilized in the service of disability rights as a political movement, to suggest that it is similar to *convenience* undermines the *agentive political will* that access (in the context of inclusive design) suggests. That is, where *access* suggests attending to those needs that are required for participation, *convenience* suggests (perhaps extraneous) labor performed to prioritize the time, ease, and comfort of others. Indeed, when accessibility accommodations are misread as requests for convenience, they are often maligned. Furthermore, *convenience* in English tends to suggest an experience of *something already laid out, a passive appreciation*, whereas *access* tends to carry a connotation of *equity, advocacy, and active agitation*.[5] Where convenience is received and appreciated, access is fought for and won. As Lauren Berlant (2022) observes, in North America, we associate inconvenience with ways in which other people impinge on our agentive sovereignty or freedom. This gets at another problem with the concept of convenience: convenience for whom? Providing access for others has been persistently represented as an inconvenience to nondisabled others, for business owners, and so on; in this way, in/convenience as a term has implicit associations with ableist resistance to disability access and inclusion movements. In English, then, to speak about in/convenience does not approach the political potency of claims about in/access. I argue that the reverse is true in Russian: although *dostupnost'* remains the formal term for legal codes referring to accessible design, complaints about inaccess are most potently formulated as complaints about inconvenience. In this way, *inaccess stories* might even be rightly called inconvenience stories in Russian, as *udobstvo* better indexes political complaint about the built environment in colloquial speech than *dostupnost'*.

Pothole Talk: Infrastructures and the Politics of In/convenience

In conversations about infrastructural barriers among the nondisabled population of the city, one element seemed to attract the most attention: potholes. In the first few months of my fieldwork researching disability and social exclusion in Petrozavodsk, Russia, I noticed that I could not escape them. If I was not stepping around them as I hurried across a street, or being jostled over them in a taxi or *marshrutka*, friends, acquaintances, and taxi drivers were talking about them. Like the weather, potholes were the favored conversation for small talk and idle conversation. Potholes were a part of the shared conditions of life to which chitchat might always turn, either in moments of forging passing solidarity with strangers, or bemoaning the status quo between gossip and catching up with friends or colleagues. Like Tania's comment that the roads in Finland were so smooth, suggesting that the roads in Russia were not, talk about potholes and bad roads in Petrozavodsk indexed an imagined elsewhere, where the government demonstrated that it cared for its citizens by caring for the roads.

People remarked on and complained about potholes. Taxi drivers, noticing my accent, made wry jokes and apologies about the "state of our roads." Friends updated one another about what they had heard about the schedule of public works projects: *this fall they will repave Nevskii, next spring they are scheduled to do Kirovskii.* By the time the spring rolled around, I found that I was the one cracking pothole jokes to cab drivers, who would guffaw and turn to look at me with raised eyebrows, clocking the unusual combination of my foreign accent and local style of banter.

One summer afternoon in 2012, not long after arriving in the field but long before I had become fluent in pothole chitchat, I was cutting through a courtyard on my way to a neighborhood grocery. The courtyard was dusty and dirty, with large, shallow, dried-up "lakes"—less pothole than wide craters. Another time, when my friend Masha and I passed through the same courtyard on the way to walk along the embankment of Lake Onego, the large, forest-lined lake that defines the city's perch in the Karelian wilderness, we joked, "Oh, here we are—Lake Onego!" "It's so much smaller than I pictured it." "I didn't realize it was so close to my house!"

But that afternoon on the way to the grocery store, I paused, noticing a decal sticker on the rear window of a nearby Lada: *Kakaia Vlast', Takie i Dorogi.*

Like many short phrases, its meaning was clear, but it resisted adequate translation. As I continued my walk, I filtered through possible renditions of the phrase in English:

> Such power, and such roads
> Such is the government, such are the roads
> What a government, and what roads

The word *vlast'* in Russian references both the sovereign power of a ruler or a system of government. It indicates a power that emanates from the center in a political science sense, or in common usage, regime or, simply, "the government." In the plural, *vlasti* could mean, "the ones in power" or "the authorities." This usage was complicated by the grammatical structure of the comparative clause "*kakaia . . . takie,*" which does not have a clear counterpart in English, making translations inevitably awkward.

> "However the _____, so is the _____"
> "What _____, and what _____"
> "As is the _____, so goes the _____"
> "Such _____, and such _____"

Significantly, the phrase leaves the judgment about what the state of the roads are to the reader, interpellating the reader of the sticker into a shared complaint, a conspiratorial affinity. To any Russian reading the bumper sticker, the implication is clear: *Bad roads, bad government.* As the days went on, I noticed, the bumper sticker affixed to cars around the city and found numerous examples in online photos.

When people in Petrozavodsk talk about potholes, they frequently used the word *iama*, meaning *hole, pit,* or *wallow.* There is not a word like the English *pothole*, a noun dedicated to the particularity of holes in the road needing repair. Aside from *iama*, a pothole might be described in Russian as *rytvina* (rut, groove, gulch) or *vyboina* (dent, corrugation, or the pot-shaped forms in river rocks, usually called potholes in English). This array of Russian synonyms belies a condition of permanency that is quite different from the American understanding of the word "pothole," which implies a temporary problem that by definition needs to be fixed. In Petrozavodsk, when people talk about *iamy*, they are talking about of the municipal lack of attention to roads. They are describing a situation in which nothing could go smoothly, both literally and metaphorically.

Pothole talk is a discursive register reserved for sharing woes, principally, complaints that may not have an answerable response. These are complaints that are posed as a manner of gesturing to a gap between a lived reality and an imagined good life (Chua 2014). In writing about Russia, many scholars have described a "culture of complaint," observing that "complaining is a popular form of communication in present-day Russian society" (Muravyeva 2014, 93–94). In many cases, scholarly discussion of a Russian culture of complaint refers to an array of habits of written complaint that address the inadequacies of the state to representatives of the state (Muravyeva 2014, 94). But in thinking about pothole talk, I am interested in performative complaint, voiced grievances, the purpose of which is not always a resulting change but rather a bond of commiseration. Specifically, this is not a complaint to authorities, but rather, a voicing of dissatisfaction to another citizen (Ries 1997).

While the genres of complaint that Ries documents, and that I observe, seem to offer no solution per se, they may also do important work of creating openings for other possibilities. Scholars have argued that complaint, including Russian patterns of complaint, say as much about a desired "ideal state" that is implicitly referenced, as a contrast to the undesirable circumstances described, as they do about the current state of affairs (Muravyeva 2014, 99). In my interlocutors' complaints, the imagined ideal state is often sketched as already in existence somewhere. That is, complaints are grounded in a diffuse sense that things are different elsewhere, abroad. Descriptions of Russian infrastructural inadequacy—ramps, potholes, or otherwise—are posited in relation to some imaginary West. The bumper sticker suggests that somewhere, because the government is good, so, too, are the roads.

The recitation of litanies and the telling of absurdist tales and ironic jokes is part of a cultural ritual of social communion. People gather around kitchen tables, in taxi cabs, in cafes or over cups of tea at the breakroom table, and share these stories. Through these enacted rituals of complaint, Ries argues, her interlocutor "identified herself with the moral community created through shared suffering and difficulty, thus effacing the boundaries between her social group and the Russian people as a whole" (1997, 91). To talk about potholes is to build affinity through shared circumstance. Ries argues that these modes of Russian talk (she is talking about the Perestroika era, but I find her definition of the genre helpful, even though a great deal of time has passed) offer not only the constitutive meaning of articulating claims about what is not right, or what has not been properly executed by those in power (e.g., the bumper sticker is a mode of activism in its own right) but also serves the function of bringing people together in moral objection to the status quo. Ries suggests that litany and Russian tales serve to create a "generalized social bond" (1997, 87).

In fact, in Petrozavodsk, complaints about *iami* or potholes were made with no intention of pursuing an "official" resolution to the problem. Rather, the complaints function to build camaraderie, establishing a "we" who suffers, while "they" (*vlasti - the ones in power*) do nothing. Ries suggests that suffering and tales that recount instances of suffering have special meaning in Russian discourse. She argues that talk about difficult social circumstances, of getting through a difficulty, had to do with "belonging in some kind of moral community—a community that shared suffering. As ritual recitations, litanies invoked and created access to that belonging" (Ries 1997, 87). In an ethnographic account of neoliberal post-Soviet Russian treatments for alcohol, Eugene Raikhel documents a similar pattern by which clinicians make claims about the "double morality" of a post-Soviet situation in which citizens are expected to be upstanding and engage in self-managing practices even while the state "took everything away and didn't return anything" (2016, 52–53). Raikhel notes that the tendency of interlocutors to offer "sweeping accounts of the Soviet past" may be influenced by an awareness of the ethnographer's foreignness, but observes that they are also undergirded by a real "longing for social norms and institutional structures" (2016, 53). Rituals of complaint enacted in a wide variety of cultures might also work to enhance social bonds by interpellating the speaker and listener into shared community. Inaccess stories, as a kind of litany, might be thought of as a discursive mode of establishing the moral personhood of a speaker.

Describing Metonyms of an Imagined Otherwise

Accessible infrastructure is not just the implementation of a particular technology. Rather, as we have seen in previous chapters, it is a complex network of heterogeneous actors who must come together to facilitate what Moser and Law call "good passages," moments when components and networks fit, and movement through space *works*. As Moser and Law write, addressing a disability studies audience, "to repeat the standard lesson from STS: if the networks are in place, if the prostheses are working, then there is ability. If they are not, well then, as is obvious, there is dis/ability. [. . .] Dis/ability is about specific passages between equally specific arrays of heterogeneous materials" (1999, 201). Interrogating colloquial language in my interview transcripts, I found that interlocutors spoke about good passages as peaceful, unhindered, comfortable, and, normal. Good passages are convenient, but not *just* convenient. Returning to the attributes of access in inaccess stories told by my interlocutors and in pothole talk alike, good passages might also be *spokoino* (peaceful), *normal'no* (normal), and comfortable (*komfortno*). The same descriptors, cast more broadly, might also describe an imagined good life.[6]

The consideration of good passage as a way of thinking about mobility, infrastructure, and movement through space further reinforces the relationship between potholes on the road and poorly constructed ramps (as discussed in previous chapters) as two material expressions of corruption or a failure of the state to care for citizens. Although I included the word *spokoino*, or peaceful, in the taxonomy of attributes at the beginning of the chapter, I left it unexamined. I turn to it now to consider it in relation to both disability access and roads. *Spokoino* is a common Russian word, and one that is not designated as referring specifically or officially to disability. It was often used not only by people with disabilities but by other residents of Petrozavodsk to refer to experiences in Finland in which a commonplace experience, such as taking the bus, walking on the sidewalk, or driving over the roads, went unexpectedly smoothly. *Spokoino*, often translated as calm or peaceful, can also mean placid or tranquil, as a calm body of water, smooth and uninterrupted. Interestingly, a definitive and ethnographically sourced dictionary of Russian from the late 1800s, the entry for *spokoi* (the shortest form of the word) defines the meaning in part as "absence of disturbance, worries; convenience of life, abundance and care [in the sense of maintenance], services" (Dal' [1880–1882] 2003, 294).[7] The entry for the adjectival form, *spokoinyi*, includes the synonyms *udobnyi, lovkii*, easy, nimble or efficient, and an example: "A peaceful *road, even, level or flat; a* peaceful *carriage* [here he uses the word *koliaska*, which in current usage means wheelchair or baby carriage, though in Dal's definition, it means, simply, something that rolls], *free of jumps and jolts. A* peaceful *place, comfortable"* (Dal' [1880–1882] 2003, 294).[8]

In this sense, the constellation of meanings—in which the word *spokoi* refers to comfortable, peaceful, and unbothersome surroundings, especially built environments and infrastructures—has existed at least since Dal's time, the second half of the nineteenth century. This association between access in its current incarnation and a more general sense of freedom from disturbance while moving through space, or across infrastructure, invokes an idiomatic gripe—*Russia has two problems: idiots and roads.*[9] In the Russian imaginary stretching back to the 1800s then, roads are perceived as a problem. Whole swaths of text in Gogol's *Dead Souls* are devoted to descriptions of traveling over muddy, rutted roads in horse-drawn carriages. In this way, even reflected in a presidential comment, maligning Russia's roads is both a national pastime, and somehow linked to some amorphous concept of prototypical, essential Russianness. As an anthropologist, I am not suggesting some definable quality of "essential Russianness" with this phrase, but rather that in popular imagination or everyday discourse, discussion of potholes and poorly cared-for roads indexes a deeply rooted shared mythology about the governance of the Russian nation and the national territory.

I note an important temporal dimension to these moral complaints about bad infrastructure and failed design. The consideration of roads and other forms of infrastructure as peaceful to travel on overlaps conceptually with the question of convenience: Good passage is considerate of the traveler's time. A road rife with potholes delays the traveler. The state's responsibility for temporal inconveniences endured by citizens has particular meaning in the post-Soviet context, in the sense that a feature of state socialist autocracy in living memory for interlocutors was a disregard for the time that citizens spent waiting in line. Verdery (1996) argues that the temporal demands that the Soviet-era socialist state placed on Romanian citizens to receive essential goods and services amounted to a kind of political control, a temporal experience of socialist autocracy defined by queueing. In this way, to point out being made to wait, or being placed on a list (for which there is no reaching the top), or to be delayed in travel because of faulty infrastructure, or to be coerced into a public service interaction that takes longer than necessary, is a kind of complaint about the state of the state. Thus, we might consider a special genre of inaccess stories to be those about temporal failures of accessible infrastructure, the hindering of good passage that is inconvenient because it causes the protagonist to lose time. The temporal inconvenience of interdependent access is one valence of what disability studies scholars call crip time (Samuels 2017; Kafer 2013; McRuer 2018; Hickman 2014).

Anya, the psychologist and powerchair user, told me an inaccess story about crip time that worked to both describe disabled people's frustration and ingenuity in the face of paternalistic systems and to voice a complaint about the moral ineptitude of a government that created a system that did not work. This was a secondhand inaccess story, related to Anya by a friend who lived in Saint Petersburg with whom she communicated with online. The friend sometimes used a paratransit service available to disabled people in Saint Petersburg known as a Sots-Taxi (social service taxi). Although complaints about paratransit were common everywhere, in this case, Anya's friend's complaint was rooted in a paternalist slant of the Sots-Taxi service policy: It was only available to take people to and from social service appointments. Although buses and trams with fold-down ramps began appearing in Saint Petersburg in the 2010s, a large portion of the transit system included the metro (accessible only by long, steep escalators that could not accommodate wheelchairs) and taxi-buses, known as *marshrutki*, which required the passengers to climb and squeeze into twelve-passenger vans. Anya explained that friend used the Sots-Taxi service all the time, but had to be clever to come up with destinations. On the occasion in question, Anya's friend wanted to go from her home to the theatre.

> So where she lived wasn't far from a medical clinic on one side, and not too far from a cemetery on the other side. So in order to get to the theater, she had to go from the clinic to some kind of social service destination. So my friend says to me, "Today I took a really fantastic trip to the theater . . . This was my route: clinic, graveyard, theater, and then on the way back, graveyard, clinic . . . [laughs] Not bad! (*Normal'no!*)" . . . But why can't she order a taxi to go straight from her house to the theater? [imitating her friend] "Why would I need to go through the graveyard to get to the theater? Are you telling me that this is normal (*normal'no*)?!" So I ask my friend, "Well, so how was it?" And she goes, "Ohh, not bad (*normal'no*)."

Anya's friend observed that while the state understood essential transportation for disabled people to be only that transportation related to medical and social service appointments, in fact, activities like attending the theater were also essential for human well-being. As such, she felt no guilt in manipulating the system to her own advantage to get where she wanted to go using one of the few accessible options available, even if it was not exactly "normal" in terms of the roundabout route. In this way, Anya's story was both an inaccess story rooted in disability expertise, which built affinity through the description of shared disability culture (crip time unfolding through the travails of public transportation), and a commentary about the state of public infrastructure in

Saint Petersburg. Asking, "Are you telling me that this is normal?!" Anya's description of her friend's absurdist bus ride posited the actual normal conditions of travel or good passage as being out of reach. The phrase *normal'no* in this story was used both to describe the "not bad" valence of a way to move through the world that worked (sort of) and to contrast lived experience of navigating public services and access infrastructure in Russia with an imagined otherwise-elsewhere where wheelchair users were afforded the same freedom of movement as other public transit users.

The built environment both produces and reproduces social relations, and social relations in turn produce the built environment. The dialectical relationship between social relations and the built environment has been thoroughly discussed in Western critical theory (e.g., Lefebvre 2005) and was at the core of the Soviet constructivist enterprise. By building the right physical environment, Soviet planners, architects, and designers surmised that they might in turn produce social relations and subjectivities more conducive to socialism. Soviet infrastructure was thus built with a centrally planned logic intended to benefit the collective over the individual, to maximize the productive capacity of workers, and to facilitate communalism and interdependencies that were imagined as conducive to building a socialist consciousness (Collier 2011). In the context of postsocialist politics of everyday Marxism, ethnographers observe that interlocutors regard the phrase *bytie opredelaet soznanie* (being determines consciousness) as a truism, that is, the notion that the material world creates the conditions that develop political subjectivity is an obvious statement (Murawski 2022). It follows from everyday Marxism that if the proletariat lives in squalor and is constantly surround by *uncultured* material surrounds (the infrastructural base), the socialist political consciousness will not develop. And furthermore, it is obvious that it is the responsibility of the state to produce the material infrastructure that might foster socialist consciousness. Resisting the possibility of a functioning infrastructure, and instead observing infrastructure as always produced in terms of special interests or government whim, was also a way of rejecting empty promises in narratives of democratization and development. By describing a state of Russian exceptionalism, in which roads are always worse on the Russian side of the Finnish border (they are), and ramps are always empty symbols (they sometimes are), interlocuters like Tania and Anya also align themselves with a moral universe in which development and good passage come at the expense of other kinds of sacrifice. Talk that reproduces Russia as a territory of inaccess is talk that reproduces Russianness as outside of a Western telos of modernist development. In this way, the metonymic relation between the constitutive meaning of the design of the material world and the semiotic meaning of the design are mobilized in pothole talk and inaccess stories to point to failures of the Russian state to meet the social contract by fulfilling the needs of citizens according to a "normal" standard of life, or an imagined good life.

Vernacular Styles of Complaint

Artyom, describing the experience of leaving his house and taking public transportation while regaining mobility after a surgery, emphasized that his experience was shaped by the need to consider in advance what would be most convenient for him. Like theorists of access in the North/West, with this turn of phrase, Artyom emphasized the ways in which nondisabled people are unaware of the burden that inaccessible infrastructure places on those with mobility impairments, and the expertise, time, and effort that disabled people expend when moving through public space designed without their bodies in mind. Yet, by emphasizing convenience as the valence of experience, Artyom situated his description in relation to colloquial Russophone conventions rooted in styles of complaint about infrastructural failure and the responsibility of the state to care for citizens—styles that have no direct parallel in anglophone lexicons of access.

When Tania described the smooth, litter-free roadways across the international border in nearby Finland, she drew a comparison to the state of roadways in Petrozavodsk. Her commentary follows a long history of complaints about Russian roadways that are imbricated with Western European assessments of Russian infrastructure as backward and insufficiently modern. Her description of little houses with green grass lawns—available just across the border, but seemingly not in Russian Karelia—mobilized signifiers of middle-class Euoramerican modernity, as if to say that accessible infrastructure belonged to a geopolitical formation that existed elsewhere, just not here. The imagined good life indexed by Tania in this comment cataloged accessible infrastructure not as a luxury but as a quotidian necessity. In her description, the public roadways and private infrastructures that facilitated good passage were like the Western domestic consumer goods that Fehérváry's interlocutors coveted: they are at once symbols and functional objects.

Cripping vocabularies of access through the attention to global access friction in the Russian context suggest possible new directions for disability studies discussions about access. The Russian emic concept of barriers and infrastructure always already indexes a relationship to power—or that which configures infrastructure. We see that the performative power of inaccess stories and litanies of complaint that do not offer possible solutions (and in fact elaborate a lack of faith in government) can serve to build social affinity. Additionally, I suggest that the de facto location of US discursive practice as the normative model for activism and social change may lead global advocates to miss subtle modes of allegiance building and imaginaries of other possible worlds. When disability studies asks, "*for whom* does infrastructure work?" relations of power are always invoked. Cultural training may predispose Western theorists, however, to think of the systems of oppression structuring the "for whom" as always related to minority identities. In contrast, the Russian word *vlast'* appears in moments when speakers seek to emphasize the *moral* corruption of pursuing financial gain for its own sake, or power for its own sake (Ries 1997). Infrastructure works *for* those in power, an insight that might be useful for Western disability advocates to explore further at home.

Lexicons for and about disability and access lend another tool to area studies research on political subjectivities of postsocialism. There may be more nuance to endemic vocabularies of disability access than the global rhetoric—that moves in friction—suggests. In this way, convenience, as a paradigm, *udobstvo*, might be considered a more political concept than access in Russophone discourse. In making this argument, I am follow others (Phillips 2011; Shaw 2017; Galmarini 2016) in suggesting that the theoretical and topical lens of disability studies offers another entry point to considering postsocialist political subjectivity. Thinking with the Soviet politics of convenience in relation to the built environment suggests that claims about inaccessible infrastructure in the built environment in Russia in the 2010s—while ostensibly an imported foreign discourse—adhere to an endogenous discourse not only about what the state owes to citizens but also about the significance of infrastructure as an indicator of a healthy society (*zdorovoe obshchestvo*) and the promise of a political imaginary of a livable future.

CONCLUSION
Heroes and Protagonists of Russian Crip Futures

One late morning in early March 2013, Sergei—who had so poignantly remarked that his experience of post-Soviet education as a disabled person was like being a guinea pig—came to my apartment for an interview. Always a proper guest, he had a box of cookies tucked under his arm as he made his way across the drive, navigating the compacted snow that had refrozen into muddy gray ice. Approaching the front door of the building, he held out his arms for balance as he stepped carefully with his distinctive gait, crouching a bit with knees slanted toward each other. Inside the door in the vestibule, he held the wall for a moment to regain balance, remarking that he preferred to walk without a cane, even though it was harder. His winter attire stowed away and a pair of house slippers proffered, we made our way to the kitchen down the hall.

I recorded a long interview as we drank tea with sun streaming in the window over Sergei's cookies laid out on a plate. Our conversation meandered through memories of the past and Sergei's description of how he spent his days now that he was done with school and university. He was still unemployed but was taking in piecemeal graphic design work from home. Sergei liked to spend time alone in his room, or alone in the family apartment when his parents went to the dacha in the summer to tend to their garden plot. Reflecting on those moments spent alone, Sergei began talking about the movies he liked to watch: With unlimited internet, he could stream almost any film, dubbed into Russian, for free (pirated on the Russian internet, but with an array of clickbait ads). The interview ended with him describing his recent predilection for watching war movies, and the difference between Russian and US films. He told me about a film in which the main character died in the final frames: The man was shot, and then the credits rolled.

> S: With American movies, a lot of the time, the main character (*geroi*) gets his motivation from fighting the enemy, and then he goes out of his mind from grief, andddd, then what? In the end everyone triumphs, right? In our Russian films, you know, it's more realistic. They tend show that even the enemy can be, sort of, we can do something deep with the character, right? So that you feel bad for them in the end [for our Russian film characters].
>
> And my mom, she says, "I don't understand it!" about this. They say that Russian films are brutal (*zhestokye*). They say that Americans don't like brutal films. And she says, that in American films, at the end, the main character always ends up with his hands raised in victory. Not, as a symbol of [relief of] having gotten through it, but just the opposite, triumph, that he was always going to come out victorious [. . .]
>
> C: Well, yes, in our American films . . . the word "hero" [in English] means that not only is he the main character, but also that he will win, you know?
>
> S: Yes, I think that's true. But in ours, there are often these shocking endings. [. . .] it's surprising when they do that. Especially in the very last moments. And everything is supposed to work out well—[switches to heavily accented English] *Kheppi Endink* [happy ending]. [then, with glee] Nope! So that's the kind of films we have. But I watch them anyway. I like it. [. . .] But on the other hand, if I watch an American film, then I like it better than ours. So . . .

When I read this transcript, I picture Sergei alone in his family apartment, watching movies on his computer. I wonder if at this very moment he is watching a US film or a Russian film, and what effect each one has on his emotional landscape. Does watching a film with a *kheppi endink* shift his horizon of what is possible in the future? I'm reminded of Sarah Ahmed's observation that, "happiness is used to justify social norms as social goods" (2019, 254). From a critical, and perhaps cynical, post-Soviet perspective, an invariably happy ending looks a lot like propaganda justifying the particular social order depicted in the story.

In telling inaccess stories, my interlocutors located themselves, or a friend, as a protagonist, at the center of a story. If inaccess stories are narratives fashioned as political complaint and a means of building interpersonal affinity, what does it mean for the narrator of the story that a protagonist—*geroi*—need not win, that a happy ending is not necessarily how stories resolve in the

Russian cultural imaginary? What does it mean to be the hero of an inaccess story, when, by definition, the hero experiences an insurmountable barrier? What does it mean to reckon with the understanding that pursuing the social good may not bring happiness, especially when social goods do not align with dominant social norms?

Inaccess Stories, Global Access Friction, Metonyms and National Narratives

As the notion of access moves through networks of global connection, it is refracted through dimensions of meaning in local contexts. In Petrozavodsk in the 2010s, standards of access (and expectations about meeting those standards) traveled across national, linguistic, and cultural borders. Moving in global friction means that the meaning of access might encounter a mismatch that is both incommensurable and generative. As we have seen, accessible design appears in advocacy work and complaints based in disability expertise; as a symbol of modernity in state discourses; and as a symbol of infrastructural failure mobilized as part of broader political critique.

Accessible design as a concept, initially imagined as a material modality by which to accommodate difference and facilitate political and social inclusion, cannot avoid cooptation. Like all technologies, accessible design is morally neutral. The imagined moral good of accessible design is subject to the complexity of human biases, markets, and incentives that may foil implementation. In fact, its symbolic address can be fetishized and coopted by capital and can be mobilized as national metonym by ablenationalism. The disability studies scholar Robert McRuer writes: "Contemporary capitalism no longer deploys a logic of 'totalizing normality'; instead, neoliberal capitalism focuses on and markets constant change, flexibility, 'difference,' and, indeed, freakiness. Put differently, neoliberal capitalism arguably embraces the freaky or abnormal, domesticating or taming it as it sells it back to us (2014, 188).

Thus, I argue that accessible design in Russia can be repackaged and sold to the population in new ways. As in Michele Friedner's (2015) consideration of deaf inclusion in India, accessible design in Russia becomes an object of value, manipulated by corporations and marketers to sell products. For example, in the fall of 2012, while I was conducting fieldwork Russia, a friend who worked at a local branch of Sberbank, the oldest and largest bank in Russia, told me offhandedly that he had heard that the corporate higher-ups at work were in the process of retrofitting design elements at Sberbank branches to make the

ATM vestibules and lobbies "accessible for the disabled." By the following spring, small tile ramps appeared where there used to be a step at some Sberbank branches around the city. Then, in December 2016, the bank staged a holiday season press event to launch newly updated ATM technology, billed as fully accessible to people with disabilities. Although the event claimed to promote access for disabled people, no disabled people were pictured in the launch event coverage. Instead, the bank's CEO German Gref demonstrated the ATM interface himself. Apparently nondisabled, Gref donned a suit designed to "simulate" disability. Such so-called empahthy suits are comprised of a vest, goggles, and other elements to limit the wearer's vision, hearing, and other senses. These suits are manufactured and sold to train medical personnel to feel empathy for aging and disabled patients.[1] Gref's performance, however, did not seem to promote empathy for the experience of disability, but instead, seemed designed to harness value produced through the association of accessibility with modernity and ease. Gref, on behalf of Sberbank, was engaging in accessible design appropriation, or cripwashing.

In this way, disability access images, material objects, and vocabularies move into Russian daily life is through the generative power of cripwashing, mobilized to produce ablenationalist sentiment. This recognition is striking, given the widely discussed homophobic political rhetoric and legislation that has unfolded in the Russian Federation since the early 2010s, which has led to an understanding of Russia as resistant to homonationalism. Yet ablenationalism, in the examples of the second kind of inaccess story described throughout this text, garner significant cultural caché. That is, we might consider whether without pinkwashing as a means of distracting from or creating displays of nationalist affective harmony through pretenses of inclusion, cripwashing remains available and becomes a dynamic by which the Russian state generates good feeling for neoliberal citizens. Ablenationalism works as an alternative to homonationalism—an (often empty) emblem of teleological social progress.

The inaccess stories told and reposted on Instagram of the wheelchair on the ledge, the images of bad ramps, and the journalist's attention to wheelchair access at the theater may ignore disability expertise. Yet, by pointing to the empty gesture of Russian cripwashing, they effectively work to unveil the hypocrisy of Russian neoliberal politics of "inclusion." Meanwhile, the actual convenience of disabled Russian citizens remains largely unaddressed, while symbols of accessible design adorn post offices and town halls, locations where emblems of inclusion are likely to inspire nationalist pride in the country's advancing development.

The alleged acceptance and tolerance for disabled people's access needs symbolized by images of accessible design in Russian public space did produce some social recognition for some of my more socially accomplished interlocutors, for example, Rudak and Anya received various forms of recognition for their professional and creative accomplishments. But at the same time, Putin's reconsolidation of social services disrupted a generation of disability expertise in the non-profit sector, and disabled people became subject to new forms of social exclusion as shifting political ground depoliticized and dismantled their claims for rights and political agency, in favor of discourses of rehabilitation that individualize, pathologize, and imagine disability as a totalizing identity, leaving ableism and social stigma uninterrogated.

Reading Russian ablenationalism in this way demonstrates the importance of thinking with disability theory for global critique. Homonationalism and queer theory have arrived in the Euroamerican academy and are widely understood as an important lens by which to understand social dynamics *in general*; however, disability theory has too often been understood to be a conceptual lens that applies to theorizing only the "exceptional" experiences of disabled people. I join others in arguing that disability theory, by attending to and theorizing the work that the categories of disability and accessible design do in the service of complex global systems of neoliberal capital and colonial nationalism. Global disability studies, therefore, is not only a consideration of disabled experiences transnationally, but a tool in the toolkit of critiques of global capitalism that seek to theorize complex workings of power. In this text, I have attempted to offer an example of disability anthropology in which disability theory offers an essential contribution to critical studies of contemporary geopolitics and lifeworlds that advance social theory.

To think ethnographically about disability and access in Petrozavodsk in the twenty-first century requires thinking about global friction and the ways that inclusion or access take on particular vernacular meanings in a specific time and place. This ethnography did not start out as an ethnography of globalization, or an ethnography of spatial relationships or infrastructure. It began with simple questions about social and political participation and about the meaning of the word *invalid* in contemporary Russia. Yet, arriving in Petrozavodsk and raising these questions, I was part of a much bigger flow of ideas about rights, knowledge, participation, and justice that has moved from the United States into post-Soviet worlds. In this book, I have worked to document how these ideas are taken up and take on meaning in vernacular vocabularies and lifeworlds in ways that would be unpredictable and difficult to parse from a Euroamerican point of view. Accessible design cannot be disentangled from the political imaginaries that infrastructure and design propose.

Western discourse has frequently described democracy or political participation as inaccessible in a Russian context. By aligning their critique with this context, Russian dissidents mobilize images of inaccessible disability access, insufficient infrastructure, and the absence of good passage to demonstrate the ways in which the Russian state ignores and dismisses the quotidian needs of its citizens. The absence of *blagoustroistvo* (well-appointed construction) for these purveyors of inaccess stories without disability expertise is metonymic of an attempt to curtail the political agency of the Russian people through persistent inconvenience that dissuade political consciousness. Like the production of temporal inconvenience in socialist Romania, wherein the necessity of constantly waiting in line came to be understood as a way to stymy dissent, as theorized by Katherine Verdery, disrepair and slow renovation of public infrastructure in Russia appears to citizens as an intentional inconvenience that hinders the capacity for consciousness to develop and social movements to organize and emerge. Registering public complaint about infrastructural failure through the circulation of images of bad ramps, Russian citizens demonstrate that they understand this failure to be paramount to political repression. The familiar narrative that reminds others that happy endings exist elsewhere, in Hollywood, but not in Russia, is mobilized: the image of a man in a wheelchair on a ledge, unable to go anywhere, resonates with the nondisabled citizens as a metaphor for the absence of viable avenues for political action.

Although disability studies asks us to be wary of the mobilization of metaphor and tropes about disability in service of other topics, Russian resistance to autocracy holds no such allegiance. Inaccess stories about bad ramps circulate in global access friction as evidence that something, something profoundly public and essential, needs to be fixed.

In this way, global access friction describes a contemporary transnational conjecture in which accessible design circulates in local vernaculars and proliferates without interrupting ableist hegemony. Disabled people struggle to create islands of access, even as accessible design as a concept and rhetorical tool become available as a commonplace idea that conjures "are we there yet?" sentiments from nondisabled subjects. Even while my disabled interlocutors drew on endemic Russophone vocabularies to describe experiences of access intimacy and frustrations of inaccess, inaccess stories without disability expertise circulated, and captured the attention of Russophone counterpublics, who in turn reposted and reproduced images of inaccessible accessibility elements as a political complaint distinct from the disability advocacy movements. Returning to the example of our journalist, and his political critique communicated through the failure of accessibility renovations to provide meaningful access, I suggest that his attention to the inaccessibility of the built environment was both about the specificity of injustice faced by disabled people and also about the failure of infrastructure in general. His performance of inaccess, thereby, underscored the ways in which the discourse of disability access moves in friction as a term with different—but generative—stakes for different political actors.

Sergei observed that narratives end in a variety of ways. When I reflect on his commentary about happy endings, I'm struck by the ambivalence with which he imagined his future. In several instances, he struggled to imagine what his future might hold other than more of the same: playing music and watching movies in his room, helping his parents, and taking on piecemeal graphic design work. After growing up in the first post-Soviet generation, subject to the shifting political ground of the post-Soviet period, it was hard to know what kind of story he was living in. In our interviews, he was actively seeking clues about what kinds of futures and subjectivities might be possible. The political topography remained uncertain and was continuously shifting throughout the research and writing of this book. The terms on which access and inclusion could be discussed depended on geopolitical changes beyond Sergei's control. As he told me, he tried to live life in the moment, suspending concrete plans.

What Can Be Done?

So, what now? What do disability studies scholars and disability advocates do with the knowledge that this powerful tool—accessible design—has been coopted and circulated in ablenationalist displays? Or with the realization that accessible design presumes a tenuous kind of liberal democratic governance and that the implementation of accessible design relies on neoliberal global capitalist extraction to create patchwork access?

Invariably, ethnography as a research method sets out to raise and complicate questions. In this book I have tried to make a case for disability anthropology as a tool for advancing a robust global disability studies as a conversation that attends not only to what ought to be but also to what actually *is* in the world. What other kinds of inaccess stories circulate? What other endemic lexicons of access are simmering below the surface of the polished global vocabulary of barrier-free design? In what ways might these lexicons be liberatory, and in what ways might they be limiting? What kinds of metonymic meanings does accessible design, traveling in global friction, take on in other locations and linguistic repertoires? What happens when ramps are present but wheelchair-users are not? What happens when wheelchairs are present, but wheelchair-users are not? What kinds of disability experience and expertise are obfuscated by the fixation on accessible design that creates material infrastructure? What possibilities for political critique in repressive autocracy does metonymic communication offer? What can crip strategies for sustaining subjugated access vernaculars, and political potentialities therein, reveal?

I ask these questions not to suggest that disability studies situated in the global North/West should advance knowledge by extracting knowledge practices from elsewhere, but to encourage the expansion of a global disability studies that locates conversations about the political topography of disability as social difference beyond and outside of the Euromerican context. Just as global feminist scholarship has demanded that advocacy unfolds on manifold incommensurable terms, recognizing that the location of hegemonic capital in the institutions of the global North/West does not mean that those so empowered deserve epistemic primacy. Rather, following the queer feminist tradition, imagining a global disability studies means moving the center.

During my fieldwork and writing, the center has in fact moved in Euroamerican disability studies as a field. The disability justice movement in the United States and Canada has indelibly shifted the conversation about advocacy and scholarship. Disability Justice activists raised a profound critique of a rights-based disability advocacy paradigm that grew out of spaces and communities that called on legal structures to work for disabled people against ableism. Instead, the disability justice paradigm argues that legal rights benefit only the most privileged, and centers on the modes of survival created by poor, queer, and racialized disabled folks, in recognition that the settler-colonial neoliberal state is premised on their disenfranchisement through intersecting systems of oppression (Sins Invalid 2015). In tandem, a growing consideration of debility troubles the category of disability itself, resituating disability as a privileged identity based on access to social service and medical care, and a Euroamerican paradigm. Thinking in allyship with disability justice, and building on Jasbir Puar's work in this vein, we might ask what kinds of debility are not only ignored by accessible design but also perpetrated by the same regimes that create ablenationalist displays?

During my years of work on this project, disability studies in Russia (located in sociological gender studies or medical sociology) first seemed to find new strength, but then suffered setbacks, especially in terms of opportunities to be in conversation with global colleagues. Putin's reconsolidation of power limited the capacity of disability studies scholars in Russia to collaborate with foreign colleagues and funders, the global pandemic reduced travel and thus crosspollination of ideas, and the Euroamerican response to Russia's aggression in Ukraine further limited the ways that Russian scholars and activists could participate in global conversation or receive international attention (given a political climate in anglophone Europe and North America that is reticent to elevate the "Russian"). The opposition to Russian imperialism in Euroamerican scholarly conversations may lend more space in anglophone disability studies to

Eastern European and Central Asian post-Soviet voices. Meanwhile, scholars working in the North American academy have made tremendous advances in history and cultural studies of disability in Slavic studies, including the formal establishment of a disability studies interest group in the Association for Slavic Eastern European and Eurasian Studies for the first time in 2022, new scholarly projects in Eastern Europe, and a new generation of graduate students who enter their advanced studies more familiar with disability studies paradigms than was typical in previous eras. Yet, as this book goes to press, new anti-DEIA rhetoric alleged cost-cutting measures from the 2025 Trump administration threaten the capacity for academic freedom to study, present, and publish on topics related to gender, race, sexuality, and disability.

Reflecting on this shifting terrain, it is clear that this book captures an ethnographic moment that was, in retrospect, fleeting: a period between the end of the immediate post-Soviet transition and the rise of a new era of geopolitical animosity marked by the 2022 invasion of Ukraine (foretold by the 2014 annexation of Crimea), followed by the destabilization of US foreign policy in Trump's second presidency. The fieldwork that I conducted in 2012 as a foreigner with a US passport in Russia would be impossible to carry out in 2025 as this book goes to press.

As I write this conclusion, disability advocacy communities in Russia continue to claim space in public discourse, to host film festivals, and to promote inclusive sports. At the same time, soldiers and civilians are disabled, displaced, and debilitated in the war in Ukraine and Russia. What new access frictions will arise as this new geopolitical catastrophe unfolds? How will the politics of disability politics shift yet again, dislodging new generative mismatches that propel different epistemological constellations of disability expertise?

Sergei's observations about film endings have stayed with me over the many years it has taken me to write this book. The question of what it means to be a main character in Russian or US movies (hero or *geroi*) suggests to me a consideration of the political imaginaries that scaffold the stories we tell about our experiences and the stories we consume about our societies. Sergei's musings seem tied to the capacity of a protagonist to take charge of their own fate, to claim a place in the tides of history. Throughout this book, I have sought to attend to stories and vernaculars of disability expertise in which disabled Russian adults play the role of protagonists, and to tell a story about disability access in global context while resisting dominant teleologies. However, irrespective of the extent to which I have managed to achieve these ambitions, in the process, I have come to the realization that the vernacular meanings of access remain available for cooptation and will continue to be coopted, circulating further afield on the friction of slanted and metonymic meanings, traveling beyond the control of the original bearers of access expertise, rasping in the turmoil of geopolitical change.

Acknowledgments

It is humbling to reflect on the far-reaching network of people who have made this work possible. I am grateful for their labor, hospitality, camaraderie, support, and willingness to share stories and points of view. I am grateful for the formal support of numerous institutions and grant-funding programs that made it possible to carry out the research, writing, and revision of this book, and, equally important, for the informal support of intellectual and personal community that made the slow trot of writing and revising a thinkable feat.

I conducted an early phase of research that laid the groundwork for this book in the Department of Anthropology at Macalester College in Saint Paul, Minnesota, including research conducted as part of a School for International Training program in Buryatia, Irkutsk, and Saint Petersburg, Russia, in 2005. I am grateful to mentors Jim von Geldern, Arjun Guneratne, Joan Ostrove, Dianna Shandy, and Cindy Wu who encouraged me and helped me to formulate my way of thinking between anthropology, disability studies, and Russian studies.

The present work began in earnest in 2009 at the Department of Anthropology at the University of North Carolina at Chapel Hill (UNC), which continued until 2015. I am grateful for the grant support for language study and for funding from the National Science Foundation Fellowship Program, which made this initial fieldwork feasible. I also received support from the Sexuality Studies Program at UNC, and held a Kennan Institute Summer Research Fellowship at the Woodrow Wilson Center in Washington, DC, in 2015. I am grateful to my mentors at UNC, especially Jocelyn Chua, Arturo Escobar, Sue Estroff, and Michele Rivkin-Fish. In particular, I am grateful to the late Bill Lachicotte, whose work on disability remained largely unpublished, but whose teaching on anthropology of disability and collegial invitation to think with him about how to invent a disability anthropology course, grounded my ambitions and provided a container for thinking expansively. Michal Osterweil was a beacon of how to live ethically as a scholar-activist in an imperfect world. Comrades Adam Leeds, Tomas Matza, and Tamar Shirinian at nearby Duke University made me feel seen and heard and eager to contribute to the ethnography of the former Soviet Union. I'm grateful to my colleagues in anthropology, cultural geography, communication, social movements, Russian history, and public health for the late-night reading sessions, coffee shop writing dates, commitment to found texts, wine-infused read-alouds, potlucks, social media musings, and swimming adventures that built the Carrboro community that sustained us all, through the hard times and the good, and whose thinking pushed my own. These colleagues include, especially, but not only, Nadya Belenky, Ori Burton, Mike Dimpfl, Shoshana Goldberg, Aaron Hale-Dorrell, Sara Juengst, Anna Kirey, Stevie Larson, Kendra Lopes, Pavi Vasudevan, and Lindsey West-Wallace (and all the other mischief-makers who made these years magic).

I am grateful to a number of mentors in Russia who hosted me and provided visa support. In light of the current political situation, I will not name them here, but without their administrative labor and kind encouragement, this book would not have been possible. I am also grateful for the love, friendship, care, and logistical supported extended to me by numerous friends, loved ones, host families, and other kin in Karelia and other parts of Russia (some of whom are no longer there, others who are, and some who have passed away). I am also grateful to the numerous teachers, instructors, and patient friends who encouraged me along my long slow journey to Russian proficiency, reminding me to use the dative case more (rather than the very American nominative first-person singular), insisting that I spend the time to properly learn to roll my *r*, and inventing creative ways to drill grammatical endings.

From 2015 to 2017, I continued to work on this book through publications and conference papers. This work was possible thanks to a position at the University of California–San Diego, hosted in the Department of Communication as part of the UC Collaboratory for Ethnographic Design. I am also grateful to the UC San Diego Department of Anthropology for welcoming me as an occasional instructor and interlocutor in a variety of seminars, and to the Medical Anthropology working group and the Russian Studies working group, both of which read and commented on work that eventually became a part of this book. I am grateful to mentors, writing companions, and friends from my time in California, including Joe Hankins and Keith Murphy (whose comments on my *American Ethnologist* article in progress were what we might call the definition of "clutch"), Elana Zilberg, Amelia Glazer, Louise Hickman, Yelena Gluzman and Christina Aushana, Patrick Anderson, Lilly Irani, Ari Heinrich, Mara Green, Utpal Sandasara, and numerous others.

Throughout this trajectory, I was in ongoing conversation with disability studies as an interdisciplinary field, and my thinking was deeply informed by the then-active in-person conferences of the Society for Disability Studies. Likewise, the Disability Research Interest Group of the American Anthropological Association became an important space for meeting colleagues and organizing as well as envisioning what our corner of the discipline might be in the future. I was especially informed by the Cripping Development Conference organized by Kateřina Kolařova and Kathi Wiedlack in Prague in 2013. I am especially grateful to mentors Pam Block, Faye Ginsburg and Rayna Rapp (a.k.a. the entity known as Fayna), Devva Kasnitz, Robert McRuer, Karen Nakamura, and Sarah Phillips for welcoming me into the field and handing me leadership roles before I knew which way was up. I am deeply in awe of and beholden to fellow contributors to the Critical Design Lab, especially Aimi Hamraie, who convenes the space, and Louise Hickman and Jarah Moesch, among others. I have the deepest gratitude for doing this work in conversation with cotravelers and close colleagues Svetlana Borodina, Michele Friedner, Anastasia Kayiatos, Christine Sargent, Zoë Wool, and others. In Russia, I am grateful to Elena Iarskaia-Smirnova for her work to create Russophone disability studies and include me in those conversations. Likewise, I am grateful to the Russian area studies community at ASEEES (Association for Slavic, Eastern European, and Eurasian Studies), Soyuz, and elsewhere, especially José Alaniz, Fran Bernstein, Alexei Golubev, Anastasia Kayiatos, Larisa Kurtović, John Little (whose work on Soviet disability history unfortunately remains unpublished), Michał Murawski, Claire Shaw, and others. I am grateful to medical anthropology, design anthropology, and post-Soviet anthropology mentors, colleagues, and friends at AAA and SfAA, including Alexei Yurchak and Serguei Oushakine, who have each been supportive from afar, and Lyndsey Beutin, Cal Biruk, and Erika Hoffman-Dilloway, who brought me into a circle of raucous hope and scholarly praxis.

In 2017–2018, I was at Yale University at the MacMillan Centre for International and Area Studies and the Department of Anthropology, during which time I was actively writing this book. I received essential feedback on a talk integrating new material about design thinking in Russia that I presented as part of the Slavic Department colloquium; that has indelibly shaped the argument of this book. I am especially grateful to Marijeta Bozovic, Greta LaFleur, Jess Newman, Eda Pepi, and Doug Rogers for making space to share that year.

In 2018, I joined the faculty at the University of Toronto Scarborough and the Graduate Department of Anthropology at the University of Toronto. This privileged role has allowed me to continue to revise this book, through the support of generous research leave and an active intellectual community. I am grateful to my colleagues in sociocultural anthropology for their generous comments on a near-complete version of the introduction to this book in our work-in-progress series. I have benefited from support for new faculty at the Centre for European and Eurasian Studies, as well as the center's lively academic event series, including the opportunity to host several interlocutors. At the University of Toronto Scarborough, I am grateful to my undergraduate students in my Disability Studies and Health Humanities courses for asking tough questions, bringing their own intersectional praxis into the classroom, and showing up through the years of the global pandemic. I am especially grateful to my colleagues and graduate students at our fledgling Centre for Global Disability Studies, who have buoyed me on through difficult years with camaraderie and intellectual community. I have been honored to share time and space with outstanding graduate students at the University of Toronto. The direction of this book was particularly influenced by Gyuzel Kamalova, Vanessa Maloney, and Hannah Quinn, each of whom offered feedback on my work in progress and influenced my thinking in our disability anthropology seminar and disability anthropology working group. Thank you also to Miggy Esteban and Elaine Cagulada, whose critical thinking and lyrical work in disability studies advances the field as a whole, and with whom I've been lucky to share intellectual community. I am grateful to several research assistants who worked with me on this and other projects, especially those whose native knowledge of Russian was a welcome resource. I am grateful to my senior colleagues who saw a place for disability studies at the University of Toronto and University of Toronto Scarborough, and to fellow faculty for creating collegial spaces to write and offer feedback on works in progress. I'm especially grateful to colleagues Andrea Allen, Susan Antebi, Chloe Atkins, Rob Austin, Hilary Brown, Andrea Charise, Nais Dave, Nisrin Elamin, Vini Furuie, Kate Holland, Katie Kilroy-Marac, Anne McGuire, Andrea Muehlebach, Aparna Nair, Natalie Oswin, Ed Schatz, Dana Seitler, Michelle Silver, Alison Smith, Janelle Taylor, Tanya Titchkosky, Holly Wardlow, Katherine Williams, and Zoë Wool.

I am grateful to those who have taken the time and energy to invite me to share this research in campus talks, and whose generous engagement has advanced this book, especially the following: Michele Friedner and Eugene Raikhel at University of Chicago, Ilya Utekhin at EUSP, Julie Hemment and Krista Harper at UMASS Amherst, Sarah Sharma at UofT's then McLuhan Centre, Kristin Bright at Middlebury, and Jessica Hardin and colleagues at RIT. I am likewise grateful to those who have invited me to be an interlocutor in other ways, including Eli Elinoff, Elizabeth Guffey, and colleagues in Berlin. Chapter 2 of this book is closely related to an article previously published in *American Ethnologist*, and I am grateful for permission to publish here, and to the journal editors and numerous anonymous reviewers for encouraging and pushing forward that article, which influenced the present work in important ways. Furthermore, I am very grateful to the numerous collaborators who made my earlier book, *I Was Never Alone or Oporniki: An Ethnographic Play on Disability in Russia* (University of Toronto Press 2020), and the play script on which it is based, a living reality. The insights from that work, as well as shared ethnographic source material, shaped this book profoundly. Thank you especially to Anne, Carli, and Stephen.

I am deeply grateful and full of respect for the outstanding work of administrative staff in each of these institutional locations who make the university run despite the many pressures from all sides that quite simply make us all want to give up sometimes. Thank you.

I have enormous respect for my editors at Cornell University Press, and the many people in the press's extended production line whose labor has made the creation of this book possible. Thank you especially to Ellen and Jim for taking an interest in this project and carrying it through the review process.

Writing a monograph as a single author obscures the depth of communal care and social worlds that make this vocation thinkable and possible. This work would never have come into being without the family and friends who have made me feel at home as I have crisscrossed two continents in pursuit of a way to bring this book into being. Thank you.

It would absolutely be possible to continue revising this book forever, but the period of research now recedes swiftly into the past, and the only option is to launch this book into the world, come what may.

Notes

INTRODUCTION

1. Throughout this text, I use both person-first (person with a disability) and identity-first (disabled person) language, in recognition of the fact that language terminology is evolving over time and diverges in translation. I have tried to approximate as closely as possible a term that fits with how a disabled interlocutor/interlocutor with a disability would refer to themselves, though given that an entire chapter of this text is devoted to the incommensurability and divergence of disability terminology between Russian and English, this can never be more than an approximation. In many cases, I have offered a few words as to what I know of a person's diagnosis; I offer this not out of a desire to reify medical categories, but rather as a shorthand for readers familiar with disability community to grasp something about the kinds of impairments and disabling experiences the described person may encounter. I hope that a reader will understand that the insufficiencies of language here are very much part and parcel of the work of disability ethnography, that representation in text is imperfect, and that I have tried to reduce ableist bias in language wherever possible.

2. Hamraie and Fritsch also refer to frictions as "productive" in the abstract sense (2019, 2).

3. *Disability expertise* draws on the longstanding consideration in disability studies of the paternalistic attitude toward disabled people that ableism engenders, and the move to flip the ableist view that disabled people are in need of help (Finkelstein 1975). The concept of disability expertise is not intended as a either a euphemistic nicety or a totalizing positive reclamation of pride, but rather as an orientation derived from complex subject position. Sometimes this manifests as "a productive experience of difference [. . .] a marker of innovation operating at the materialist edge of species innovation" (Mitchell and Snyder 2017, 26–27); at other times, no such innovation or benefit arrives, only embodied knowledge of how ableism operates. I also discuss disability expertise in the section of this chapter about disability anthropology, as well as in my 2020 article.

4. Reporting on the photo project, Davies (2019) explains:

> Known by his alias *Vreditel Li*? (or "Is That a Pest?"), the Samara-based artist and his team took over a disused apartment block on the outskirts of the city. After taking two days to drill holes into the building's outer wall, they attached brackets in order to create a platform on the fourth floor of the five-storey building. Props were lowered down from the roof using a rope, while the artist himself wore a cleverly-hidden harness. The performance sees the artist sitting in a wheelchair trapped by the steps—and the dizzying drop—beneath him. According to the team, the piece was designed to highlight the challenges faced by twelve and a half million disabled people in Russia today. "For my disabled neighbour, the staircase is an insurmountable obstacle—which is why we so rarely see people with disabilities out and about," *Vreditel Li* wrote on his Instagram page. "But the staircase is just the first step in a series of urban obstacles. There are unusable ramps, poor-quality materials, falling tiles, subways, and many other dangers within our daily environment."

The @vreditel_li art collective Instagram account was still active as this book was going to press. *Vreditel'* is a Russian word (styled for social media without the transliterated soft sign) meaning pest or vermin, with a specific political history related to the Soviet criminal category of *vreditel'stvo* (subversive acts or economic sabotage), used in a contemporary context (sometimes ironically) to describe those who sabotage others or ruin property. The artists called the series of photos *gorodskaia sreda*, which could be translated in several ways: *municipal surroundings* (emphasizing the governmentality manifest in the built environment), or, perhaps more simply, *cityscape* (with a sort of ironic bent). The photos of the wheelchair user and impossible ramp were one iteration of a project called 1m2, which also includes various other scenes taken on the same ledge.

Interestingly, both of these examples suggest an orientalizing vantage on the purported subject. We might consider the social forces that would also characterize accessible design or wheelchair users as seductive, simple, backward, or uncivilized, and other descriptors.

5. I use the term *Euroamerican*, following Ingstad and Whyte (2007), to designate a particular nexus of geopolitical power and attendant imperialism of related cultural formations.

6. The Russian Federation during the 2010s was a globally connected economic, social, cultural, and political space. The 2010s are in this way distinct. They follow the period of post-Soviet transition in the 1990s and early 2000s characterized by exploitative economic shock therapy, shortages, poverty, and instability. In contrast, the 2010s opened with a feeling of optimism and a sense of political and economic stability distinct in recent memory. The economic stability allowed for increased flow of consumer goods and cultural objects into and out of Russia as well as for the possibility for travel abroad for some classes, a situation quite different from just ten years earlier.

7. Nina Anatoliievna is a pseudonym. I use pseudonyms throughout for interlocutors, except in cases in which the person in question is a public figure, in which case, I use their real name, usually a last name. In most cases, I use a first name or the casual (shortened) version of a first name. When I refer to people of a more senior generation, I often use a first name and patronymic. These choices are intended to follow standard practices of expressing respect in Russophone address.

8. A complaint in medical practice refers to the "symptoms and ailments reported by a patient" (Chua 2012, 221), and Chua, as a medical anthropologist, identifies the practice of reporting one's symptoms and ailments as a particular register of speech or social performance. I consider inaccess stories in relation to Chua's observation, in that they, too, are a kind of speech act; however, in inaccess stories, it is not symptoms of disability as a medical condition being reported, but rather the social and relational concerns of living with a disability in a particular context.

9. Related to the separation of access objects from access knowledge is the way that the labor of actually disabled designer-activists becomes devalued. Scholars and activists argue that disabled designers are frequently excluded from the accessible design industry (see Jackson and Williamson 2023). Designs by disabled people may instead get coded as lay innovation or patient hacking, capitulating the dominant logics of medical paternalism.

10. Defining design requires distinguishing design from three neighboring fields: art, architecture, and engineering. Professionals in each of these fields may engage in a process of design, or *do* design work, yet, the professional terrain of design is distinct from each field. Design is distinct from art partially in terms of the disciplinary distinctions of professional training; but, perhaps most fundamentally, art can exist for art's sake, aesthetics over application. Design, as understood in contemporary

professional usage, designates this shared attention to both aesthetics and function in the process of making. Architecture has to do primarily with the design of human dwellings and spaces on a civic and structural level. Engineering often involves the work of researching, devising, and determining how to structure an object, infrastructure, or system, but unlike design, art, and architecture, the aesthetic properties of the engineered object are secondary to concepts of efficiency and function. (The resulting object does work; its function is more important than its form; its value derives from its function; and attention to aesthetics is an inefficiency.) These definitions are useful, too, in distinguishing the *anthropology of design* (see Hartblay, Hankins, and Caldwell 2018) from anthropology of art, architecture, or infrastructure.

11. I use the metageographic descriptor "global North/West" in opposition to "global South/East" as an indicator of geopolitical hegemonies that accounts for both the post–Cold War move away from the rubric of a first, second, or third world, and the ways in which a global North/global South paradigm fails to capture material histories of state socialism. This use follows critical feminist scholars writing about post-Soviet and postsocialist Europe, including Suchland (2011) and Wiedlack and Neufeld (2014, 2016).

12. "Cripwashing" has been proposed as the corollary to ablenationalism that pinkwashing is to homonoationalism (Moscoso and Platero 2017).

13. I am hardly the first to use a version of this approach to study disability ethnographically, but rather I join a rich history of scholars working in this tradition.

14. Several minority languages are in use in the Karelian Republic—Karelian (a dialect of Finnish), Veps (a minority indigenous group), and various languages that Central Asian and Caucasian migrant workers spoke among themselves or at home—but I rarely encountered these languages in daily life, and Russian was the native language of all of my primary interlocutors. In a few cases, the novelty of my role as a US researcher who spoke Russian was elevated as spectacle—I was profiled in two human interest interviews—one published online, and one in print in a local newspaper. I am a white person of Slavic and Ashkenazi descent. I grew up in the Northeast United States the child of first- and third-generation immigrants, respectively. My father's parents spoke Polish in their home (although his father's first language was Yiddish), and throughout my childhood, we were in contact with the Polish side of his family, especially in the late 1980s and early 1990s, when Poland reopened to the West. My mother's grandparents and great-grandparents spoke Slovak and Ukrainian, and family holidays were marked with Eastern European cuisine. With this family background, no one was surprised when I opted to study Russian in high school. My ethnicity also meant that as I moved through public spaces in Russia, I was not usually identified as a foreigner until someone heard that I spoke Russian with a foreign (although not identifiably American) accent.

1. "I CAN DO IT MYSELF"

1. *Dacha* is a Russian summer house. Although the word could refer to the summer palaces and mansions of the Russian gentry and royalty in the pre-Soviet era, the Soviet dacha was more of a practical necessity. Many families were allotted small gardening plots outside of the city, constructing small huts, and growing food there. For many Petrozavodsk families, those with dachas relied on the food they produced to survive the lean years of the 1990s, canning cabbage and pickles and carrots and tomatoes, and storing potatoes on city apartment balconies. Today in Karelia, dachas might be newly constructed lake houses for the wealthy and upper middle class, or they might be inherited gardening plots or small hunting cottages for those without the means to conduct a full renovation. Many families will spend whole weeks or every weekend at the dacha

throughout the summer season, or take advantage of the warm weather to send half the family from a cramped apartment to the unheated summer home.

2. Disability inclusion activists in Petrozavodsk in my experience (or elsewhere in Russia as far as I know), have not been subject to the accusations of "foreign" ideological influence that feminist and LGBTQ activists have (see Healey 2018; Kondakov 2022), although some disability activists are also feminist or LGBTQ activists. In cases in which disability has been represented as shameful, it has largely been in the context of longstanding endogenous tropes, sometimes remixed with global cultural imagery (e.g., see Wiedlack and Neufeld 2016).

3. "In theory," explain Benevolenski and Toepler, "Russian nonprofits have principally had access to government and municipal contracts as well, as contracting laws did not favor one legal form or auspice over the other. However, in the implementation of these provisions, public funds for social services were almost exclusively awarded to public institutions in fields like health, education, and human services" (2017, 69).

4. "Working on the self" and notions of psychosocial development have a complex history in Soviet theories and practices that dovetail with contemporary neoliberal self-work as understood in the global North/West. For a discussion of Soviet influence on contemporary Russian concepts of working on the self, see Hellbeck (2001); Raikhel (2016); and Matza (2018), among others.

2. INACCESSIBLE ACCESSIBILITY

1. Parts of this chapter are similar to the article "Good Ramps, Bad Ramps" published in *American Ethnologist* in 2017.

2. The phrase "disability things" was coined by Katherine Ott, a curator at the National Museum of American History of the Smithsonian Institute. See the project "Everybody: An Artifact History of Disability in America" (2013) for an example of how her work uses material culture and technology to discuss the complexity of disability. Ott also published a chapter about the concept in an edited volume (Ott 2014). The phrase was a point of departure for a series of panels at the Society for Disability Studies conference for two years running (2013 and 2014), at which disability studies and design scholars unpacked the cultural associations in a given object that is often characterized as a disability thing but does not necessarily have to be (prosthetic limbs), or is not usually considered to be a disability thing but in fact may be (the iPhone). Thanks to Aimi Hamraie for their help tracking the origin of this concept.

3. The notion of good passage is one that I carry over from the article "Good Passages, Bad Passages" in which Ingunn Moser and John Law (1999) blend science studies and disability theory to argue that as cyborgs, humans rely on the confluence of a variety of technologies and material and human factors to facilitate smooth communication or passage from one state, stage, or place to another. For those of us negotiating nonnormative bodies, however, the links between the elements in these exchanges and passages do not align; and passage is rocky, incomplete, tumultuous, slow, or difficult. In crip culture, the choreography of discrete design elements and social factors into a "good passage" is a goal rather than an expected occurrence. Here I have used the phrase "smooth passage" to emphasize the concept of unevenness and friction.

4. Robert McRuer reported a similar phenomenon regarding a lone curb cut installed in a sidewalk outside of the British Embassy in Mexico City—although installed with much fanfare, McRuer argued that the curb cut did little to facilitate access in the city, nor to assuage the disabling and debilitating conditions of life in the city more broadly (McRuer 2013, 2018, 135–136).

5. People drink the water from the springs, which is also gathered and used for mineral baths. Each of the three springs has a its own composition of minerals, which are said to be healing for specific ailments.

6. Imgur is an online image aggregating site that allows readers to give a news item an up or down vote to signify whether a given content item should be promoted or get buried. The site's algorithm processes shares and response to provides constant new content to its readers. Imgur was designed to generate viral image memes and draws an international user base (Garber 2014).

7. Whether the ratification of the treaty holds an meaning for disabled Russians, or represents a manner by which the Russian government sought an easy acknowledgment and legitimization as the sole entity of justice in the territory of the Russian Federation is another story. For a critique of the role of the United Nations Convention on the Rights of Persons with Disabilities in non-Western contexts, see Meekosha and Soldatic (2011).

8. Thanks to Kevin Gotkin, Aimi Hamraie, and other members of the Critical Design Lab for a discussion of "forness" as a term to think with in Ahmed's book, which influenced this section.

3. HOUSING FATES

1. While streets elsewhere were named for monarchs, national heroes, and natural features (Oak Street, Lake Street), in the Soviet Union, the most ubiquitous streets names were those referencing Communist Party leaders, Soviet military heroes, and socialist heroes (from Karl Marx to Yuri Gagarin).

2. *Stiob* is a Russian word referencing a kind of performative ironic or sarcastic speech, described in detail by Alexei Yurchak (2006) in his account of the late-Soviet period in Saint Petersburg, Russia, and elsewhere. Like sarcasm, *stiob* involves voicing or enacting a rhetorical position or concept accurately, but unfaithfully, to draw attention to its absurdity. Like performances of ironic disbelief by Jon Stewart and Stephen Colbert in the United States in the early 2000s, *stiob* is a humorous form of speaking from the subject position that one is simultaneously mocking (Yurchak and Boyer 2010).

3. Of course, floor and building plans are reused in capitalist construction as well. The material and ideological production of the plans and the buildings, however, are predicated on the idea of a universal needs.

4. Throughout this text, I distinguish between post-Soviet and postsocialist, in the sense that post-Soviet is a time period and postsocialist is a global conjuncture (e.g. see Mladenev 2017; Gille 2010; Fraser 1997). However, recent scholarly attention to the Soviet and post-Soviet built environment suggests a potential different interpretation of the post-Soviet *parti*. Stephen Collier (2011) has explored the ways in which the built environment of the Soviet infrastructure has led to particular and culturally located configurations of public infrastructure, which are now repurposed into privatized and state-owned infrastructures that follow logics and arrangements of responsibility unique to post-Soviet space. Jane Zavisca (2012) has argued that the spatial confines of the Soviet family apartment, and the limited availability of housing in those now-aging apartment units in Russia today, create particular constraints on kinship and reproduction.

5. Readers who have also read *I Was Never Alone* (Hartblay 2020) will recognize this exchange as the eponymous excerpt from Portrait IV in that book.

6. For a discussion of the phrase "needed by nobody" in Russian, see Höjdestrand (2009).

7. At the same time, in 2012, Vera was saving money and hoping that if her husband sold an apartment that he owned in Saint Petersburg, they might be able to buy another apartment, leaving her parents to their own apartment.

8. This review of archival material was conducted by the author in collaboration with Gyuzel Kamalova, as of press time, under review for separate publication.

9. See, for example, Novopolianskii, D. *"Razmyshleniia nad pis'mami: Neotlozhnyi Dolg"* [Musings on Letters: An enduring duty]." *Pravda*, April 15, 1975, 6. https://www .eastview.com/resources/gpa/pravda/. For further discussion of veteran experience and organizing, see Edele (2008); Bernstein (2015); and Krylova (2001).

10. See Sazhko, P. *"Udoben li magazin?: kak razvivat'sia torgovle* [Is the store convenient?: how to develop commerce]." *Pravda*, No. 233, February 2, 1972, 3. https://www .eastview.com/resources/gpa/pravda/.

4. NORMAL, CONVENIENT, COMFORTABLE

1. Although the anglophone terms *accessible* and *barrier-free* may be used interchangeably in disability advocacy work, there are some differences. The phrase *barrier-free environment* came into widespread global usage following its use in architectural discourse, and subsequently in the United Nations disability rights documents and treaties. This term distinctively refers to a concept of removing barriers to access related to the so-called social model of disability. *Accessible* is clearly the preferred term in the landmark Americans with Disabilities Act (ADA) legislation and is widely used in the United States and Canada. It strikes me that barrier-free may be preferred in the international context because it is more readily translated across languages. The concept of barriers is also more closely aligned with the British context and the origin of the social model (Oliver 2009(1996)).

2. Galina's description of the disability law in Russia was extremely precise. She wrote:

> The first legal acts that named *dostupnaia sreda* were the Presidential Decree of the RF from October 2, 1992 number 1156 "On measures for the creation of access for disabled people in daily surroundings" [*O merakh po formirovaniu dostupnoi dlia invalidov sredy zhiznedeiatel'nosti*] and in Legal Act of the RF from March 25 1993 Number 245 with an identical name. These were strengthened and further developed in the Federal Law Number 181 from November 24, 1995, with changes and amendments from August 8 2001, "On the social protection of *invalidov* in the Russian Federation." In articles 14, 15, 16 the state declared the creation of accessible infrastructures and the necessity of free access of *invalidov* to information and related measures of responsibility for realization of the items laid out in the Law in 1990 starting with that they translate books, such as Kalmet Kh. U. "Living surroundings for the disabled" 1990. [. . .]
>
> The first standards [*normy*] for the implementation of accessibility [*obespecheniu dostupnosti*] in elements of infrastructure [*infrastruktura*] appeared in the USA at the start of the 1970s. Fairly soon after many other countries have made it mandatory to agree with accessibility standards [*trebovaniia dostupnosti*] for elements of the built environment [*ob"ektov sredovogo okruzheniia*] for individuals with limitations [*lits, imeushchikh ogranicheniia*]. The first standards [*normativom*] for barrier-free construction [*bezbari'ernogo stroitel'stva*] to appear were RSN 70–90, which have existed [*deistvovavshii*] since 1991. It follows to note that the law "On the social protection of the disabled" from 1991 prohibited the development and building of venues not equipped with elements of access for *invalidov*. (Galina Gorbatykh, personal communication, 2014)

3. So far in my review, the categories remain distinct and correspond to the anglophone concepts. However, the focus on "approach on foot" adheres more clearly to *dostup*, and the concept of modern infrastructure aligns more closely with *udobstvo*.

Preobrazhenskiy's etymological dictionary (1951(1910–1926), 408–409) includes *dostup*, *dostupnyi*, *dostupnost'*, and *nedostupnyi* under the entry for the root *stupat'* (to step), of Slavic origin. Müller's *English Russian Dictionary* (1965) in the entry for access offers *dostup* as the first translation, and *prokhod* and *podkhod*, nouns from verbs describing approach on foot, as the second. Müller's entry does include "ease of surroundings in a renovation" as the second definition of accessibility, suggesting the obvious and clear cognate concept to the subsequent anglophone usage in disability politics.

4. I thank Aparna Nair for this point.

5. I thank Larisa Kurtović for this point.

6. When interlocutors describe the gap between reality and an imagined good life, one interpretation is to consider how their inaccess stories are a complaint about corruption, or the moral failure of others, particularly those in power. Anthropologists understand *corruption* as a conceptual category that is instrumental in meaning-making at local and global levels (Gupta 2005, 2012; Haller and Shore 2005). When people narrate quotidian transgressions of social norms and in so doing outline the moral field of appropriate conduct as actors negotiating the rules governing social and political life, they are often making complaints about the category we understand as corruption (Haller and Shore 2005, 8). Although my interlocutors' complaints might also be understood as narratives of corruption (Gupta 2005), I hesitate to use this category because Western accusations of Russian corruption have become overdetermined, and scholars argue that they flatten social and moral experience (Rivkin-Fish 2005a; Ledeneva 1998). Still, the confluence of infrastructure, power, and complaint do offer a compelling association.

7. "*Udobstva zhizni, dostatok" i ukhod", usluga*" (Dal' [1880–1882] 2003, vol 4 294).

8. "*Spokoinaia doroga, rovnaia; spokoinaia koliaska, netriaskaia. Spokoinoe pomyshchen'e, udobnoe*" (Dal' [1880–1882] 2003, vol 4 294).

9. This refrain is sometimes attributed to the writer Gogol (who indeed wrote much about driving carriages over rutted and potholed roadways), or to the historian and writer Karamzin, as well as to others. A Russian-language internet search turns up numerous circular blog posts pondering the origin of the phrase. I should note the potential for unpacking the deployment of "*durak*" here: specifically, the suggestion that moronic or stupid people (*duraki*) are seemingly harmless, at the same time that low intelligence or illogical reasoning are a "problem" that society must work to resolve just as poor roads ought to be fixed. But that's a topic for another project.

CONCLUSION

1. The suit was reportedly imported from the United Kingdom specifically for the event. The suit suggests that Gref was engaging in what critical disability studies calls "disability simulation"—donning limiting apparel (such as a blindfold) to simulate the experience of a disability, or temporary use of an assistive technology, for example, spending an hour or a day using a wheelchair to get around. The premise that disability simulation may be used to promote access and understanding is refuted by critical disability studies scholars and disabled advocates, who argue that such exercises often serve to reify difference and reinforce incorrect assumptions and attitudes of pity among nondisabled participants (Nario-Redmond, Gospodinov, and Cobb 2017; DAVT 2018).

References

Abilis Foundation. 2014. http://www.abilis.fi/.

Adams, Vincanne, ed. 2016. *Metrics: What Counts in Global Health.* Critical Global Health: Evidence, Efficacy, Ethnography. Durham, NC: Duke University Press.

Ahmed, Sara. 2019. *What's the Use? On the Uses of Use.* Durham, NC: Duke University Press.

Asimov, Isaac. 1966. *Understanding Physics.* New York: Dorset.

Bell, Chris. 2017. "Is Disability Studies Actually White Disability Studies?" In *The Disability Studies Reader,* edited by Lennard J. Davis. New York: Routledge. 406–415.

Benevolenski, Vladimir B., and Stefan Toepler. 2017. "Modernising Social Service Delivery in Russia: Evolving Government Support for Non-Profit Organisations." *Development in Practice* 27 (1): 64–76. https://doi.org/10.1080/09614524.2017.1259392.

Berlant, Lauren Gail. 2022. *On the Inconvenience of Other People.* Writing Matters! Durham, NC: Duke University Press.

Bernal, Victoria, and Inderpal Grewal. 2014. *Theorizing NGOs: States, Feminisms, and Neoliberalism.* Durham, NC: Duke University Press.

Berne, Patty. 2020. "What Is Disability Justice?" Sins Invalid. June 16. https://www.sinsinvalid.org/news-1/2020/6/16/what-is-disability-justice.

Bernstein, Frances. 2013. "Prosthetic Promise in Late-Stalinist Russia." In *Disability in Eastern Europe and the Former Soviet Union: History, Policy and Everyday Life,* edited by Michael Rasell and Elena Iarskaia-Smirnova. New York: Routledge. 42–66.

———. 2015. "Prosthetic Manhood in the Soviet Union at the End of World War II." *Osiris* 30 (1): 113–33. https://doi.org/10.1086/682969.

———. 2024. "Arms Race: The Cold War Story of a Bionic Arm." In *Technologies of Mind and Body in the Soviet Union and the Eastern Bloc,* edited by Anna Toropova and Claire Shaw. London: Bloomsbury. 197–216.

Biehl, João, and Torben Eskarod. 2005. *Vita: Life in a Zone of Social Abandonment.* Berkeley: University of California Press.

Borodina, Svetlana. 2020. "Needed Subjects: An Ethnography of the Formation of the Inclusion Complex in Russia." PhD diss., Rice University. https://www.proquest.com/docview/2568260252/abstract/1F578D2FA94749AAPQ/1.

———. 2021. "Strategies of Disability Activism in Soviet and Post-Soviet Russia." *Current History* 120 (828): 274–79. https://doi.org/10.1525/curh.2021.120.828.274.

———. 2023. "Russia's Domestication of Disability Inclusion." *Problems of Post-Communism,* 1–11. https://doi.org/10.1080/10758216.2023.2176322.

Bowker, Geoffrey C, and Susan Leigh Star. 1999. *Sorting Things out: Classification and Its Consequences.* Cambridge, MA: MIT Press.

Buchli, Victor. 1997. "Khrushchev, Modernism, and the Fight against 'Petit-Bourgeois' Consciousness in the Soviet Home." *Journal of Design History* 10 (2): 161–76. https://www.jstor.org/stable/1316130.

Callon, Michel. 1991. "Techno-Economic Networks and Irreversibility." In *A Sociology of Monsters: Essays on Power, Technology and Domination,* edited by John Law, 132–64. Sociological Review Monograph 38. London: Routledge.

Canguilhem, Georges. 1989. *The Normal and the Pathological*. New York: Zone.

Chakrabarty, Dipesh. 2000. *Provincializing Europe: Postcolonial Thought and Historical Difference*. Princeton, NJ: Princeton University Press.

Charlton, James I. 2010. "Peripheral Everywhere." *Journal of Literary and Cultural Disability Studies* 4 (2): 195–200. https://doi.org/10.3828/jlcds.2010.15.

Chua, Jocelyn Lim. 2012. "The Register of 'Complaint.'" *Medical Anthropology Quarterly* 26 (2): 221–40.

Chua, Jocelyn Lim. 2014. *In Pursuit of the Good Life: Aspiration and Suicide in Globalizing South India*. Berkeley: University of California Press.

Church, Richard L., and James R. Marston. 2003. "Measuring Accessibility for People with a Disability." *Geographical Analysis* 35 (1): 83–96. https://doi.org/10.1111/j.1538-4632.2003.tb01102.x.

Collier, Stephen J. 2011. *Post-Soviet Social: Neoliberalism, Social Modernity, Biopolitics*. Princeton, NJ: Princeton University Press.

Dal', V.I. (Vladimir Ivanovich). (1880–1882) 2003. *Tolkovyi slovar' zhivogo velikorusskogo iazyka: v chetyrekh tomakh* [Lexical dictionary of the living greater-Russian language: in four volumes]. Moscow: *Spravochnoie Izd*. In Russian.

Dale, Robert. 2013. "The Valaam Myth and the Fate of Leningrad's Disabled Veterans." *Russian Review* 72 (2): 260–84. https://doi.org/10.1111/russ.10691.

Davidov, Veronica. 2017. *Long Night at the Vepsian Museum: The Forest Folk of Northern Russia and the Struggle for Cultural Survival*. Toronto: University of Toronto Press.

Davies, Katie. 2019. "Watch This Artist Take to the Skies to Make a Vertiginous Statement on Disabled Rights." *Calvert Journal*. July 15. https://www.calvertjournal.com/articles/show/11264/art-performance-statement-disability-building-midair-samara-russia.

Davis, Lennard. 2006. *The Disability Studies Reader*. 2nd ed. New York: Routledge.

DAVT. 2018. "Disability Simulations." *Disability Alliance at Virginia Tech* (blog). September 11, 2018. https://disabilityalliancevt.wordpress.com/disability-simulations/.

Djumagulova, Chinara. 2004. *Inclusive Education Development in Central Asia*. Bishkek: Save the Children UK.

Dokumaci, Arseli. 2018. "Disability as Method: Interventions in the Habitus of Ableism through Media-Creation." *Disability Studies Quarterly* 38 (3). https://doi.org/10.18061/dsq.v38i3.6491.

Driakhlitsina, Svetlana Anatolevna. 2009. "The Specificities of Socialization of Young People with Impairment of the Spinal-Movement System: A Sociological Study in the Republic of Karelia" [*Osobennosti sotsializavtsii molodezhi s narusheniem oporno-dvigatel'nogo apparata (Po dannym sotsiologicheskogo issledovaniia v Respublike Kareliia)*]. PhD diss., Saint Petersburg State University.

Dunham, Vera. 1989. "Images of the Disabled, Especially the War Wounded, in Soviet Literature." In *The Disabled in the Soviet Union Past and Present, Theory and Practice*, edited by William McCagg and Lewis H. Siegelbaum. Pittsburgh, PA: University of Pittsburgh Press. 151–164.

Edele, Mark. 2008. *Soviet Veterans of World War II: A Popular Movement in an Authoritarian Society, 1941–1991*. Oxford: Oxford University Press.

Erevelles, Nirmala. 2011. *Disability and Difference in Global Contexts Enabling a Transformative Body Politic*. New York: Palgrave Macmillan.

Escobar, Arturo. 2018. *Designs for the Pluriverse: Radical Interdependence, Autonomy, and the Making of Worlds*. Durham, NC: Duke University Press, 2018.

Essig, Laurie. 1999. *Queer in Russia: A Story of Sex, Self, and the Other*. Durham, NC: Duke University Press.

"EveryBody: An Artifact History of Disability in America." 2013. Smithsonian National Museum of American History. http://everybody.si.edu/.

Fefelov, Valerii. 1986. *V SSSR invalidov net!* [There are no disabled in the USSR!]. London: Overseas Publications Interchange Ltd. http://hdl.handle.net/2027/mdp .39015051172834.

Fehérváry, Krisztina. 2009. "Goods and States: The Political Logic of State-Socialist Material Culture." *Comparative Studies in Society and History* 51 (2): 426–59. https://doi.org/10.1017/S0010417509000188.

Fehérváry, Krisztina. 2013. *Politics in Color and Concrete: Socialist Materialities and the Middle Class in Hungary.* New Anthropologies of Europe. Bloomington: Indiana University Press.

Finkelstein, Vic. 1975. "Fundamental Principles of Disability." Remarks to the Union of the Physically Impaired Against Segregation [later created as a pamphlet]. The Disability Archive, Centre for Disability Studies at the University of Leeds. https://disability-studies.leeds.ac.uk/wp-content/uploads/sites/40/library /finkelstein-UPIAS-Principles-2.pdf.

Fitzpatrick, Sheila. 2000. *Everyday Stalinism: Ordinary Life in Extraordinary Times.* Oxford: Oxford University Press.

Forlano, Laura, and Anijo Mathew. 2014. "From Design Fiction to Design Friction: Speculative and Participatory Design of Values-Embedded Urban Technology." *Journal of Urban Technology* 21 (4): 7–24. https://doi.org/10.1080/10630732.2014. 971525.

Foucault, Michel. 1970. *The Order of Things: An Archaeology of the Human Sciences.* London: Tavistock.

Forlano, Laura, and Anijo Mathew. 2015. "From Design Fiction to Design Friction: Speculative and Participatory Design of Values-Embedded Urban Technology." In *Urban Informatics: Collaboration at the nexus of policy, technology and design, people, and data.* Kristene Unsworth, Andrea Forte, Richardson Dilworth, eds. London: Routledge.

Fraser, Nancy. 1997. *Justice Interruptus: Critical Reflections on the "Postsocialist" Condition.* New York: Routledge.

Friedner, Michele. 2015. *Valuing Deaf Worlds in Urban India.* New Brunswick, NJ: Rutgers University Press.

——. 2018. "Beyond the Social." *Cambridge Journal of Anthropology* 36(1): 107–12. https://doi.org/10.3167/cja.2018.360108.

——. 2022. *Sensory Futures: Deafness and Cochlear Implant Infrastructures in India.* Minneapolis: University of Minnesota.

Fröhlich, Christian. 2012. "Civil Society and the State Intertwined: The Case of Disability NGOs in Russia." *East European Politics* 28 (4): 371–89. https://doi.org/10 .1080/21599165.2012.718269.

Fry, Tony. 1999. *A New Design Philosophy: An Introduction to Defuturing.* Sydney, Australia: University of New South Wales Press.

Galis, Vasilis. 2011. "Enacting Disability: How Can Science and Technology Studies Inform Disability Studies?" *Disability and Society* 26(7): 825–38. https://doi.org /10.1080/09687599.2011.618737.

Galmarini, Maria Cristina [also Galmarini-Kabala]. 2016. *The Right to Be Helped: Deviance, Entitlement, and the Soviet Moral Order.* DeKalb: Northern Illinois University Press.

——. 2017. "Ability to Bear Rights or Ability to Work? The Meaning of Rights and Equality for the Russian Deaf in the Revolutionary Period." *Historical Research* 90 (247): 210–29. https://doi.org/10.1111/1468-2281.12154.

———. 2021. "A Common Space of International Work: Disability Activism, Socialist Internationalism, and the Russian Union of the Blind." *Russian Review* 80 (4): 624–40. https://doi.org/10.1111/russ.12334.

———. 2024. *Ambassadors of Social Progress: A History of International Blind Activism in the Cold War.* NIU Series in Slavic, East European, and Eurasian Studies. Ithaca ; London: Northern Illinois University Press, an imprint of Cornell University Press.

Garber, Megan. 2013. "Imgur: The Biggest Little Site in the World." December 4, 2013. http://www.theatlantic.com/technology/archive/2013/12/imgur-the-biggest-little-site-in-the-world/281872/?7.

Gatrell, Peter. 2005. "Prisoners of War on the Eastern Front during World War I." *Kritika: Explorations in Russian and Eurasian History* 6 (3): 557–66. https://doi.org/10.1353/kri.2005.0036.

Gibson-Graham, J. K. 2006. *The End of Capitalism (as We Knew It): A Feminist Critique of Political Economy.* Minneapolis: University of Minnesota Press.

Gill, Carol J. 1995. "A Psychological View of Disability Culture." *Disability Studies Quarterly* 15(4): 16–19. https://kb.osu.edu/handle/1811/86490.

Gille, Zsuzsa. 2010. "Is There a Global Postsocialist Condition?" *Global Society* 24(1): 9–30.

Ginsburg, Faye, and Rayna Rapp. 2013. "Disability Worlds." *Annual Review of Anthropology* 42(1): 53–68. https://doi.org/10.1146/annurev-anthro-092412-155502.

Gleeson, Brendan. 1999. *Geographies of Disability.* London: Routledge, 1999.

Golubev, Alexey. 2020. *The Things of Life: Materiality in Late Soviet Russia.* Ithaca, NY: Cornell University Press.

Gorbatykh, Galina. Master's thesis.

Gupta, Akhil. 2005. "Narratives of Corruption Anthropological and Fictional Accounts of the Indian State." *Ethnography* 6 (1): 5–34. https://doi.org/10.1177/1466138105055663.

———. 2012. *Red Tape: Bureaucracy, Structural Violence, and Poverty in India.* Durham, NC: Duke University Press.

Hacking, Ian. 1986. "Making Up People." In *Reconstructing Individualism: Autonomy, Individuality, and the Self in Western Thought*, edited by Thomas C. Heller and Christine Brooke-Rose. Stanford, CA: Stanford University Press.

Haller, Dieter, and Cris Shore, eds. 2005. *Corruption: Anthropological Perspectives.* Anthropology, Culture, and Society. Ann Arbor, MI: Pluto.

Hamraie, Aimi. 2013. "Designing Collective Access: A Feminist Disability Theory of Universal Design." *Disability Studies Quarterly* 33 (4). https://doi.org/10.18061/dsq.v33i4.3871.

Hamraie, Aimi. 2017. *Building Access: Universal Design and the Politics of Disability.* Minneapolis: University of Minnesota Press.

Hamraie, Aimi. 2020. "Mapping Access Methodology." Critical Design Lab. https://www.mapping-access.com/mapping-access-methodology.

Hamraie, Aimi, and Kelly Fritsch. 2019. "Crip Technoscience Manifesto." *Catalyst: Feminism, Theory, Technoscience.* 5(1): 1–33. https://catalystjournal.org/index.php/catalyst.

Hartblay, Cassandra. 2006. "An Absolutely Different Life: Locating Disability, Motherhood, and Local Power in Rural Siberia." Undergraduate honors thesis, Macalester College. http://digitalcommons.macalester.edu/anth_honors/1/.

———. 2012. "Accessing Possibility: Disability, Parent-Activists, and Citizenship in Contemporary Russia." Master's thesis, University of North Carolina at Chapel Hill.

———. 2014. "A Genealogy of (Post-)Soviet Dependency: Disabling Productivity." *Disability Studies Quarterly* 34 (1). https://dsq-sds.org/article/view/4015/3538.

———. 2017. "Good Ramps, Bad Ramps: Centralized Design Standards and Disability Access in Urban Russian Infrastructure." *American Ethnologist* 44 (1): 9–22. https://doi.org/10.1111/amet.12422.

———. 2020. *I Was Never Alone or Oporniki: An Ethnographic Play on Disability in Russia.* Toronto: University of Toronto Press.

Hartblay, Cassandra, Joseph D. Hankins, and Melissa L. Caldwell, eds. 2018. "Keywords for Ethnography and Design." *Theorizing the Contemporary* (blog). *Society for Cultural Anthropology*, March 29, 2018. https://culanth.org/fieldsights/1363-keywords-for-ethnography-and-design.

Healey, Dan. 2018. *Russian Homophobia from Stalin to Sochi.* New York: Bloomsbury Academic.

Hellbeck, Jochen. 2001. "Working, Struggling, Becoming: Stalin-Era Autobiographical Texts." *Russian Review* 60 (3): 340–59. https://www.jstor.org/stable/2679665.

Hemment, Julie. 2004. "The Riddle of the Third Sector: Civil Society, International Aid, and NGOs in Russia." *Anthropological Quarterly* 77 (2): 215–41. http://muse.jhu.edu/journals/anthropological_quarterly/v077/77.2hemment.html.

———. 2007. *Empowering Women in Russia: Activism, Aid, and NGOs.* Bloomington: Indiana University Press.

Hendren, Sara. 2017. "Notes on an Inclined Plane—Slope:Intercept." In *Disability, Space, Architecture: A Reader,* edited by Jos Boys. Abingdon, UK: Taylor and Francis.

Hickman, Louise, dir. 2014. *Taking the Bus in Crip Time.* Experimental documentary. Digital film. 11 minutes.

Hickman, Louise, and David Serlin. 2018. "Towards a Crip Methodology for Critical Disability Studies." In *Interdisciplinary Approaches to Disability,* edited by Katie Ellis, Rosemarie Garland-Thomson, Mike Kent, Rachel Robertson. London: Routledge. https://doi.org/10.4324/9781351053228-13.

Höjdestrand, Tova. 2009. Needed by Nobody: Homelessness and Humanness in Post-Socialist Russia. Ithaca: Cornell University Press.

Human Rights Watch. 2013a. *Barriers Everywhere: Lack of Accessibility for People with Disabilities in Russia.* http://www.hrw.org/reports/2013/09/11/barriers-everywhere-0.

———. 2013b. *Laws of Attrition: Crackdown on Russia's Civil Society after Putin's Return to the Presidency.* Edited by Konstantin Baranov. New York: Human Rights Watch.

Hunt-Kennedy, Stefanie. 2020. *Between Fitness and Death: Disability and Slavery in the Caribbean.* Disability Histories. Urbana: University of Illinois Press.

Iarskaia-Smirnova, Elena. 2001. "Social Change and Self-Empowerment: Stories of Disabled People in Russia." In *Disability and the Life Course: Global Perspectives,* edited by Mark Priestley. New York: Cambridge University Press.

Iarskaia-Smirnova and Romanov. 2013.

Imrie, Robert. 1996. *Disability and the City: International Perspectives.* London: P. Chapman.

Ingstad, Benedicte, and Susan Reynolds Whyte. 2007. *Disability in Local and Global Worlds.* Berkeley: University of California Press.

Irani, Lilly. 2010. "HCI on the Move: Methods, Culture, Values." In *CHI'10 Extended Abstracts on Human Factors in Computing Systems,* 2939 (42). ACM Digital Library.

———. 2019. *Innovators and Their Others: Entrepreneurial Citizenship in Indian Development.* Princeton, NJ: Princeton University Press.

Jackson, Liz, and Bess Williamson. 2023. "On Brand: When Design Museums Discover Disability." In *Curating Access: Disability Art Activism and Creative Accommodation,* edited by Amanda Cachia. New York: Routledge.

Kafer, Alison. 2003. "Compulsory Bodies: Reflections on Heterosexuality and Able-Bodiedness." *Journal of Women's History* 15 (3): 77–89. https://doi.org/10.1353/jowh.2003.0071.

——. 2013. *Feminist, Queer, Crip.* Bloomington: Indiana University Press.

Kaganovsky, Liliya. 2008. *How the Soviet Man Was Unmade: Cultural Fantasy and Male Subjectivity under Stalin.* Pittsburgh: University of Pittsburgh Press. https://doi.org/10.2307/j.ctt9qh907.

——. 2024. "Embodied Technologies: Lilya Brik's The Glass Eye (1929) and Esfir Shub's Today (1930)." In *Technologies of Mind and Body in the Soviet Union and the Eastern Bloc,* edited by Anna Toropova and Claire Shaw. London: Bloomsbury Academic.

Katsui, Hisayo, and Virpi Mesiäislehto. 2022. *Embodied Inequalities in Disability and Development.* Stellenbosch, South Africa: African Sun Media.

Kay, Rebecca. 1999. Russian Women and Their Organizations : Gender, Discrimination, and Grassroots Women's Organizations, 1991–96. New York: St. Martin's Press.

——. 2007. *Gender, Equality and Difference during and after State Socialism.* New York: Palgrave Macmillan.

Kikkas, Kaido. 2001. "Lifting the Iron Curtain." In *Disability and the Life Course: Global Perspectives,* edited by Mark Priestley, 113–22. New York: Cambridge University Press.

Kim, Eunjung. 2011. "'Heaven for Disabled People': Nationalism and International Human Rights Imagery." *Disability and Society* 26 (1): 93–106. https://doi.org/10.1080/09687599.2011.529670.

——. 2014. "The Specter of Vulnerability and Disabled Bodies in Protest." In *Disability, Human Rights and the Limits of Humanitarianism,* edited by Michael Carl Gill and Cathy J. Schlund-Vials. Surrey, UK: Ashgate.

——. 2017. *Curative Violence: Rehabilitating Disability, Gender, and Sexuality in Modern Korea.* Durham, NC: Duke University Press.

Knox, Jane E., and Alex Kozulin. 1989. "The Vygotskian Tradition in Soviet Psychological Study of Deaf Children." In *The Disabled in the Soviet Union: Past and Present, Theory and Practice,* edited by William O McCagg and Lewis Siegelbaum. Pittsburgh, PA: University of Pittsburgh Press.

Kohrman, Matthew. 2005: *Bodies of Difference: Experiences of Disability and Institutional Advocacy in the Making of Modern China.* Berkeley: University of California Press.

Kolarova, Katerina, and Martina Winkler. 2021: *Re/Imaginations of Disability in State Socialism: Visions, Promises, Frustrations.* Frankfurt: Campus Verlag.

Kondakov, Alexander Sasha. 2022. *Violent Affections: Queer Sexuality, Techniques of Power, and Law in Russia.* London: UCL Press.

Kruglova, Anna. 2017. "Social Theory and Everyday Marxists: Russian Perspectives on Epistemology and Ethics." *Comparative Studies in Society and History* 59 (4): 759–85. https://doi.org/10.1017/S0010417517000275.

Krylova, Anna. 2001. "'Healers of Wounded Souls': The Crisis of Private Life in Soviet Literature, 1944–1946." *Journal of Modern History* 73 (2): 307–31.

Kullman, Kim. 2016. "Prototyping Bodies: A Post-Phenomenology of Wearable Simulations." *Design Studies* 47: 73–90. https://doi.org/10.1016/j.destud.2016.08.004.

Kulmala, Meri. 2010. "'Women Rule This Country': Women's Community Organizing and Care in Rural Karelia." *Anthropology of East Europe Review* 28 (2).

Kuppers, Petra. 2014. *Studying Disability Arts and Culture: An Introduction.* Basingstoke: Red Globe.

Kurki, Tuulikki. 2013. "From Soviet Locality to Multivoiced Borderland: Literature and Identity in the Finnish-Russian National Borderlands." *Region: Regional Studies of Russia, Eastern Europe and Central Asia* 2 (1): 95–112.

Lampland, Martha, and Susan Leigh Star, eds. 2009. *Standards and Their Stories: How Quantifying, Classifying, and Formalizing Practices Shape Everyday Life.* Ithaca, NY: Cornell University Press.

Larkin, Brian. 2013. "The Politics and Poetics of Infrastructure." *Annual Review of Anthropology* 42: 327–43.

Latour. 1987. *Science in Action: How to Follow Scientists and Engineers Through Society.* Harvard University Press.

Ledeneva, Alena V. 1998. *Russia's Economy of Favours: Blat, Networking, and Informal Exchange.* Cambridge Russian, Soviet and Post-Soviet Studies 102. Cambridge, UK ; New York, NY, USA: Cambridge University Press.

Lefebvre, Henri. 2005. *The Production of Space.* Oxford: Blackwell.

Linton, Simi. 2005. "What Is Disability Studies?" *PMLA* 120 (2): 518–22. https://www.jstor.org/stable/25486177.

Magid, Jill. 2002. "System Azure Security Ornamentation." http://www.jillmagid.com/projects/system-azure-security-ornamentation.

Matza, Tomas Antero. 2018. *Shock Therapy: Psychology, Precarity, and Well-Being in Postsocialist Russia.* Durham, NC: Duke University Press.

McRuer, Robert. 2006. *Crip Theory: Cultural Signs of Queerness and Disability.* New York: New York University Press.

——. 2013. "Cripping Development." Conference Presentation.

——. 2014. "Normal." In *Keywords for American Cultural Studies*, edited by Bruce Burgett and Glenn Hendler, Second edition. New York: New York University Press.

——. 2016. "Curb Cuts: Crip Displacements and El Edificio de Enfrente." *Somatechnics* 6 (2): 198–215. https://doi.org/10.3366/soma.2016.0191.

——. 2018. *Crip Times: Disability, Globalization, and Resistance.* New Directions in Disability Studies. New York: New York University Press.

Meekosha, Helen, and Karen Soldatic. 2011. "Human Rights and the Global South: The Case of Disability." *Third World Quarterly* 32 (8): 1383–97. https://doi.org/10.1080/01436597.2011.614800.

Melnikova, Ekaterina. 2009. "Global Postsocialism on a Local Scale: The Soviet Migrants at Karelia and Their Past." *Anthropology of East Europe Review* 27 (2): 86–100.

Merry, Sally Engle. 2016. *The Seductions of Quantification: Measuring Human Rights, Gender Violence, and Sex Trafficking.* Chicago Series in Law and Society. Chicago: University of Chicago Press.

Meyers, Stephen. 2016. "NGO-Ization and Human Rights Law: The CRPD's Civil Society Mandate." *Laws* 5 (2): 21. https://doi.org/10.3390/laws5020021.

Mitchell, David T., and Sharon L. Snyder. 2001. *Narrative Prosthesis: Disability and the Dependencies of Discourse.* Ann Arbor: University of Michigan Press.

——. 2015. *The Biopolitics of Disability: Neoliberalism, Ablenationalism, and Peripheral Embodiment.* Ann Arbor: University of Michigan Press.

Mitchell, David T., Susan Antebi, and Sharon L. Snyder, eds. 2019. *The Matter of Disability: Materiality, Biopolitics, Crip Affect.* Ann Arbor: University of Michigan Press.

Mladenov, Teodor. 2015. "Neoliberalism, Postsocialism, Disability." *Disability and Society* 30 (3): 445–59.

——. 2017. "Postsocialist Disability Matrix." *Scandinavian Journal of Disability Research* 19 (2): 104–17. https://doi.org/10.1080/15017419.2016.1202860.

——. 2018. *Disability and Postsocialism.* New York: Routledge.

Mol, Annemarie. 2002. *The Body Multiple: Ontology in Medical Practice.* Durham, NC: Duke University Press.

Moscoso, Melania, and R. Lucas Platero. 2017. "Cripwashing: The Abortion Debates at the Crossroads of Gender and Disability in the Spanish Media." *Continuum* 31 (3): 470–81. https://doi.org/10.1080/10304312.2016.1275158.

The Moscow Times. 2019. "Russian Artist Takes to Apartment Wall to Highlight Country's Social Issues." The Moscow Times. July 19, 2019. https://www.themoscowtimes.com/2019/07/19/russian-artist-takes-apartment-wall-highlight-countrys-social-issues-a66486.

Moser, Ingunn, and John Law. 1999. "Good Passages, Bad Passages." *Sociological Review* 46 (2): 196–219.

Müller, Vladimir Karlovich. 1965. *English-Russian Dictionary. 70 000 Entries.* 11th ed. Moscow: Soviet Encyclopaedia Pub. House.

Mullins, Philippa. 2021. "'But We Are Always at Home': Disability and Collective Identity Construction on Runet." *Digital Icons* 21. https://www.digitalicons.org/issue21/but-we-are-always-at-home-disability-and-collective-identity-on-runet/.

Muravyeva, Marianna. 2014. "The Culture of Complaint: Approaches to Complaining in Russia: An Overview." *Laboratorium* 6 (3): 93–104.

Murawski, Michał. 2022. "Falshfasad: Infrastructure, Materialism, and Realism in Wild-Capitalist Moscow." *American Ethnologist* 49 (4): 461–77. https://doi.org/10.1111/amet.13104.

Murphy, Keith. 2015. *Swedish Design: An Ethnography.* Expertise: Cultures and Technologies of Knowledge. Ithaca, NY: Cornell University Press.

Murphy, Keith M., and Eitan Y. Wilf, eds. 2021. *Designs and Anthropologies: Frictions and Affinities.* School for Advanced Research Advanced Seminar Series. Albuquerque, New Mexico: University of New Mexico Press.

Nakamura, Karen. 2006. *Deaf in Japan: Signing and the Politics of Identity.* Ithaca, NY: Cornell University Press.

———. 2013. *A Disability of the Soul: An Ethnography of Schizophrenia and Mental Illness in Contemporary Japan.* Ithaca, NY: Cornell University Press.

Nario-Redmond, Michelle R., Dobromir Gospodinov, and Angela Cobb. 2017. "Crip for a Day: The Unintended Negative Consequences of Disability Simulations." *Rehabilitation Psychology* 62 (3): 324–33. https://doi.org/10.1037/rep0000127.

Neinvalid.ru. 2015. *Spustya god posle paralimpiadyi v Sochi ne rabotaet ni odin gorodskoy podemnik dlya invalidov* [One year after the Olympic games in Sochi, not a single public lift remains in working order]. March 4, 2015. http://neinvalid.ru/spustya-god-posle-paralimpiadyi-v-sochi-ne-rabotaet-ni-odin-gorodskoy-podemnik-dlya-invalidov/

Novopolianskii, D. 1975. "*Razmyshleniia nad pis'mami: Neotlozhnyi Dolg*" [Musings on Letters: An enduring duty]. *Pravda.* April 15, 1975, 6. East View Pravda Digital Archive. https://www.eastview.com/resources/gpa/pravda/.

———. 1977. "*Tebe, veteran*" [To you, veteran]. *Pravda.* February 21, 1977. East View Pravda Digital Archive. https://www.eastview.com/resources/gpa/pravda/.

Oliver, Michael. 2009 (1996). "The Social Model in Context." In *Rethinking Normalcy: A Disability Studies Reader,* edited by Tanya Titchkosky and Rod Michalko, 19–30. Toronto: Canadian Scholars' Press.

Ott, Katherine. 2014. "Disability Things:" In *Disability Histories,* edited by Susan Burch and Michael Rembis, 119–35. University of Illinois Press. http://www.jstor.org/stable/10.5406/j.ctt6wr5rt.11.

Osobaia Sem'ia. 2009. "Interaction of social organizations and municipal services in the sphere of the socialization of children and young people with disabilities in the Republic of Karelia [*Vzaimodeistvie obshchestvennykh organizatsii i munitsipal'nykh uchrezhdenii v oblasti sotsializatsii detei i molodykh liudei s invalidnost'iu Respublike Kareliia*]." Seminar materials. In Russian. Petrozavodsk: Karelian Regional social organization for parents with disabled children, A Special Family [*Osobaia Sem'ia*].

Overboe, James. 2016. "'Difference in Itself': Validating Disabled People's Lived Experience." *Body and Society*, June. http://journals.sagepub.com/doi/10.1177/13570 34X99005004002.

Oxford English Dictionary. 2014. "Accessible, Adj." Oxford University Press. https://doi.org/10.1093/OED/1203427411.

Perspektiva (Association of Regional Disability Organizations). 2017. "Moscow: An Accessible or Inaccessible City?" [*Moskva: dostupnyi ili nedostupnyi gorod?*]. *News* (blog). *Perspektiva*, August 12, 2017. https://perspektiva-inva.ru/news/moskva -dostupnyj-ili-nedostupnyj-gorod/.

Phillips, Sarah D. 2008. *Women's Social Activism in the New Ukraine: Development and the Politics of Differentiation*. Bloomington: Indiana University Press.

———. 2009. "'There Are No Invalids in the USSR!' A Missing Soviet Chapter in the New Disability History." *Disability Studies Quarterly* 29 (3).

———. 2011. *Disability and Mobile Citizenship in Postsocialist Ukraine*. Bloomington: Indiana University Press.

Preobrazhensky, A. G. 1951 (1910-1926). *Etymological Dictionary of the Russian Language*. Columbia Slavic Studies. New York, NY: Columbia University Press. https://doi.org/10.7312/preo91046.

Puar, Jasbir. 2013. "Rethinking Homonationalism." *International Journal of Middle East Studies* 45 (2): 336–39. https://doi.org/10.1017/S002074381300007X.

———. 2017. *The Right to Maim: Debility, Capacity, Disability*. Durham, NC: Duke University Press.

Raikhel, Eugene. 2016. *Governing Habits: Treating Alcoholism in the Post-Soviet Clinic*. Ithaca, NY: Cornell University Press.

Ralph, Laurence. 2014. *Renegade Dreams: Living through Injury in Gangland Chicago*. Chicago; London: University of Chicago Press.

Rasell, Michael, and Elena Iarskaia-Smirnova, eds. 2013. *Disability in Eastern Europe and the Former Soviet Union: History, Policy and Everyday Life*. New York: Routledge.

Reid, Susan E. 2006. "The Meaning of Home: 'The Only Bit of the World You Can Have to Yourself.'" In *Borders of Socialism*, edited by Lewis H. Siegelbaum, 145–70. New York: Palgrave Macmillan US. https://doi.org/10.1007/978-1-4039-8454-8_8.

———. 2018. "Communist Comfort: Socialist Modernism and the Making of Cozy Homes in the Khrushchev Era." In *The Routledge Companion to Modernity, Space and Gender*. New York: Routledge.

Ries, Nancy. 1997. *Russian Talk: Culture and Conversation during Perestroika*. Ithaca, NY: Cornell University Press.

———. 2009. "Potato Ontology: Surviving Postsocialism in Russia." *Cultural Anthropology* 24 (2): 181–212.

Rivkin-Fish, Michele. 2005a. "Bribes, Gifts, and Unofficial Payments: Towards an Anthropology of Corruption in Post-Soviet Russia." In *Corruption: Anthropological Perspectives*, edited by Dieter Haller and Cris Shore. Ann Arbor, MI: Pluto. 47–64

———. 2005b. *Women's Health in Post-Soviet Russia: The Politics of Intervention*. Bloomington: Indiana University Press.

Romanov, Pavel, and Elena Iarskaia-Smirnova. 2006. *The Politics of Disability: The Social Citizenship of Disabled People in Contemporary Russia* [*Politika invalidnosti: sotsial'noe grazhdanstvo invalidov v sovremennoi Rossii*]. Saratov: Nauchnaia kniga.

Romberg, Kristin. 2018. *Gan's Constructivism: Aesthetic Theory for an Embedded Modernism*. Oakland: University of California Press.

Rosenberg, Steve. 2012. "Russia Expels USAID Development Agency." *BBC News*, September 19, 2012. http://www.bbc.com/news/world-europe-19644897.

Roudakova, Natalia. 2017. *Losing Pravda: Ethics and the Press in Post-Truth Russia*. Cambridge: Cambridge University Press.

Ryazanov, Eldar, dir. 2002. *The Irony of Fate, or Enjoy Your Bath*. DVD.

Samuels, Ellen. 2017. "Six Ways of Looking at Crip Time." *Disability Studies Quarterly* 37 (3). https://doi.org/10.18061/dsq.v37i3.5824.

Sazhko, P. *"Udoben li magazin?: kak razvivat'sia torgovle* [Is the store convenient?: how to develop commerce]." *Pravda*, No. 233, February 2, 1972, 3. https://www .eastview.com/resources/gpa/pravda/.

Schalk, Samantha Dawn. 2018. *Bodyminds Reimagined: (Dis)Ability, Race, and Gender in Black Women's Speculative Fiction*. Durham, NC: Duke University Press.

———. 2022. *Black Disability Politics*. Durham, NC: Duke University Press.

Serlin, David. 2015. "Constructing Autonomy: Smart Homes for Disabled Veterans and the Politics of Normative Citizenship." *Critical Military Studies* 1 (1): 38–46. https://doi.org/10.1080/23337486.2015.1005392.

Shakespeare, Tom. 2006. "The Social Model of Disability." In *The Disability Studies Reader*, edited by Lennard Davis, 2nd ed. New York: Routledge. 197–204.

Shaw, Claire L. 2017. *Deaf in the USSR: Marginality, Community, and Soviet Identity, 1917–1991*. Ithaca, NY: Cornell University Press.

Sins Invalid. 2015. "10 Principles of Disability Justice." Sins Invalid. https://www .sinsinvalid.org/blog/10-principles-of-disability-justice.

Smith, Mark B. 2010. *Property of Communists: The Urban Housing Program from Stalin to Khrushchev*. DeKalb: Northern Illinois University Press.

Sobchak, Kseniya. 2019. "Kseniya Sobchak [Ксения Собчак] on Instagram: "Get Acquainted with the Photos of This Cool Guy @vreditel_li. . ." [Знакомьтесь-Это Фотографии Классного Парня @vreditel_li . . ."]." Instagram. July 27, 2019. https://www.instagram.com/p/B0ayjGPANQ4/.

Sperling, Valerie. 1999. *Organizing Women in Contemporary Russia: Engendering Transition*. Cambridge: Cambridge University Press.

Spradley, James. 1979. *The Ethnographic Interview*. New York: Holt Rinehart and Winston.

Stiker, Henri-Jacques. 1999. *A History of Disability*. Ann Arbor: University of Michigan Press.

Suchland, Jennifer. 2011. "Is Postsocialism Transnational?" *Signs: Journal of Women in Culture and Society* 36 (4): 837–62. https://doi.org/10.1086/658899.

Suchman, Lucy. 2018. "Design." *Fieldsights* (blog). *Society for Cultural Anthropology*, March 29, 2018. https://culanth.org/fieldsights/design.

Tchueva, Ekaterina. 2008. *"'Mir posle voiny': Zhaloby kak instrument regulirovaniia otnoshenii mezhdy gosudarstvom i invalidami Velikoi Otechestvennoi Voiny"* [World after the war: complaints as an instrument of regulating the relationships between the state and the disabled in the great patriotic war]. In *Sovetskaia sotsi-alnaia politika: stseny i deistvuiushchie litsa, 1940–1985* [Soviet Social Policy in 1940–1985: Scenes and Actors], edited by Elena Iarskaia-Smirnova and P. V. Romanov, 96–120. *Biblioteka Zhurnala issledovanii sotsial'noi politiki*. Moskva: TSentr sotsial'noi politiki i gendernykh issledovanii.

Titchkosky, Tanya. 2011. *The Question of Access: Disability, Space, Meaning*. Toronto: University of Toronto Press.

Trotter, William R. 1991. *A Frozen Hell: The Russo-Finnish Winter War of 1939–1940*. Chapel Hill, NC: Algonquin.

Tsing, Anna. 2005. *Friction: An Ethnography of Global Connection*. Princeton, NJ: Princeton University Press.

Turchenko, Mikhail. 2017. "The Rise and Fall of Local Self-Government in Petroza-vodsk." *Demokratizatsiya: The Journal of Post-Soviet Democratization* 25 (2): 155–73.

Tysiachniouk, Maria, Svetlana Tulaeva, and Laura A. Henry. 2018. "Civil Society Under the Law 'On Foreign Agents': NGO Strategies and Network Transformation." *Europe-Asia Studies* 70 (4): 615–37. https://doi.org/10.1080/09668136.2018.1463512.

United Nations Enable. 2004. "Accessibility for the Disabled: A Design Manual for a Barrier Free Environment." Accessed February 14, 2023. https://www.un.org/esa /socdev/enable/designm/index.html.

Utekhin, Ilya, Alice Nakhimovsky, Slava Paperno, and Nancy Ries. 2006. "Communal Living in Russia." A Virtual Museum of Soviet Everyday Life. http://kommunalka .colgate.edu/.

Varga-Harris, Christine. 2015. *Stories of House and Home: Soviet Apartment Life during the Khrushchev Years*. Ithaca, NY: Cornell University Press.

Verdery, Katherine. 1996. *What Was Socialism, and What Comes Next?* Princeton, NJ: Princeton University Press.

von Geldern, James. 1995. *Mass Culture in Soviet Russia : Tales, Poems, Songs, Movies, Plays, and Folklore, 1917–1953*. Bloomington: Indiana University Press.

Washington Group on Disability Statistics. 2017. Accessed April 7, 2017. http://www .washingtongroup-disability.com/.

Wates, Anna, and Hari Byles. 2015. "Gender and Disability, Asking Difficult Questions, University of Sheffield." *Journal of Literary and Cultural Disability Studies* 9 (1): 107–12. https://muse.jhu.edu/pub/105/article/577411.

Watkin, Jessica. 2022. "Disability Dramaturgy: Performance, Care and Community." PhD diss., University of Toronto.

Welland, Sasha. 2018. "Aesthetics." *Fieldsights* (blog). *Society for Cultural Anthropology*, March 29, 2018. https://culanth.org/fieldsights/aesthetics.

Wiedlack, Katharina, and Maria Neufeld. 2014. "Lost in Translation? Pussy Riot Soli-dary Activism and the Danger of Perpetuating North/Western Hegemonies." *Religion and Gender* 4 (December): 145. https://doi.org/10.18352/rg.9215.

——. 2016. "Dangerous and Moving? Disability, Russian Popular Culture and North/ Western Hegemony." *Somatechnics* 6 (2): 216–34. https://doi.org/10.3366/soma .2016.0192.

Yurchak, Alexei. 2006. *Everything Was Forever, Until It Was No More: The Last Soviet Generation*. Princeton, NJ: Princeton University Press.

Yurchak, Alexei, and Dominic Boyer. 2010. "American Stiob: Or, What Late Socialist Aesthetics of Parody Reveal about Contemporary Political Culture in the West." *Cultural Anthropology* 25 (2): 179–221.

Zavisca, Jane R. 2012. *Housing the New Russia*. Ithaca, NY: Cornell University Press.

Zubovich, Katherine. 2021. *Moscow Monumental: Soviet Skyscrapers and Urban Life in Stalin's Capital*. Princeton, NJ: Princeton University Press.

——. 2024. *Making Cities Socialist*. New York: Cambridge University Press.

Index

Page numbers followed by letters "f" and "t" refer to figures and tables, respectively.

www.ingramcontent.com/pod-product-compliance
Lightning Source LLC
Chambersburg PA
CBHW032351280326
41935CB00008B/527